Pro/ENGINEER®
Advanced Tutorial
Release 2001

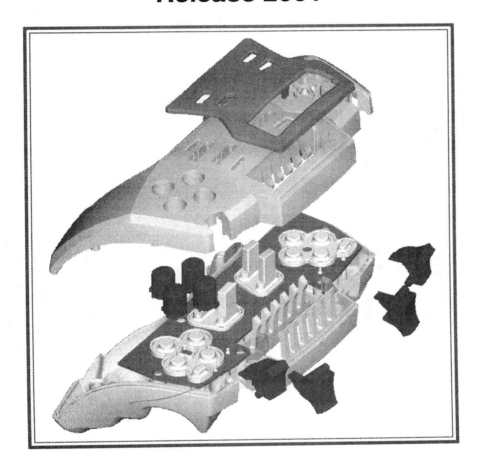

Roger Toogood, Ph.D., P. Eng.
Mechanical Engineering
University of Alberta

PUBLICATIONS

Schroff Development Corporation

www.schroff.com

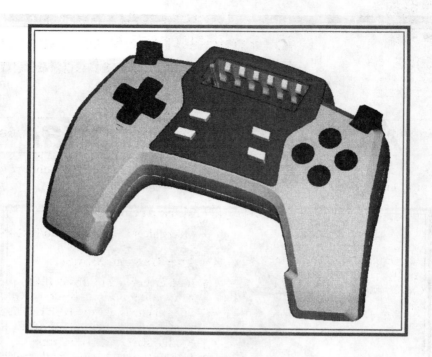

ON THE COVER

AIRPLAY™ is a Radio Wireless controller for PlayStation® game consoles. AIRPLAY™ was designed using Alias/Wavefront® and Pro/ENGINEER® by Eleven Engineering Inc., #2011, 10155 - 102St, Edmonton, Alberta. Mechanical design team: Jason Gosior, Kip Hampson, John Sobota, Andy Yu, Roger Toogood. See **http://www.airplayer.net**. Used by permission.

AIRPLAY™ is a trademark of XI Intellectual Capital Inc. (Patents Pending)

PlayStation® is a registered trademark of Sony Computer Entertainment Inc.

Alias® is a registered trademark of Alias/Wavefront, a division of Silicon Graphics Limited.

Pro/ENGINEER® is a registered trademark of Parametric Technology Corporation.

SDC
TRAINING
INSTITUTE

Quality CAD training
for Pro/ENGINEER professionals
from a distinguished faculty

Training Institute Faculty

Mark Archibald, Ph.D.
Professor, Dept. of Mechanical Engineering
Grove City College
Author of *Mechanical Engineering Design with Pro/ENGINEER*

Yves Gagnon, M.A.Sc.
Professor, Dept. of Mechanical Engineering Technology
Okanagan University College
Author of *Pro/MECHANICA Structure: Elements & Applications*

David S. Kelley, Ph.D.
Assistant Professor, Dept. of Computer Graphics Technology
Purdue University
Author of *Pro/ENGINEER Instructor 2001*; *Pro/ENGINEER Assistant 2001*; *Pro/ENGINEER Instructor*

Randy Shih, M.S.
Professor, Dept. of Mechanical Engineering
Oregon Institute of Technology
Author of *Parametric Modeling withPro/ENGINEER*

Roger Toogood, Ph.D., P.Eng.
Associate Professor, Dept. of Mechanical Engineering
University of Alberta
Author of *Pro/ENGINEER Tutorial*; *Pro/ENGINEER Advanced Tutorial*; *Pro/MECHANICA Structure Tutorial*

Jack Zecher, M.S., P.E.
Professor, Dept. of Mechanical Engineering Technology
Indiana University-Purdue University Indianapolis
Author of the *MultiMedia CD* that accompanies Roger Toogood's *Pro/ENGINEER Tutorial*

Training Institute Courses

These courses are offered only a few times during the year on a first come-first serve basis.

Mark Archibald, Ph.D.

Mechanical Design with Pro/ENGINEER	5 days

Yves Gagnon, M.A.Sc.

Introduction to Pro/ENGINEER	5 days
Advanced Pro/ENGINEER	4 days
Fundamentals of Pro/SHEETMETAL	2 days
Fundamentals of Pro/SURFACE	2 days
Pro/INTRALINK User Course	2 days
Finite Element Analysis with Pro/MECHANICA	4 days

David S. Kelley, Ph.D.

Introduction to Pro/ENGINEER	5 days
Pro/ENGINEER Fundamentals	3 days
Introduction to Drawing Mode	2 days
Surface Modeling	2 days
Advanced Modeling Techniques in Pro/ENGINEER	3 days

Randy Shih, M.S.

Introduction to Pro/ENGINEER	5 days

Roger Toogood, Ph.D., P.Eng.

Pro/ENGINEER Fundamentals	5 days
Pro/MECHANICA (Structure) Fundamentals	3 days

Jack Zecher, M.S., P.E.

Introduction to Pro/ENGINEER	3 days

About the **SDC** Training Institute

1. Training is offered for the following software:
    Pro/ENGINEER   Pro/SURFACE
    Pro/SHEETMETAL   Pro/INTRALINK
    Pro/MECHANICA

2. All of the Institute faculty are active in writing books for PTC software and bring a wealth of real world and training experience to the classroom.

3. All Institute courses are taught at the customer's location. This eliminates travel expenses and reduces scheduling conflicts.

4. All courses offered by the Institute are the unique creations of the Faculty members and reflect their individual style and perspective. Please visit our web site for detailed information about the course in which you have an interest.

Consult our web site for details and for the latest course offerings:

www.SDCpro.com

Pro/ENGINEER 2001 Advanced Tutorial

Preface

The purpose of this tutorial is to introduce users to some of the more advanced features, commands, and functions in Pro/ENGINEER. The style and approach of the previous Tutorial have been maintained. Each lesson concentrates on a few of the major topics and the text attempts to explain the "Why's" of the commands in addition to a concise step-by-step description of new command sequences. Familiarity with the basic operation of Pro/E is assumed, and material presented in the previous tutorial is taken for granted. In a few places in this Tutorial, those commands are reviewed to put the discussion in context with the extensions and options presented here.

The material covered in this Tutorial represents an overview of what are felt to be commonly used and important functions. These include customization of the working environment, advanced feature creation (sweeps, round sets, draft and tweaks, UDF's, patterns and family tables), layers, Pro/PROGRAM, and advanced drawing and assembly functions. The Tutorial is not exhaustive, and there are many areas and options in Pro/E that could not be included due to space limitations. Nonetheless, it is hoped that the selection of the material presented here will satisfy a broad range of users wishing to expand their understanding of the program and learn additional features on their own.

The **Advanced Tutorial** consists of eight lessons. Each lesson should be studied using a live Pro/E session in order to fully experience and absorb the material. Most of the material in the lessons is reinforced by repetition, on the grounds that "practice makes perfect." Each lesson should take from 2 to 3 hours to complete. Additional exploration of the program is strongly encouraged throughout.

This **Advanced Tutorial** has been written and tested using Pro/Engineer 2001-Preproduction Build 2001020 running under Windows NT 4.0 (SP 6).

About the Project

A continuing theme through the lessons is the creation of parts for a medium-sized modeling project. Project parts are given at the end of each lesson that utilize functions presented in that lesson. Final assembly is performed in the last lesson. The project consists of a small three-wheeled utility cart. The entire cart project (part creation and final assembly) should take from 20 to 30 hours to complete (not including drawings). A Quick Reference chart for all the project parts is included immediately after the Table of Contents (page ix). Mark this page!

In today's litigious culture, it seems necessary to mention that the cart design is purely for the demonstration of modeling techniques in Pro/ENGINEER. The cart design has been developed entirely by the author and any resemblance to an existing device is unintentional and coincidental. The cart and its components have not been subject to any engineering analysis, for example to determine its load carrying capacity or safety factors. Its suitability to any particular task or manufacturing process is therefore unwarranted and the author cannot take responsibility for the performance of an actual physical realization of the model.

Acknowledgments

This Tutorial would not have been possible without the support and patience of my family who have tolerated (although not always quietly!) my determination to complete the work to the exclusion of other important activities. So to Elaine, Kate, and Jenny: a great big THANKS! And let's go get some ice cream.

Stephen Schroff at SDC has also been continually supportive and enthusiastic about this and other projects. A better publisher could not be imagined.

I would like to acknowledge all the people who have sent comments on the previous Tutorial. These have often provided a necessary motivation for going the extra step.

Thanks are due to John Sobota, President, Eleven Engineering Inc., for permission to use the images of AIRPLAY™ on the cover.

And, as always, thanks are due to our good and true friends, Jayne and Rowan, whose enthusiasm and good wishes are a constant source of energy.

I hope you enjoy the Tutorial.

RWT
Edmonton, Alberta
29 June 2001

TABLE OF CONTENTS

Lesson 1 : The Pro/E Interface and Customization

Lesson 2 : Helical and Variable Section Sweeps

Lesson 3 : Advanced Rounds and Tweaks

Lesson 4 : Patterns and Family Tables

Lesson 5 : User Defined Features (UDF's)

Lesson 6 : Pro/PROGRAM and Layers

Lesson 7 : Advanced Drawing Functions

Lesson 8 : Assemblies

PROJECT PARTS QUICK REFERENCE

Part Name	Description	Page
arm_brack	bracket on horizontal side tube for suspension arm	1 - 21
arm_lower	lower wheel suspension arm	2 - 22
arm_upper	upper wheel suspension arm	2 - 22
arm_vbrack	bracket on vertical side tube for suspension arm	1 - 21
cargo	cargo bin	3 - 23
fram_low_rgt	lower frame tube member on right side	2 - 23
fram_upp_rgt	upper frame tube member on right side	2 - 24
frame_front	front frame member	7 - 41
front_axle	front wheel axle	6 - 23
front_pillar	front wheel assembly pillar	7 - 40
front_spr_plate	circular plate to support front spring	1 - 20
front_spring	front wheel spring	2 - 21
front_wheel	front wheel	6 - 23
front_wheel_brack	front wheel mounting bracket	6 - 23
handle	front handle	5 - 22
handle_pin	axle pin for front handle	1 - 20
hex_bolt	generic part for hexagonal shoulder bolt	4 - 28
hubcap	wheel hubcap	3 - 23
lugnut	nut to attach wheel to axle	3 - 23
mount	side wheel axle mounting plate	5 - 23
pillar_cap	cap on top of front wheel assembly pillar	7 - 40
spring	main side wheel suspension spring	3 - 25
stud	original part to define stud UDF	5 - 24
tubing	generic part for square tubing	4 - 27
wheel	main side wheel	4 - 27
wheel_axle	side wheel axle	5 - 24

This page left blank.

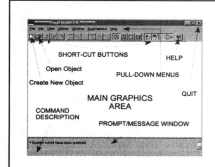

Lesson 1

Pro/E Customization Tools and Project Introduction

Synopsis:

Configuration settings; customizing the screen toolbars and menus; mapkeys; part templates; introduction to the project

Overview

This lesson will introduce tools for customizing your Pro/E configuration and working environment and show you how to create some useful shortcuts for accessing Pro/E commands. The major customization tool is the use of one or more configuration files (default file: *config.pro*). The lesson also includes managing and creating your own custom toolbars and mapkeys. We'll also see how you can create your own part templates.

The major project used in this tutorial is introduced and the first four parts are presented.

Configuration Files (*config.pro*)

By now, you should be familiar with the commands for environment settings that are available in

Utilities > Environment

These aspects of the Pro/Engineer working environment (and much more!) can also be controlled using settings stored in configuration files (*config* files for short). Pro/E has several hundred individual configuration settings. All settings have default values that will be used if not specifically set in a *config* file.

The most important *config* file is a special file called *config.pro* that is automatically read when Pro/E starts up a new session. You can also read in (and/or change) additional configuration settings at any time during a session. For example, you may want to have one group of settings for one project you are working on, and another group for a different project that you switch to during a single session. In this tutorial, we will deal only with the use of the single configuration file, *config.pro*, loaded at start-up.

Several copies of *config.pro* might exist on your system, and they are read in the following order when Pro/E is launched:

♦ *config.sup* - this is a protected system file which is read by all users but is not available for modification by users. Your system administrator has control of this file.
♦ Pro/E loadpoint - this is read by all users and would usually contain common settings determined by the system administrator such as search paths, formats, libraries, and so on. This file cannot normally be altered by individual users.
♦ user home directory - unique for each user (Unix)
♦ startup directory - the current or working directory when Pro/E starts up. To find where this directory is, select *File > Open* and observe the directory name in the top box[1]

Settings made in the first copy (*config.sup*) cannot be overridden by users. This is handy for making configuration settings to be applied universally across all users at a Pro/E installation (search paths for part libraries, for instance). An individual user can modify entries in the last two copies of *config.pro* to suit their own requirements. If the same entry appears more than once, the last entry encountered in the start-up sequence is the one the system will use. After start-up, additional configuration settings can be read in at any time. These might be used to create a configuration unique to a special project, or perhaps a special type of modeling. Be aware that when a new configuration file is read in, some options may not take effect until Pro/E is restarted. This is discussed more a bit later.

Settings in *config.pro* are composed of two entries in the following form:

config_option_name   config_option_value

Option values can be composed either of text, single numbers, or series of numbers. A complete listing and description of all *config* options is contained in the on-line help. With the Help page visible in your browser, select

Contents > Pro/ENGINEER Foundation > Using Configuration File Options

This gives a (very long) list of all the options, with a short description of each. Note that the default value is indicated in italics. You will have a hard time remembering the meaning of all these options, let alone their names! Fortunately, the dialog window for working with configuration files contains a one line description of any selected option. There is also a new search capability for finding option names. Although this makes finding the options much easier, you are encouraged to explore the on-line help - you might find just the setting you need to make your life easier!

Your system may have a standard configuration file available for you to use as a basis for your own work. Look for the *config.pro* file in the **pro_stds** ("standards") directory in the Pro/E installation.

---

[1] In Windows, right click on the Pro/E icon on the desktop (if it exists), select **Properties > ShortCut** and examine the **Start In** text entry field.

Before we proceed, if you have access to this file, copy it to your start-up directory, along with the file *config.win* (this is a file containing customized screen layout settings which are discussed later). Now launch Pro/E, or if it is already up erase everything currently in session and set your working directory to your normal start-up directory.

The Configuration File Editor

You can access your current configuration file using

Utilities > Options

This brings up the **Options** window. If your system has options set already, these will appear in the window. If not, the central area of the window will be blank, as in Figure 1. We'll discuss the operation of this dialog window from the top down.

The **Showing** pull-down list at the top will let you choose from a number of configuration groups (Current Session, your start-up config.pro, or elsewhere)

Deselect the check box just below the **Showing** pull-down box. After a couple of seconds, a complete list of all the Pro/E configuration options will appear. The first column shows its name, and the second column shows its current value. An entry with an asterisk indicates a default value.

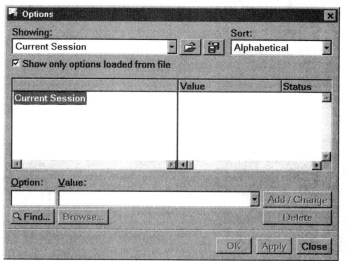

Figure 1 The Options window for setting and editing configuration files

Browse down through the list. There are a lot of options here! Note that the options are arranged alphabetically. This is because of the setting in the **Sort** pull-down menu in the top-right corner. Change this to *By Category*. This rearranges the list of options to group them by function. For example, check out the settings available in the **Environment** and **Sketcher** groups. Fortunately, there are a couple of tools to help you find the option name you're looking for. Let's see how they work.

Check the box beside "Show only options loaded from file" and select *Sort(Alphabetical)*. Note that the options listed here are only those that are different from the default settings.

Adding Settings to *config.pro*

Assuming you have a blank *config.pro*, let's create a couple of useful settings. At the bottom of the **Preferences** window are two text boxes for entering option names and values. If you know the name of the option, you can just type it in to the first box. One of the most common settings is to turn off the (annoying!) beep that Pro/E emits from time to time. In the text box below **Option**, enter the option name *bell*. In the pull-down list under **Value**, select *No*. Note that the option name is not case sensitive and the default value is indicated by an asterisk in the pull-down list. Now select the ***Add/Change*** button on the right. The entry now appears in the data area. A bright green star in the **Status** column indicates that the option has been defined but has not yet taken effect.

Now enter a display option. The default part display mode in the graphics window is **Shaded**. Many people prefer to work in hidden line mode - let's make it the default on start-up. Once again, we will enter the configuration option name. As you type this in, notice that Pro/E anticipates the rest of the text box based on the letters you have typed in. After typing the "dis" characters, the rest of the option will appear; just hit the Enter key. The option name and value we want are

> **display**   **hiddenvis**

Now select ***Add/Change*** as before (or just hit the Enter key after typing the "h").

Another common setting is the location of the Pro/E trail file. As you recall, the trail file contains a record of every command and mouse click during a Pro/E session. The default location for this is the start-up directory. Theoretically, trail files can be used to recover from disastrous crashes of Pro/E, but this is a tricky operation. Most people just delete them. It is handy, therefore, to collect trail files for each session in a single directory, where they can be easily removed later. There is an option for setting the location of this directory. Suppose we don't know its specific name. Here is where a search function will come in handy.

At the bottom of the **Preferences** window, click the ***Find*** button. This brings up the **Find Option** window (Figure 2). Type in the keyword *trail* and select

> ***All Categories > Find Now***

Several possibilities come up. The option we want is listed as **trail_dir**. Select this option and ***Browse*** to a suitable location on your system for the value. Perhaps something like *c:\temp*. Then select ***Add/Change***. The new entry appears in the Preferences window. In the Find Option window, select ***Close***.

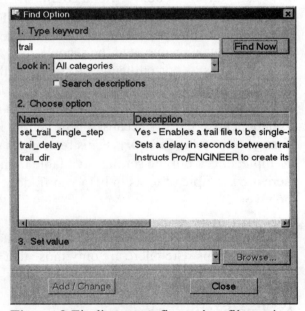

Figure 2 Finding a configuration file option

For some options, the value is numeric (eg setting a default tolerance, number of digits, or the color of entities on the screen). In these cases, you can enter the relevant number (or numbers separated by either spaces or commas). For example, under **Option**, enter the name

system_hidden_color. Then under **Value**, enter the numbers **60 60 60** (separated by spaces). These give the values of red, green, and blue (out of 100). Equal values yield gray; this setting will brighten the hidden lines a bit from the default value. Select *Add/Change*.

We have now specified four options. To have them take effect, select the *Apply* button at the bottom. The green stars change to small green circles in the Status column.

Note that you can resize the column widths by dragging on the short vertical column separator bars at the top of the display area. At the far right is a long (scrollable) one-line description of the option.

For practice, enter the options shown in Figure 3. The order that the configuration options are declared does not matter (the exception is mapkeys, discussed below). Check the on-line help for a description of these configuration settings and feel free to add new settings to your file. Investigate settings for search paths, libraries, default editors, default decimal places, import/export settings, and so on.

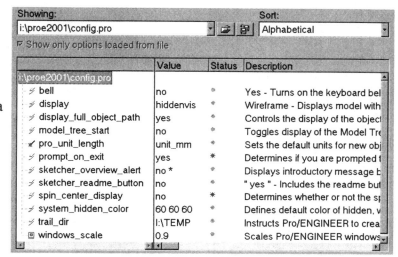

Figure 3 Settings in *config.pro*

Notice the icons in the first column beside the option names. These mean the following:

        ⚡ (lightning) - option takes effect immediately

        ✦ (wand) - option will take effect for the next object created

        ▣ (screen) - option will take effect the next time Pro/E is started

If you are using a *config* file from a previous version of Pro/E you may see a "stop sign" (actually a red circle with a line through it), which means that the option is no longer used.

Try to add an illegal option name. For example, in Release 2000i there was an option **sketcher_readme_alert**. Type that in to the **Option** field. When you try to set a value for this, it will not be accepted (the *Add/Change* button stays gray). Pro/E only recognizes valid option names! Thus, if you mistype or enter an invalid name, this is indicated by not being able to enter a value for it.

We will be making more changes to this *config.pro* a bit later in this lesson when we discuss mapkeys.

Saving Your *config.pro* Settings

To store the settings we have just created, select the *Save As* button ▦ at the top of the **Options** window. At the bottom of the new window, type in the desired name for the file - in this case *config.pro* and select *OK*.

Deleting Configuration Options

With the configuration file name visible in the Showing field at the top, highlight one of the options and select *Delete*. Selecting *Apply* automatically saves the new settings. *Close* the window.

Loading a Configuration File

To load a new configuration file, select the *Open File* button beside the **Showing** list. Select the desired file and then *Open*. Note that these settings will be read in but not activated immediately (note the green star). Select the *Apply* button and observe the green star.

Now select *Close* in the **Options** window.

Checking Your Configuration Options

Because some settings will not activate until Pro/E is restarted, many users will exit Pro/E after making changes to their *config.pro* file and then restart, just to make sure the settings are doing what they are supposed to. Do that now. This is not quite so critical since the window shows you with the lightning/wand/screen icons whether an option is active. However be aware of where Pro/E will look for the *config.pro* file on start-up, as discussed above. If you have saved *config.pro* in another working directory than the one you normally start in, then move it before starting Pro/E. On the other hand, if you have settings that you only want active when you are in a certain directory, keep a copy of *config.pro* there and load it once Pro/E has started up and you have changed to the desired directory. To keep things simple, and until you have plenty of experience with changing the configuration settings, it is usually better to have only one copy of *config.pro* in your startup directory.

Note that it is probably easier to make some changes to the environment for a single session using *Utilities > Environment*. Also, as is often the case when learning to use new computer tools, don't try anything too adventurous with *config.pro* in the middle of a part or assembly creation session - you never know when an unanticipated effect might clobber your work!

Customizing the Interface

In addition to the environment settings, there are several ways of customizing the Pro/E interface: using *config.pro*, toolbars, menus, and mapkeys. An example of a customized interface is shown in the figure at the right. When you modify the interface layout, your changes will be saved in a *config.win* file in a directory of your choice (usually the current working directory). It is possible and permissible to have several different *config.win* files in different directories, each with a different customization of the screen to suit the work you may be doing on files in that directory.

In this section, we will introduce methods to customize the toolbars and menus.

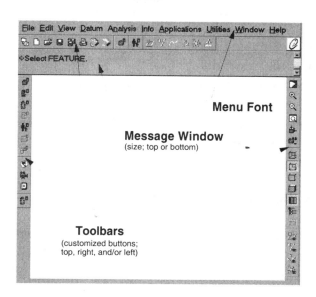

Figure 4 A customized screen layout

Toolbars

With the cursor on the top toolbar, hold down the right mouse button. This brings up the menu shown in Figure 5. This shows the toolbar groups currently displayed (see check marks); the groups can be toggled to include/exclude them from the display. Each group contains a set of functionally-related shortcut buttons.

Figure 5 *Toolbar* toggle menu

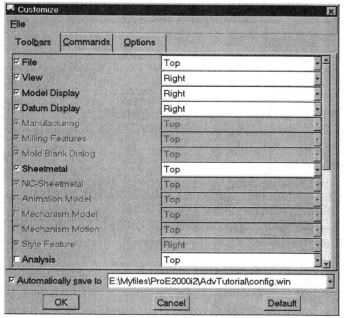

Figure 6 The *Toolbars* tab in the **Customize** window

At the bottom of this pop-up menu, select *Toolbars*. This brings up the **Customize** menu which contains a list of all available toolbars, and their location (see Figure 6). At the bottom of this window you can specify whether or not, and where, to automatically save the current layout settings. The default is *config.win* in the current working directory. As mentioned above, you can create multiple *config.win* files, and use *File > Save Settings* and *File > Open Settings* in the **Customize** window to store and recall previous files. Note that in addition to the eleven standard toolbar groups there are three initially empty groups (Toolbars 1 through 3), which you can populate with short-cut buttons using methods described below. The pull-down lists at the right allow you to place the selected toolbars at different places on the screen (left, right, top of graphics window).

Changing Toolbar Buttons

In the **Customize** window, select the *Commands* tab. (This is also available by selecting *Commands...* in the menu shown in Figure 5 or using *Utilities > Customize Screen* in the pull-down menu.) The window shown in Figure 7 will open. Groups of toolbar commands are listed in a tree structure in the **Categories** area on the left. Click on any of the group names and the available short-cut buttons will appear in the **Commands** area on the right. As you move the mouse over these buttons, a tool tip will display.

To add a button to a toolbar, just drag and drop it onto an existing toolbar at the top, right, or left. The button will be added wherever you drop it on the toolbar. To remove it, drag it off the toolbar and drop it somewhere else (on the graphics window, for example). Note that it is possible to mix and match the short-cut buttons: any button can be placed on any toolbar. For example, a button listed under the **File** category can also be added to the **View** toolbar. Buttons can also be present on more than one toolbar. The possibilities are endless!

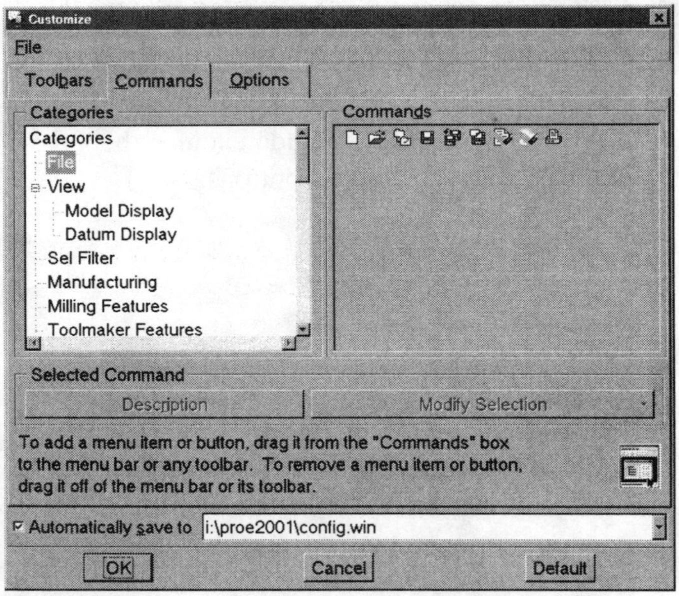

Figure 7 Choosing short-cut buttons for toolbars

While we are here, notice that at the bottom of the **Categories** list is **Mapkeys**. We will be discussing mapkeys a bit later. You can add a button representing any of your defined mapkeys to any of the toolbars. It is helpful to keep your mapkey descriptive names short for this.

At the bottom of the **Categories** list is **New Menu**. You can drag this up to the menu area at the top of the screen to create your own pull-down menus.

If you turn on one of the user toolbars (select Toolbar 1, 2, or 3 under the *Toolbars* tab), an initially empty button will appear in the designated location (top, left, or right). You can use the

Commands selector to drag any button to define your own toolbar.

Notice that the final tab in the **Customize** window is *Options*. This lets you set the position of the Command/Message window (above or below the graphics area) and some other settings.

When you leave the **Customize** dialog box, your new settings can be written to the file designated in the bottom text entry box. Each new *config.win* file is numbered sequentially (*config.win.2, config.win.3*, and so on).

Helpful Hint

It is tempting, especially if you are blessed with a lot of screen space, to over-populate the toolbars by trying to arrange every commonly used command on the screen at once. This is reminiscent of many other Windows-based CAD programs. Before you do that, you should work with Pro/E for a while. You will find that Pro/E will generally bring up the appropriate toolbars for your current program status automatically. For example, if you are in Sketcher, the Sketcher short-cut buttons will appear. Furthermore, many commands are readily available in the right-mouse pop-up menus. Thus, adding these buttons permanently to any toolbar is unnecessary and the buttons will be grayed out when you are not in Sketcher anyway - you are introducing screen clutter with no benefit.

Keyboard Shortcuts - Mapkeys

A mapkey is a short sequence of keyboard key strokes or a function key that will launch one or a series of Pro/E commands. Mapkeys are very similar to macros that can be defined in other software packages. Mapkey definitions are contained/included in your *config.pro* file, so they are loaded at start-up.

The mapkey key stroke sequence can be as long as you want; most users restrict mapkeys to only 2, or sometimes 3, characters. This gives several hundred possible mapkey sequences - more than you can probably remember effectively. Pro/E constantly monitors the keyboard for input and will immediately execute a defined command sequence when its mapkey is detected. Single character mapkeys should be avoided due to the way that Pro/E processes keyboard input. If you have two mapkeys "v" and "vd", for example, the second mapkey would never execute since Pro/E will trap and execute the first one as soon as the "v" is pressed. For the same reason, a 3-character mapkey can never have the same two first letters as a 2-character mapkey.

Ideally, you would like to have mapkey sequences that are very easy to remember, like "vd" (view default), or "rg" (regenerate). Because it is common to only use two characters, it will take some planning to decide how you want to set up your definitions to use only a couple of easy-to-remember key strokes! The mapkey should be mnemonic, but can't collide with other definitions. You don't want to have to remember that "qy" means "repaint the screen."

A practical limit on usable mapkeys is perhaps in the range of 20 to 30, although some "power users" can use over a hundred.

For this exercise, clear your session and load any single simple part file. We will not be modifying the part.

Listing Current Mapkeys

To see a list of your current mapkeys (some are defined in the *config.pro* contained in the pro_stds directory) select

Utilities > Mapkeys

This dialog window (Figure 8) allows you to define and record, modify, delete, run, and save mapkeys. Note that each mapkey has a short Name and Description. The Name will be used on any short-cut button (described below), and the Description will appear at the bottom of the main graphics window. Mapkeys that start with a "$" are function keys.

Note that mapkeys created using a previous release may differ in command syntax and it is likely that some mapkey definitions from previous releases will not function properly. However, mapkeys are easy enough to record. Before you do that, you might try to get hold of the *config.pro* file in the **pro_stds** directory mentioned above. A list of these mapkeys is in the file usually stored in

/ptc/pro_stds/mapkeys.htm

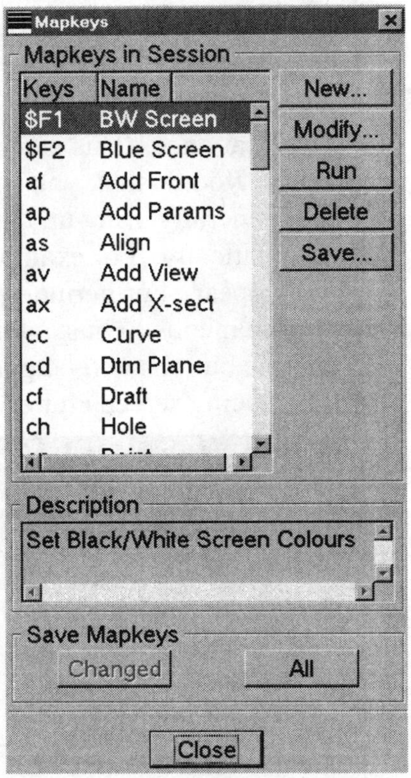

Figure 8 Accessing Mapkeys currently in session

In the following, it is assumed that you have no mapkeys defined as yet. If any of these tutorial mapkeys collide with existing mapkeys shown in the mapkeys list (Figure 8), you can modify the keyboard sequence (for example, use "dv" instead of "vd") for the new mapkey.

Creating Mapkeys

New mapkeys are created as follows. We will create a mapkey sequence "vd" that will reorient the view to the default orientation. To set this up, you will have to bring in one of your previously created parts. We will not be modifying the part.

Select the *New* button in the menu of Figure 8. The **Record Mapkey** dialog box shown in Figure 9 will open. Enter the data shown in the figure: key sequence, name, description. Now we record the command sequence:

> *Record*
> *View > Default Orientation* (in the top pull-down menus)
> *Stop > OK*

It's that easy! Spin the model with CTRL-middle. In the Mapkeys window, highlight the new mapkey "vd" and select the *Run* button. It's a good idea to check your mapkey definitions now when it is easy to modify them.

As mentioned above, mapkey definitions are saved in a configuration file (as in *config.pro*). New mapkey definitions are appended to the end of the file. If you redefine a mapkey (or use a duplicate keystroke sequence), the definition closest to the bottom of the *config* file is the one that will be used. When saving a mapkey you can choose either *config.pro* or *current_session.pro*. There are three ways to save the mapkeys using the buttons in the **Mapkeys** window:

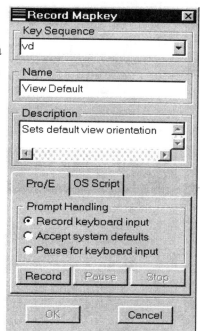

> *Save* - saves only the highlighted mapkey
> *Changed* - saves any mapkeys changed this session
> *All* - saves all mapkeys defined for session

Remember that if you save the mapkey in the *current_session.pro* or elsewhere, it will not be loaded automatically the next time you start Pro/E. To do that, you must explicitly save the mapkey definitions into the *config.pro* file.

Close the **Mapkeys** window.

Figure 9 Creating a mapkey

Minimize Pro/E and open *config.pro* using your system text editor. Scroll down to the bottom of the file to see the new line(s) that describe the mapkey. Obviously, these lines should never be separated since they are a continuation of the same sequence. It is possible, but probably not advisable, to try to edit the mapkey definitions manually - leave that to the power users! Exit your text editor and restore the Pro/E window.

Some final points about mapkeys: it is possible to set up the mapkey so that execution will pause to allow user input during the command sequence, either by picking on the screen or through the keyboard. Mapkeys can also call other mapkeys. You might like to experiment with these ideas on your own. The possibilities for customization are almost limitless!

As mentioned above, the *config.pro* file provided in the **pro_stds** directory contains several dozen mapkeys. Some of these are listed in Table 1-1 on the next page.

We will return to mapkeys after the next section.

Table 1-1 Some commonly used mapkeys

General Mapkeys		Feature Creation Mapkeys	
wc	Window Close	ct	Create Cut
wa	Window Activate	cp	Create Protrusion
rg	Regenerate	ch	Create Hole
dd	Done	cr	Create Round
qq	Quit	cc	Create datum Curve
View Mapkeys		cd	Create Datum plane
rr	Repaint	Utility Mapkeys	
sd	Shade	fr	Feature Redefine
vd	View Default	fs	Feature Suppress
vr	View Refit	fd	Feature Delete
vf	View Front	fe	Feature Resume
vb	View Back	fm	Feature Modify
vt	View Top	fi	Feature Information
vl	View Left		
vg	View Right		

Working with Part Templates

Most part files that you create contain many common elements such as datums, defined views, coordinate systems, parameters, and so on. Creating these from scratch for every new part that you start is tedious and inefficient. Prior to Release 2000i^2 a very handy model creation tool used the notion of a "start part" which contain these common elements. Users would then create a mapkey that would bring the part into session and then rename it. This made the creation of new parts very quick and efficient, with the added bonus that standard part setups could be employed.

This "start part" functionality has been built into the program using part templates. Several part templates are included with a standard Pro/E installation for solid and sheet metal parts in different systems of units. You may have a reason at some point to create your own template, which we will do here. We'll also define a mapkey to quickly bring it in session and allow you to change its name. Then you can immediately get on with the job of creating features. We will create the part template from scratch, although you could use any of the existing templates as a basis for this.

Select *File > New*. Make sure the **Part** and **Solid** radio buttons are selected. Deselect the **Use Default Template** box, and enter a name *mytemplate*. Select *OK* and in the next window, select the **Empty** template and *OK*.

Create the default datums and use *Part > Set Up > Name* to rename the datums *SIDE* (DTM1), *TOP* (DTM2), and *FRONT* (DTM3). Now set up some named views.

> *View > Orientation*

and create the following three named views:

View Name	Reference 1		Reference 2	
	Direction	Pick Datum	Direction	Pick Datum
FRONT	Front	FRONT	Top	TOP
TOP	Front	TOP	Right	SIDE
RIGHT	Front	SIDE	Top	TOP

The completed list of saved views should appear as shown in Figure 10. Feel free to add additional standard views (Left, Back, Bottom, Iso_Right, ...). Select *OK* to leave the **Orientation** dialog.

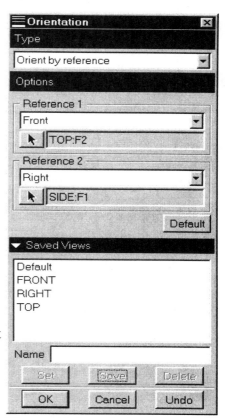

Check out our previously defined mapkey for setting the default view ("vd").

Set the part units using

> *Set Up > Units*

and picking "millimeter-Newton-Second", then

> *Set > OK > Close*

We are finished with creating the start part, so save it with the name **mytemplate.prt**. If you have write access, move the part file to the Pro/E installation directory, something like

> **\ptc\proe2001\templates**

This is the default directory where Pro/E will look for part templates. If you do not have write access to this directory,

Figure 10 Saved views in mytemplate.prt

leave the part file in your working directory. You can rename the file to remove the version number if you want, so that it appears as as **mytemplate.prt** rather than **mytemplate.prt.1**.

Creating More Mapkeys

Before we leave this new part template, let's create some more mapkeys to go directly to the named views. Select

> *Utilities > Mapkeys > New*

Use the key sequence "vt" and enter a short name like "View Top" and description "Orientation Top View". Now record the mapkey using

> *Record*
> *Saved View List* (a toolbar button) *> TOP*
> *Stop > OK*

Spin the datum planes, and select *Run* to try out the mapkey. Similarly, create and test two more mapkeys to go to the front view ("vf") and the right side view ("vg")[2]. Don't forget to save all the changed/new mapkeys in your *config.pro* file. Open up your *config.pro* to confirm that they are there.

Using the New Part Template

Erase the current part from the session[3]. Select

> *File > New*

Deselect the **Use Default Template** box, enter a name (like *test*), and select *OK*. In the **New File Options** window, scroll to and highlight the template **mytemplate**. This is the copy in the default templates directory. If you weren't able to put your file there, use the Browse button to find it in the working directory. Once the template is located, select *OK*. A copy of the template is now brought into session and given the name you specified.

Setting the Default Part Template

We can tell Pro/E to use our new template as the default by setting an option in *config.pro*.

---

[2] The mapkey "vr", which is more logical for the right view, is usually used for "View Refit"

[3] If you have stored your template part in the templates directory you must close Pro/E and restart it.

Select

Utilities > Options

and enter the Option **template_solidpart**. Set the value for the option by browsing to the template directory (or use the current working directory, wherever you have saved the template file) and selecting the part file **mytemplate.prt** we created above. Select Add/Change and then *Apply* the new setting (remember that this automatically saves the *config* file).

Creating a Mapkey to Start a New Part

Erase the current part from the session. Select

Utilities > Mapkeys > New

Enter the key sequence "cp" ("create part"), name "Create Part", and description "Create a New Part and Rename". Now select

Record
File > New

Choose *Part | Solid | OK*. Leave the default part name as **prt0001**, and the check beside Use Default Template. Now select

File > Rename

This is where we want the mapkey to stop, so select *STOP > OK* in the **Record Mapkey** dialog. In the **Rename** window, enter a new name for the part, like **test**, then select *OK* twice. We have a new mapkey called "cp", so highlight this in the **Mapkeys** dialog and save it. Close the **Mapkeys** dialog window. Open the *config.pro* file to see the listing added for this new mapkey.

To try out the mapkey, erase the new file with *File > Erase > Current*. Type "cp". Several windows will quickly open and close, and you will be left with the dialog box for renaming the part. You can now enter the desired name for a new part, which will contain the default datums, units, and named views set up above to work with the view mapkeys we created earlier. Pretty slick!

We have created a very simple part template here. You can make this as elaborate as you like with parameters, units, materials, layers, datum features and so on - even solid features. For example, if you often create parts whose base feature is a cylindrical solid, consider including this in a special template, perhaps called *cylinder.prt*. You can include as many features as you want in a template and, of course, use any of the provided part templates as a starting point for any new ones.

Adding Mapkeys to Menus and Toolbars

Mapkeys can be added to any of the existing toolbars and pull-down menus. You might like to do this for mapkeys that you do not use frequently, and are likely to forget.

To see how this is done, select the **Commands** tab in the **Customize** window (see Figure 11). At the bottom of the **Categories** list, you will find an entry called **Mapkeys**. Select this. This shows the tree structure of the pull-down menus on the left, and your currently defined mapkeys on the right. In the Mapkeys pane on the right, select the mapkey **Create Part**. The two buttons *Description* and *Modify Selection* are now active. Selecting the former shows you the description you entered when defining the mapkey. Selecting the latter allows you to modify the mapkey button image (currently a "happy face") and display. You might like to get rid of the "happy face", since all mapkeys use this same icon. You can select from a large collection of Pro/E icons, or design your own.

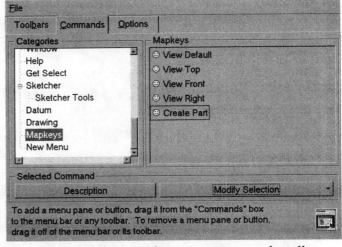

Figure 11 Adding mapkeys to menus and toolbars

Drag the Create Part mapkey in the right pane up to the *File* pull-down menu and drop it in a convenient location, as in Figure 12. Selecting this will launch the mapkey.

Another way to utilize mapkeys is to create shortcut buttons on the toolbars. Again select the Create Part mapkey in the right pane and drag it to a toolbar.

We now have three different ways to launch the Create Part mapkey:

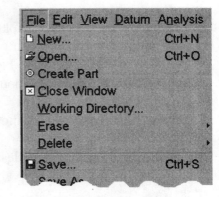

♦ from the keyboard, with "cp"
♦ from the pull-down *File* menu
♦ from the toolbar

Experiment with these to find out which one is most suitable for you. Again, remember the cautionary note about cluttering up your screen.

Figure 12 Create Part mapkey added to a pull-down menu

Introduction to the Project

The assembly project to be completed in this tutorial involves the modeling and assembly of the three-wheeled utility cart shown in Figure 12. The cart contains 26 or so parts, many of which are repeated in the assembly. The total assembly has about 75 parts (mostly bolts!). We will use the techniques introduced in the lessons to model various parts of the cart as exercises at the end of each lesson. We will average about 4 parts per lesson, so you should get lots of practice! In the final lesson, we will assemble the cart, using a number of advanced functions for dealing with assemblies. Try not to "jump the gun" on this assembly task, since the functions to be covered in the last lesson can really speed up your job of putting the cart together.

Figure 13 The assembly project - a three-wheeled utility cart

For your modeling exercises, the parts shown at the end of each lesson will illustrate the critical dimensions. A figure will also be provided to show where the parts fit into the overall assembly. **Not all dimensions are shown on each part - you can use your judgement and creativity to determine the remaining dimensions.** In this regard, please take note of the following:

   ♦   ALL UNITS ARE IN MILLIMETERS! You might set up your default part template with this setting.
   ♦   Dimensions are usually multiples of 5mm. For instance, all the plate material and the wall of the cargo box are 5mm thick. The tubing is 25mm square.
   ♦   All holes and cylinders, unless otherwise dimensioned, are $\varphi 10$. This applies to bolt holes, pins, rods, and so on.
   ♦   All holes, unless otherwise dimensioned, are coaxial with cylindrical surfaces or located on symmetry planes.
   ♦   For some of the trickier parts, in addition to the figures showing the dimensions, there will be some discussion and hints to help you get going.

When we get to the final assembly in Lesson 8, remember that it is an easy matter to modify dimensions of the various parts so that the assembly fits together. Don't be too concerned when you are modeling the parts if you have to guess at one or two dimensions. These can be modified later if the need arises.

When you are creating the parts, try to be aware of the design intent for the part and how it might eventually be placed in the assembly[4]. For example, if the part has one or more planes of symmetry, it is common practice to use the default datum planes for these. In the assembly, the **Align** constraint using these datum planes is an easy way to position the part (usually with another symmetric part).

Although a suggested part name is given, feel free to make up your own part names (although this might cause confusion in Lesson 8!). Remember that Pro/E is fussy about files that get renamed in isolation, or moved to another directory. If a part has been used in an assembly (or sub-assembly) or drawing, make sure the assembly or drawing is in session if you rename or move the part so that the related files can also be updated.

For the entire project, you will require about 10 Megabytes of disk space to store all the parts and assemblies. This does not include parts we will make during the lessons themselves, just the cart project parts. If you are not particularly careful about disk housekeeping (like deleting older version of the part files), you will require more space.

This lesson should have given you enough ideas and ammunition to allow you to customize the interface so that it will be most efficient for the type of work that you do. There are a surprising number of users who are unaware of many options available in *config.pro*. Check them out!

In the next lesson we will look at functions directly involved in model creation. These are for the creation of sweeps.

Questions for Review

1.   What is the name of the file containing your configuration settings?
2.   What is the name of the file containing your screen layout settings?
3.   When, and from where, are your configuration settings loaded? Why is there more than one location?
4.   What happens if your configuration file contains multiple entries for the same option, each with different values?
5.   How can you find out where your start-up directory is?
6.   How can you create/edit/delete configuration settings?
7.   When do configuration settings become active?
8.   Is it possible to have more than one customized screen layout?
9.   How do you place toolbars on the top/left/right edge of the graphics window?
10.   How do you add/delete shortcut buttons on the toolbars?
11.   How many empty toolbars are there?
12.   Where are the toolbar definitions saved?
13.   What is a mapkey?

---

[4] You might like to look ahead to the last lesson to see what assembly constraints are used for each part.

14. Why do you usually want to keep mapkey names short?
15. How is the mapkey name different from the mapkey sequence?
16. How do you create a new mapkey?
17. Are new mapkeys stored automatically? Where?
18. What is the purpose of a part template? Where are they stored and how do you access them?

Exercises

1. Create an assembly template. This should have named datums and named views to match your view selection mapkeys and default units to match your default part template. Make this the default template for assemblies.
2. Set up a mapkey to create a new assembly using the default assembly template.
3. Put the Create Assembly mapkey on the pull-down File menu.

Project Exercises

We're going to start off with some of the easier parts in the cart. These should give you some time to experiment with your configuration file, mapkeys, and part template. The project parts are shown in the figures below. Their location in the cart is also shown for reference in the Figure here:

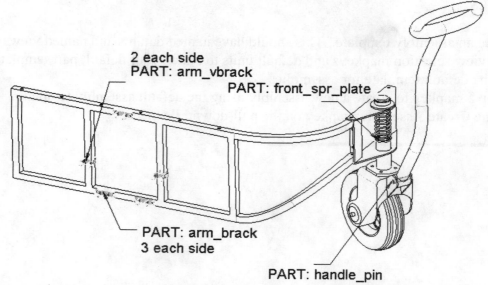

Figure 14 Project parts in Lesson #1

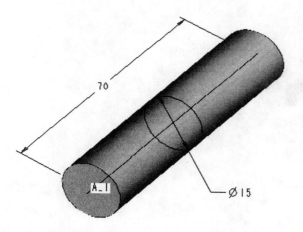

Part: *handle_pin*

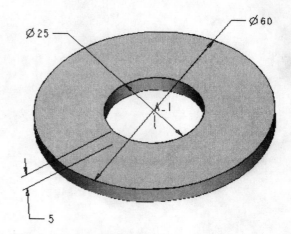

Part: *front_spr_plate*

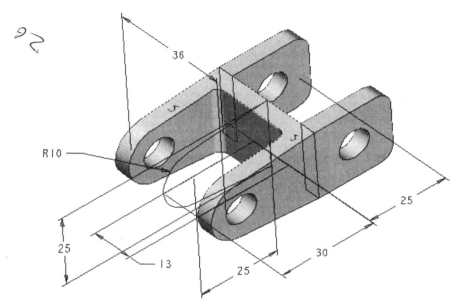

Part: *arm_vbrack*

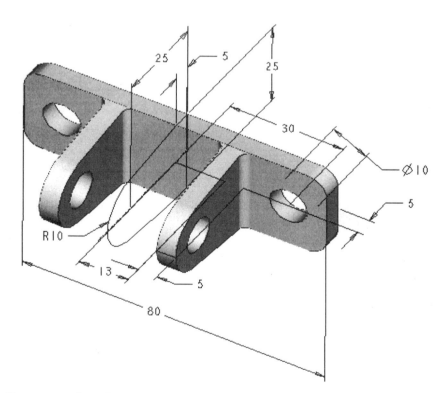

Part: *arm_brack*

NOTES:

Lesson 2

Helical Sweeps and Variable Section Sweeps

Synopsis:

Helical sweeps; pitch graphs; variable section sweeps; picking multiple trajectories; sweep parameter *trajpar*; using a *Datum Graph* to control a swept section

Overview

This lesson will introduce you to the main aspects of advanced sweeps. This includes helical sweeps and several different forms of variable section sweeps. Helical sweeps are quite special in that the trajectory, as you will have guessed, forms a helix. There are some interesting variations on this theme. Variable section sweeps are extremely flexible features, and offer quite a number of options: using multiple trajectories, relations, built-in parameters and functions (*trajpar* and *evalgraph*). We will also see how to create and use a *Graph* feature. There are numerous other options available.

The primary difficulty in modeling with variable section sweeps is identifying how to set up the references so that the sweep has the geometry you want. After some experience with them and more familiarity with the options, the job will get easier.

Helical Sweeps

A common request of students in a mechanical design course is "How can I get Pro/E to make a spring?". The answer is to use a helical sweep. This is a relatively straight forward feature that has the basic elements shown in Figure 1. These are the profile and axis, which together define a revolved surface, and a section which moves up and around the surface along a helical path.

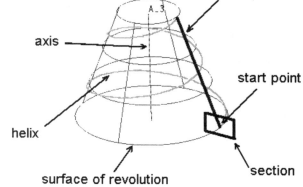

The profile is an open curve created on a sketching plane using Sketcher. The profile **Figure 1** Basic elements of helical sweep

sketch also includes the axis of the helix. Revolving the profile curve around the axis 360° produces a surface of revolution that defines the envelope of the helical trajectory of the feature. The pitch of the helix is the distance traveled along the axis in one complete revolution of the helix around the axis. The number of turns of the helix is determined by the pitch and the height of the profile along the axis of the helix. In Figure 1, this worked out to exactly two complete turns. The section is a closed curve, also created using Sketcher, with the sketching plane located at the start point of the profile. Note that the surface of revolution and helix itself do not appear in the model as a surface or curve.

There are three main attributes that define the geometry:

> ▸   Pitch: constant vs variable
> ▸   Section: orientation relative to the helix (***Thru Axis*** or ***Norm to Traj***)
> ▸   Direction: right hand or left hand helix

Some examples of helical sweeps are shown in Figure 2. Although these are all protrusions, you can also use helical sweeps to create cuts, like threads on a bolt or power screw.

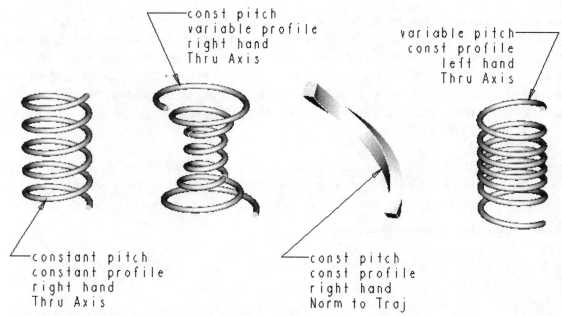

Figure 2 Some examples of protrusions using helical sweeps

In this lesson, we will create two helical sweeps. The first is a simple one, using a constant radius profile and constant pitch, to illustrate the general procedure (similar to the sweep on the far left in Figure 2). The second will be a bit more complicated, using a multi-segment profile and variable pitch (a combination of the 2ⁿᵈ and 4ᵗʰ sweeps in Figure 2).

Constant Profile/Constant Pitch

Use the start part from the previous lesson to create a part called **hsweep1**. Then,

> *Feature > Create > Solid > Protrusion*
> *Advanced | Solid | Done*
> *Helical Swp | Done*
> *Constant | Thru Axis | Right Handed | Done*

The last commands will yield a constant pitch right-handed helix. The **Thru Axis** attribute determines the orientation of the section sketch relative to the helix. **Thru Axis** means that the plane containing the section to be swept will always pass through the axis of the helix as the section is swept along the helical trajectory. The section, therefore, is not normal to the trajectory. This means that the sketching plane for the section is oriented the same as the sketch plane for the profile. The other option (**Norm to Traj**) will result in the section being defined and maintained normal to the helix as it is swept along the trajectory. In this case, the section sketching plane and profile sketching plane will be different. We will use the **Norm to Traj** option in the next exercise. Note that the difference between the resulting features will be more noticeable as the pitch to helix diameter ratio increases, as seen in the 3rd sweep of Figure 2.

We now create the sketch for the profile. Use the **FRONT** datum as the sketching plane, and the **TOP** datum as the top reference. Create the sketch shown in Figure 3. Note the direction arrow coming from the start point on the lower vertex of the sketch. Also, don't forget the axis (a centerline aligned with the SIDE datum).

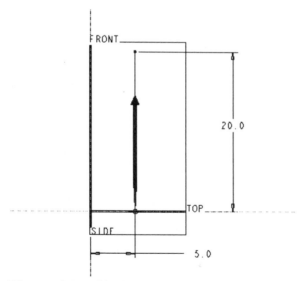

Figure 3 Profile for simple helical sweep

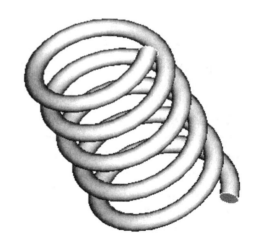

Figure 4 Finished constant pitch helical sweep

When the sketch is complete, select **Done**. Enter a pitch of **4**.

Crosshairs will appear at the start point of the trajectory. Since protrusions come towards you out of the screen, the view reorients so that you are actually looking at the back (red side) of the FRONT datum.

Create a circular sketch centered on the crosshairs having a diameter of **1.5**. Select **Done** in Sketcher, and **Preview** the feature. The feature should look like Figure 4. How many turns is the helix? Note that this is the height of the profile (20mm) divided by the pitch (4mm) - exactly 5 in this case. Save the part.

If you want to finish this spring off, you can cut the ends normal to the spring axis ("squared ends") as in a compression spring, or add hooks (perhaps using a variable section sweep covered later) for a tension spring. Investigate what happens when you try to *Feature > Modify* in order to change the spring dimensions and parameters. You might try to add relation(s) to automatically compute the pitch given the number of coils and the profile height. It wouldn't take much to set up some relations for the design of a helical coil spring. We will discuss a module of Pro/E called Pro/PROGRAM a bit later that would assist with this.

Now we'll create something a bit more complicated...

Variable Profile/Variable Pitch

Start a new part called **hsweep2**. Select

> *Feature > Create > Solid > Protrusion*
> *Advanced | Solid | Done*
> *Helical Swp | Done*
> *Variable | Norm to Traj | Right Handed | Done*

This will produce a variable pitch sweep whose section will be always normal to the helix. For the profile, use FRONT as the sketching plane, and TOP as the top reference. Sketch the profile shown in Figure 5. Using *Norm to Traj* requires that the profile be C1 continuous (all edges tangent). Since we are using variable pitch, we will create a profile with a number of vertices. The pitch will be defined at several of these vertices. The minimum number of vertices is two, with (possibly) different pitch values at each end of the profile. Our sketch contains 6 vertices, and we will define the pitch at 4 of these locations.

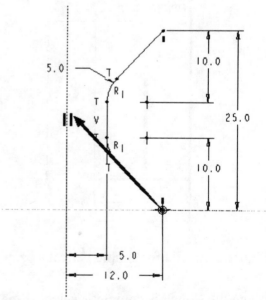

Figure 5 Profile for variable pitch helix (note continuity at corners)

When the profile sketch is complete (don't forget the centerline!), you will be asked for the pitch values at the start and end of the profile. Enter **5.0** for both of these.

A new window containing the Pitch Graph opens up, showing a horizontal line with values of 5.0 at each end. This is the graph of the pitch values along the profile (the horizontal axis represents the position along the axis of the helix). We want to add a couple of new points to the pitch graph. We can pick any of the four interior vertices on the profile at either end of the rounded corners. Select

Define > Add Point

and pick on one of the inner vertices on the profile
sketch (10 from the end). Enter a value of 2 for the
pitch at this point. Pick the other inner point and enter
a pitch value of **2** there as well. As you define pitch
values at key points along the profile, the Pitch Graph
will change shape. When these are entered, select
Done in GRAPH menu.

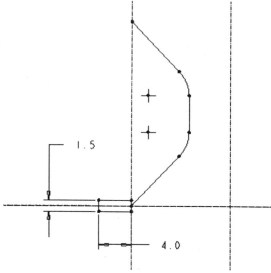

Now the screen will reorient and we can sketch the
section. If your datum planes are displayed, notice
that your orientation is a bit "off". Recall that our
section is going to be normal to the helix trajectory.
Therefore our sketch plane is at a slight angle to the
default planes. Create a small rectangle whose
vertical right edge is on the vertical crosshair as
shown in Figure 6.

Figure 6 Section for the helical sweep

Select *Done* in Sketcher and *Preview* the feature. It should look like Figure 7.

Figure 7 Variable pitch sweep

Helical Sweep Summary

We have seen two variations of the helical sweep. The main categories involve the orientation of
the section (*Thru Axis* or *NormToTraj*). In addition, for any helical sweep, we can define a
constant or variable pitch, and an arbitrarily shaped profile. For *NormToTraj* sweeps, the profile
must be composed of all tangent edges. Finally, for any helical sweep the tangent to the profile
can never be normal to the axis - the section must always advance along the axis as it is swept.

Variable Section Sweeps

For variable section sweeps, the idea is basically the same is regular sweeps: specify a trajectory and section. The main differences are that the section can change shape along the trajectory, and the orientation of the section can be determined along the trajectory in a number of ways. The trajectory can be open or closed; the section must always be closed. Variable section sweeps are one of the more complicated of the Pro/E solid creation features. The main obstacle to using them is, perhaps, in visualizing how to apply the many options in order to create your desired geometry. Remember that sweeps can be used to create solids or cuts.

In the following we will create several different parts using some of the different variations possible. The intent here is for breadth of coverage rather than extreme depth, and for you to understand the basic sweep forms and definitions of terms. Definitions of new terms will be provided when they are first used in the exercises. We will see how to create simple sweeps with a constant and variable cross section, how to use multiple sweep trajectories as references, how to modify the section using relations, and how to use a new feature (a *Datum Graph*) to provide data to control the section shape.

Pivot Dir Sweep

Bring up a start part and call it **vsweep1**. Create a 30 X 30 X 5 thick solid protrusion as shown in Figure 8.

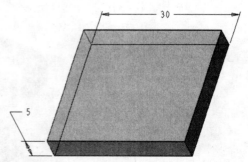

We are going to create the sweeps shown in Figure 9. Both sweeps use the same trajectory shape (a circular arc) and the same section shape (a 5 unit square). However, note the different orientations of the surfaces at the end of each sweep. These surfaces have been "pivoted" around a specific vector direction called the *pivot direction*. This is most obvious in the sweep on the left in the figure.

Figure 8 Base feature for *Pivot Dir* sweep

With *Pivot Dir* sweeps, we must supply two elements: the sweep trajectory and a reference to define a pivot direction. The meaning of the pivot direction is as follows:

> For a *Pivot Dir* sweep, the swept section will always appear normal to the trajectory when viewed along the pivot direction.

You can think of this as the section rotating ("pivoting") around the pivot direction in order to stay perpendicular to the trajectory when viewed in the pivot direction. The pivot direction can be defined by one of the following:

- selecting a plane - the pivot direction is normal to this plane (this is how the pivot direction was specified in Figure 9)
- selecting an edge or curve - the pivot direction is along the edge, or tangent to the curve at the nearest datum point

▶   selecting a coordinate system - the pivot direction is in a specified coordinate direction

In the left sweep of Figure 9, the pivot direction (labeled #1) is perpendicular to the top face of the block. If you look straight down on the block, the section is perpendicular to the circular arc trajectory. In the right sweep of Figure 9, the pivot direction is perpendicular to the right face of the block. If you look in this direction (normal to the right face), the trajectory appears ("projects") as a simple horizontal line. The section appears perpendicular (vertical) to this projection of the trajectory. Both these trajectories are planar, but general 3D curves are allowed (as long as the section does not become tangent to the trajectory!).

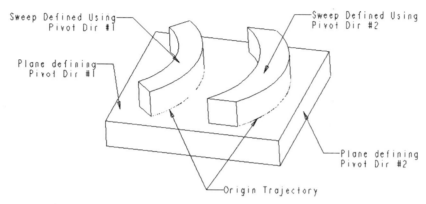

Figure 9 Location of sweep origin trajectories and *Pivot Dir* reference planes

Create a datum curve on the top of the block, starting with the toolbar icon:

Datum Curve > Sketch | Done

Use the top of the block as sketching plane, and the right face as the RIGHT sketching reference. Sketch the arc shown in Figure 10 making sure that only one horizontal dimension connects this sketch to the block. Create a copy of this using *Copy > Same Refs*, changing the 7 dimension to 22. The second datum curve is shown in Figure 11.

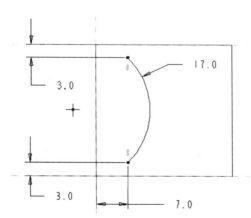

Figure 10 Datum curve for first sweep

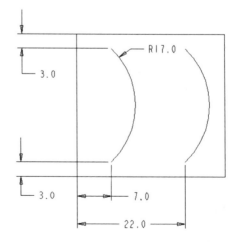

Figure 11 Copied datum curve for second sweep

Now we can get on with creating the first sweep (on the left in Figure 9).

> *Create > Solid > Protrusion > Advanced | Solid | Done*
> *Var Sec Swp | Done*
> *Pivot Dir | Done*

Check the message window and the attributes window on the right. Pro/E is asking us to define an orientation reference to define the pivot direction.

For our first sweep, make sure *Plane* is highlighted and pick the top surface of the block as the plane defining the pivot direction. The direction arrow is *Okay*.

You now must choose the *Origin* trajectory. This is the main trajectory in the feature and is required by all variable section sweeps. It operates the same as the trajectory in a simple sweep, and defines the basic nature of the sweep. The origin trajectory can be specified using any edges or curves (with some restrictions discussed below). Note that it is not necessary that a vertex of the section move along the origin trajectory - the section can be offset.

In the **VAR SEC SWP** menu, select

> *Select Traj > One By One*

Pick on the left datum curve and then middle click. A start point arrow will appear on one end of the curve. This is where we will specify the initial section for the sweep. If the start point is not at the front of the part, select *Start Point > Next* to use a different start point, and then *Accept* when the desired vertex is identified.

In the **CHAIN** menu, select *Done*. We can now specify other trajectories to define the sweep. We don't need to do that now and will leave it to some later exercises, so in **VAR SEC SWP**, select *Done*. The model rotates and we are looking at the crosshairs at the start of the sweep. For a solid protrusion, the sweep will come towards you out of the screen. Sometimes the orientation of the model is a bit strange when you are first shown the section sketching plane and the crosshair. Spin the model to orient yourself and observe where the sketching plane is relative to the origin trajectory. We want to sketch a square with a vertex on the origin of the crosshair.

Note the orientation of the sketching plane relative to the top surface of the block (pivot plane). Recall that the pivot direction is normal to the top surface, so looking straight down on the block we should see the crosshairs (or at least one of them - the other is a point when viewed from here) perpendicular to the trajectory.

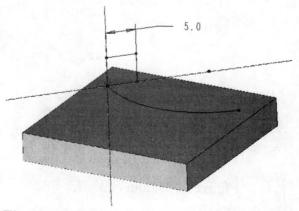

Create the sketch (a 5 unit square) shown in Figure 12 (some of the constraints are not displayed in the figure). If you are using Intent Manager, then the crosshairs are automatically designated as sketch

Figure 12 Section for first *Pivot Dir* sweep

references. Otherwise, you can align the sketch to these lines.

With a completed sketch, select **Done** in the Sketcher menu and accept the feature.

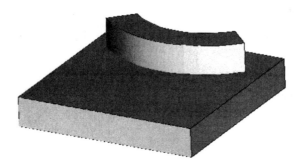

Figure 13 First sweep completed

We will create another sweep using the other datum curve, the same section shape, and a different pivot direction.

>   **Feature > Create > Solid > Protrusion**
>   **Advanced | Solid | Done**
>   **Var Sec Swp | Done**
>   **Pivot Dir | Done**

This time, use the right face of the base rectangular block to define the pivot direction. Choose the second datum curve as the origin trajectory using **Select Traj > One By One**. Again, we only need the origin trajectory for this feature; no other trajectories are necessary. Create the same 5 unit square section. The sketching plane and crosshairs are shown in Figure 14. Note the orientation of the sketch relative to the end face of the block that defines the pivot direction.

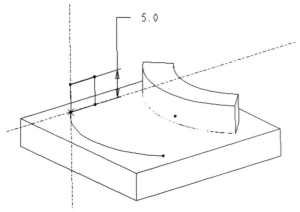

Figure 14 Section for second *Pivot Dir* sweep

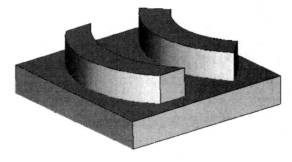

Figure 15 Second sweep completed

When you are finished with Sketcher, select **Done > Preview**. The geometry is shown in Figure 15. Note the difference in the appearance at the ends of the sweeps. Save the part.

NrmToOriginTraj Sweeps

In this exercise we will create a number of sweeps using the *NrmToOriginTraj* option. For these, the swept section stays perpendicular to the origin trajectory along its entire length. The section can still rotate around the origin trajectory, so we need to supply another reference to determine the rotation. This is called the "horizontal reference trajectory" and can be an edge or datum curve.

Also for this part, we will see how the section can be made variable along the sweep. The section shape will change automatically in order to maintain some assigned dimensions or alignments.

Start a new part **vsweep2**. For the base feature, make a ***Both Sides*** extruded protrusion off the SIDE datum using the sketch shown in Figure 16. The feature depth is 80.

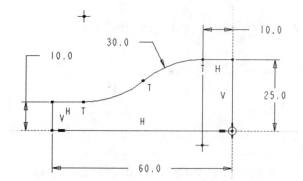

Figure 16 Sketch for base feature for *NormToOriginTraj* sweep

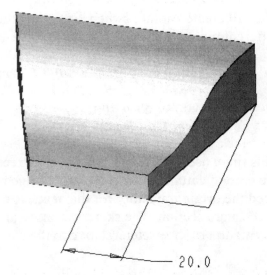

Create a cut on one end of the base feature using the dimension shown in Figure 17. Create a mirror copy of this cut to the other end of the block.

Figure 17 Creating cuts on end of base feature

Now we will create a datum curve to act as an origin trajectory by projecting the top right S-shaped edge onto the SIDE datum.

> ***Datum Curve***
> ***Projected | Done***
> ***Select | Done***
> ***Tangnt Chain***

Pick on the top right S-shaped edge. Select ***Done*** in the **CHAIN** menu. Then, with ***Datum Plane*** highlighted in the **PROJCRVREFS** menu select the SIDE datum plane. In the **PROJ TYPE** menu, select ***Norm To Surf | Done > OK***. The datum curve should appear as shown in Figure 18.

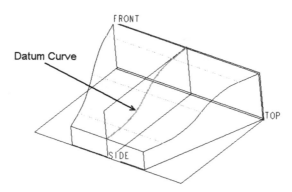

Figure 18 Datum curve for origin trajectory

Create a sweep along this datum curve (see the final shape in Figure 20)

> ***Feature > Create > Solid > Protrusion***
> ***Advanced | Solid | Done***
> ***Var Sec Swp | Done***
> ***NrmToOriginTraj | Done***
> ***Select Traj > Curve Chain***

Pick on a length of the datum curve, then in the **CHAIN OPTS** menu *Select All*. The datum
curve highlights and the start arrow appears. If necessary, change the start point to the front of
the block using *Start Point > Next | Accept*. Then select *Done*.

Now we specify another trajectory that tells Pro/E how to orient the section as it moves along the
origin trajectory, that is, specify its rotation around the trajectory. This is the "section horizontal
trajectory". In this case, we don't want the section to rotate, but we need to specify the reference
anyway in order to orient our sketch.

In the **VAR SEC SWP** menu, choose *Select Traj > Tangnt Chain* and pick the top left S-shaped
edge, then *Done*. Why this one instead of the top right edge? A hint appears below!

We will specify the other top S-shaped edge as a third trajectory to act as a dimensioning
reference for the section. In the **VAR SEC SWP** menu, choose *Select Traj > Tangnt Chain* and
pick the top right S-shaped edge, then *Done*.

Back in the **VAR SEC SWP** menu, select *Done*.

The model reorients so that we are looking at the crosshairs. You should be looking at the back
of the block (remember that the sweep will come towards you) with the crosshair going through
the horizontal reference trajectory which is on the right of your screen. If the orientation is not
clear to you, give the model a quick spin to see what you are looking at. Go back to the sketch
with *View > Sketch View* (or pick the toolbar icon to do this).

Create a symmetrical sketch with dimensions as shown in Figure 19 (note that this is not the
sketch view). The widest vertices in the sketch are dimensioned to the two reference trajectories.

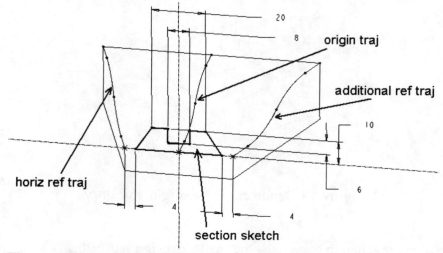

Figure 19 Section sketch for first *NrmToOriginTraj* sweep

Leave Sketcher and accept the feature. The sweep should look like the figure below. Observe the effect of (a) dimensioning the sweep to the left and right edge trajectories, and (b) using symmetry around the vertical crosshair on the origin trajectory.

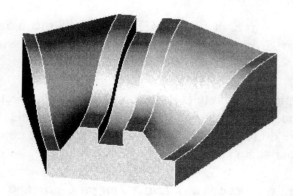

Figure 20 Completed sweep

Let's do a couple more sweeps to demonstrate some more ways to get variations in the section. We will create a couple of *NrmToOriginTraj* sweeps along the end faces of this base feature. For the first one, select the top right edge as the origin trajectory, and the lower right edge as the horizontal reference trajectory. Sketch a small triangular section with the apex on the origin trajectory and a height of 8. See Figure 21. The resulting sweep is shown in Figure 22. Note that the sweep maintains a constant angle to the side face. Furthermore, the section shape is constant along the sweep.

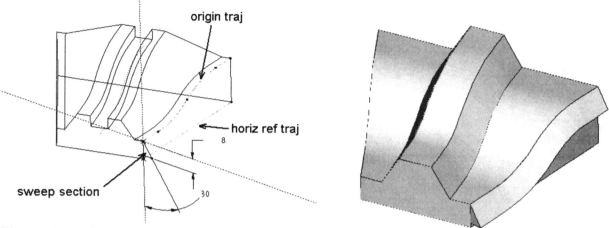

Figure 21 Trajectories and section for sweep

Figure 22 *NormToOriginTraj* sweep

Now ***Redefine*** the section so that the bottom of the triangular sketch is aligned with the horizontal reference trajectory (see Figure 23), not the lower surface of the base. In the section sketch, a small cross on the crosshair shows this alignment point.

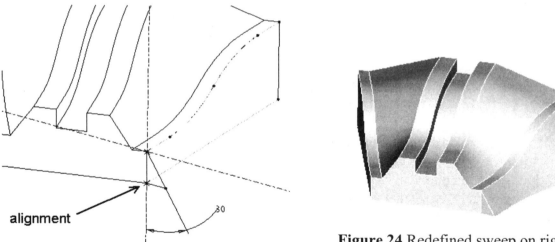

Figure 24 Redefined sweep on right face

Figure 23 Redefining the section sketch

Accept this redefined sketch and feature. The part now looks like Figure 24. The alignment is maintained as the section is swept. The angle of the sketch is maintained, and the width across the bottom grows to maintain the alignment.

Let's see what happens if we exchange the two trajectories. Create another *NrmToOrginTraj* sweep on the left face of the block. This time, use the bottom edge as the origin trajectory and the S-shaped edge as the horizontal reference trajectory (Figure 25). The sketch must be closed.

Accept this feature. Go to the top view of
the model (using the named views defined
in the start part). A subtle difference exists
between the sweeps on the left and right
ends of the block.

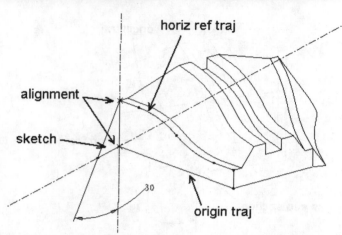

Figure 25 Another *NrmToOriginTraj* sweep

Redefine the sketch for the left-end sweep.
Explicitly dimension the horizontal width
at the base of the triangle (this should make
the angle dimension unnecessary). The
width of the triangle at the base is **5**. The
resulting geometry is shown in Figure 26.
Note that the new lower left edge is
straight. The angle of the section has
automatically adjusted to follow the S-shaped edge.

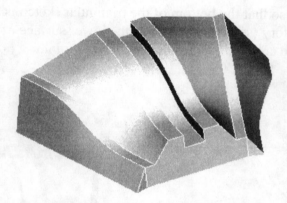

Figure 26 Final sweep on left face

A couple of things you have to watch out for when creating variable section sweeps are to use a
dimensioning scheme and values that will do the job that you want, and that will work for the
entire length of the sweep. This means you have to be careful about setting up dimensions to
other features of the part. For example, if you dimension a sketched entity to a part entity that
disappears half way along the sweep, you can expect trouble. Try to keep your sweep section
dimensions "local", ie within the sketch itself, and reference only the trajectories and section
crosshair.

As a final, and important note, remember that the *NrmToOriginTraj* trajectory must be C1
continuous (all tangent edges). There cannot be any "kinks" in the trajectory where Pro/E will
have trouble deciding on what the "normal" direction is. Also, you can expect trouble if the
section is large and straddles or is inside the curve of a trajectory with tight corners, where you
run the risk of the sweep intersecting itself.

ing Additional Trajectories

ther example of including additional trajectories in the sweep definition. These "extra" trajectories can be used to control/define the cross section shape of the sweep along the main (origin) trajectory.

Start a new part called **vsweep3**. Create three datum curves as shown in the figure at the right. The first curve is on the intersection of the SIDE and TOP datums and is 100 units long. You can sketch this using appropriate datums as sketching and reference planes. Note that datum curve #2 has equal length line segments at each end, with a circular arc in between. Datum curve #3 is a simple arc.

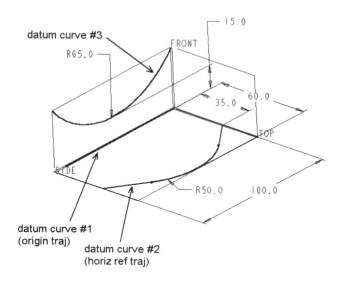

Figure 27 Datum curves

We'll create a sweep using these three curves to define how the swept section changes shape along the sweep. Select

> *Feature > Create > Solid > Protrusion*
> *Advanced | Solid | Done*
> *Var Sec Swp | Done*
> *NrmToOriginTraj | Done*
> *Select Traj > One by One*

and pick on datum curve #1 to act as the origin trajectory. Middle click. Make sure the start point is on the FRONT datum plane. Select **Done** in the **CHAIN** directory. For the horizontal reference vector, use **Select Traj > Curve Chain** and pick on datum #2, then **Select All > Done**.

At this point, we have usually skipped defining additional trajectories. This time, use **Select Traj > One By One** and pick on datum curve #3, then **Done** in **CHAIN** menu, **Done** in the **VAR SEC SWP** menu. We are now looking at the crosshair (reorient the view to figure out where you are). Create the sketch shown in Figure 28, aligning the three vertices of the sketch to the ends of the trajectories. Only one dimension is required in the sketch for the arc. Select **Done** in Sketcher, and accept the feature - see Figure 29.

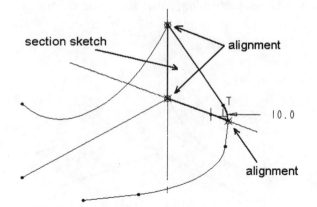

Figure 28 Sketch of section

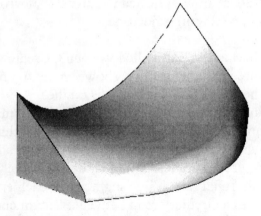

Figure 29 Completed sweep using three trajectories defined by datum curves

Looks sort of like Batman's hat! Well, maybe not...!

Once the origin trajectory and horizontal reference trajectory are determined, you can add as many additional trajectories as you want to be used in determining the section shape. You can expect that these are not totally arbitrary, since the resulting shape must still be a valid solid. For example, you cannot have a set of trajectories that would require the surfaces of the feature to pass through each other. There may also be geometries where, for example, the position or length of the horizontal reference trajectory do not allow the determination of the section orientation on the origin trajectory. Try redefining datum curve #3 in the latest part so that it extends only from the FRONT datum to the bottom of the arc.

Variable Sections using *trajpar*

In this feature, we will use relations to drive the section geometry using a built-in parameter *trajpar*. This parameter is available for all variable section sweeps. Its value is 0 at the start point and varies from 0 to 1 along the origin trajectory (regardless of how many segments it has). The feature we are going to make is shown in Figure 31. This is one single solid feature!

Start a new part called **vsweep4**. Create a single datum curve similar to datum #1 of the previous exercise (100 units long on the intersection of SIDE and TOP datums). This will be the origin trajectory

> *Feature > Create > Solid > Protrusion*
> *Advanced | Solid | Done*
> *Var Sec Swp | Done*
> *Pivot Dir | Done*

and select the TOP datum to define the pivot direction. Select the datum curve as the sweep trajectory (remember that for a *Pivot Dir* sweep, we do not need a horizontal reference trajectory). Make sure the start point is on the FRONT datum.

Sketch and dimension the section shown in Figure 30. Note the symmetry constraints on the top vertices. To get these, create a centerline on the vertical crosshair and use the symmetry option with the constraint Sketcher toolbar icon. Make sure your sketch uses this dimensioning and constraint scheme. The dimension values are shown to the right of the figure.

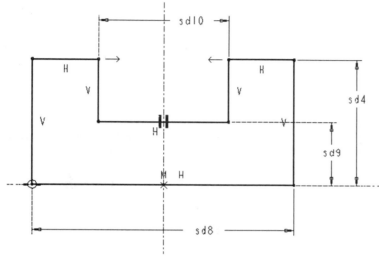

Dim	Value
sd4	30
sd8	60
sd9	15
sd10	30

NOTE: Your symbolic dimension names may be slightly different from those shown in the figure. Make a note of your symbolic names, as we will use these in some sketcher relations.

Figure 30 Section for sweep showing symbolic dimensions to use with *trajpar*

While still in Sketcher, select (in the pull-down menu)

> ### *Sketch > Relations > Add*

Enter the following relations (be sure to use your own symbolic names on the left side of the equal signs):

```
/* width of sketch
sd8 = 60 + 60*trajpar
/* height of sketch
sd4 = 30 - 20*trajpar
/* width of slot
sd10 = 55 - 25*cos(trajpar*180)
/* height of slot
sd9 = 10 + 5*cos(trajpar*180)
```

These will make the block grow wider and shorter along the trajectory, as well as modifying the width and depth of the slot. When these are entered, select *Done* in Sketcher, and accept the feature. The final shape is shown in Figure 31.

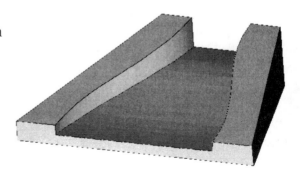

Figure 31 Completed sweep using *trajpar*

Using a *Graph* Feature to Control Section Dimensions

In the previous exercise we used explicit relations involving *trajpar* to control the section dimensions. This works well as long as the expressions don't get too complicated. For complex variations in a dimension along a sweep, it may be useful to use a *Graph* feature. In this exercise, we will use a *Datum Graph* to define a dimension on a cam to produce a desired variable offset of the follower as the cam rotates.

Start a new part called **vsweep5**. Create a *One Sided* blind protrusion on the TOP datum plane. Put a diameter 30 coaxial hole in the center, as shown in Figure 32.

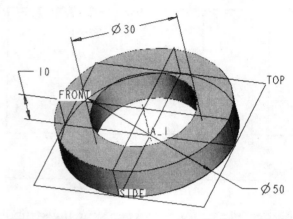

Figure 32 Base feature and hole for cam

Now select (in the pull-down menu)

Insert > Datum > Graph

Enter a name "camgraph" for the new feature. A new Sketcher window opens where we will create the graph. First create a coordinate system to identify the origin of the graph.

Sketch > Coord Sys

and place a Csys towards the lower left corner. Create horizontal and vertical centerlines through the origin of the coordinate system. Then sketch and dimension the following curve (notice the left and right ends are horizontally aligned):

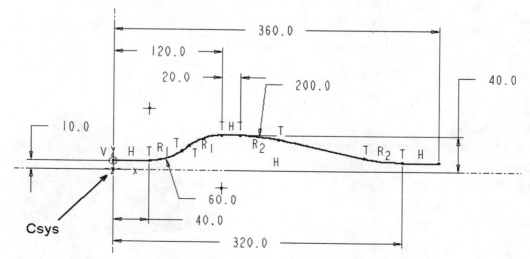

Figure 33 *Datum graph* to define cam follower displacement

In this graph, the horizontal scale (0 - 360) corresponds to the angular rotation of the cam. The vertical distance will be used to define the outer surface of the cam, resulting in a cam follower motion that will dwell-rise-dwell-return-dwell[1].

Select *Done* in the graph window. Open the model tree to see the new graph feature.

Now we create the sweep using the graph as follows

> ***Feature > Create > Solid > Protrusion***
> ***Advanced | Solid | Done***
> ***Var Sec Swp | Done***
> ***Pivot Dir | Done***

and select the TOP datum plane as the pivot direction reference. For the origin trajectory,

> ***Select Traj > Tangent Chain***

and click on the bottom outer edge of the disk. *Done*. No other trajectories are necessary.

Now create a simple sketch which is a rectangle on the outside of the disk, aligned on one edge to the cross hairs, with a height of **8**. See the dimensioning scheme in Figure 34. The width of the rectangle (sd4 in the figure) is controlled by the graph feature using a relation with a call to the built-in function *evalgraph* as follows:

```
/* use evalgraph to determine dimension
sd4 = evalgraph("camgraph",trajpar*360)
```

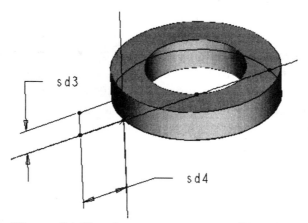

Figure 34 Sketch to create cam profile using dimension *sd4*

---

[1] This profile is not a particularly good one for a high performance cam due to the "jerk" (infinite derivative of acceleration) that occurs at the end of each arc segment. It will also work only for a knife-edge follower. However, it will illustrate the construction method.

The two arguments in the call to *evalgraph* are the graph name, and the horizontal position in the graph according to the graph scale. Note that since *trajpar* goes from 0 to 1, we have to scale up the second argument in the *evalgraph* call so that the graph is evaluated at the correct position. It is possible to apply scaling parameters to both the horizontal and vertical dimensions in the graph. You could, for example, normalize the graph so that the range in both horizontal and vertical directions was 1. Then, in the above relation you could use *trajpar* directly, and could multiply on the right hand side by a scaling factor equal to the maximum real offset in units that match the part. If you made a library of graphs this way, you would have an easy way to create similar cams of arbitrary size.

Select **Done** in sketcher and accept the feature. The final cam shape with the variable section sweep is shown in Figure 35.

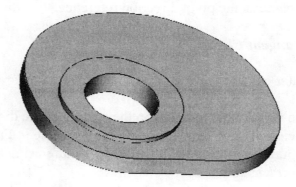

Figure 35 Completed cam

Summary of Variable Section Sweeps

Variable section sweeps require, at a minimum, three elements: an origin trajectory, a section shape, and a way to determine the orientation of the section along the trajectory. We looked at two ways of specifying the orientation: using a pivot direction, and using a horizontal reference trajectory. In addition, you can use additional trajectories to help define the variation of the section as it is swept. Other ways to do this involve sketcher relations, the trajectory parameter *trajpar*, and datum graphs.

This lesson has introduced you to the main aspects of using advanced sweeps. This included helical sweeps and several different forms of variable section sweeps. The flexibility of variable section sweeps was illustrated using multiple trajectories, relations, *trajpar*, and *evalgraph* with a graph feature. There are numerous other options available. We did not touch on *NrmToTraj* sweeps at all. You might like to experiment with these other options on your own.

In the next lesson we will look at the creation of advanced rounds, round sets, and round transitions, as well as a number of features available in the **Tweak** menu: drafts, ribs, lips, and ears.

Questions for Review

1.   What are the essential elements in a helical sweep?
2.   What options are available to define the orientation of the section in helical sweeps?
3.   What are the restrictions on the section for a helical sweep?
4.   What are the restrictions on the profile for the two major kinds of helical sweeps?
5.   What is the pitch graph and where is it used?
6.   Can you create a helix that passes through or along the axis (eg a spring that is right handed at one end but crosses over through the middle and is left handed at the other)?
7.   What happens if the pitch is small enough that the sections of a helical sweep overlap?
8.   How can the pivot direction be defined?
9.   Explain the meaning and interpretation of the pivot direction.
10.   In the tutorial part **vsweep1**, if you use the front or back vertical face of the block to define the pivot direction, the feature will fail. Why?
11.   What is the minimum number of trajectories that are required for (a) a *Pivot Dir* sweep, and (b) a *NrmToOriginTraj* sweep?
12.   What is the maximum number of trajectories that can be used with (a) a *Pivot Dir* sweep, and (b) a *NrmToOriginTraj* sweep?
13.   What do you suppose will happen if any trajectories intersect?
14.   How do you change the location of the trajectory start point?
15.   What is required to define the orientation of the section for (a) a *Pivot Dir* sweep, and (b) a *NrmToOriginTraj* sweep?
16.   What happens if the section plane at some place along a *NrmToOriginTraj* does not intersect the horizontal reference trajectory?
17.   How and where does a datum graph appear in the model tree?
18.   How is the shape of a datum graph interrogated in a relation (ie how is the graph evaluated?)
19.   Is it necessary to draw a datum graph at true scale in either, neither, or both horizontal and vertical directions? Explain.

Project Exercises

Here are some parts for the project. All involve sweeps of various kinds.

The spring that goes on the front wheel assembly is a simple helical sweep. The ends have been finished off with a variable angle revolved protrusion and a cut perpendicular to the spring axis. We need flat surfaces on each end of the spring to use in *Mate* constraints in the wheel assembly.

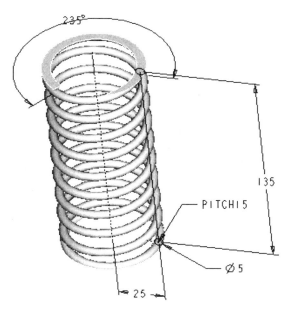

PART: *front_spring*

The two arms that support the side wheel mounting plates are shown below. Make the upper arm first using a simple sweep. Then do a *Save As* to create the part file for the lower arm. You only need to *Modify* two dimensions to create the lower arm geometry. Using techniques we will discuss in Lesson 4, you could actually create both these, and many variations, from the same part file using something called a family table.

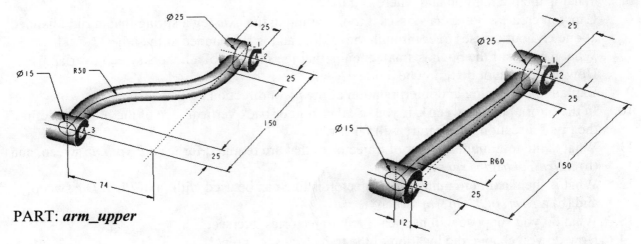

PART: *arm_upper*

PART: *arm_lower*

The main square tubing frame members are based on parts created for the right side of the cart. The left side will be created in Lesson 8, using functions in assembly mode (*Merge* and *Mirror*). First, create a default CSYS at the origin of the datum planes and dimension a set of four datum points according to the figure below. The datum point locations are indicated in the table on the following page.

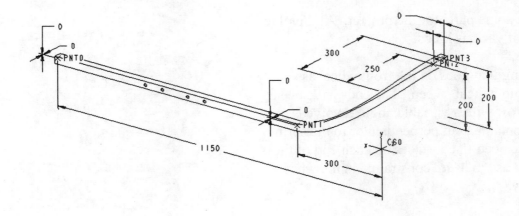

Logitech
MIN MM33´

Point	PNT0	PNT1	PNT2	PNT3
X	1150	300	0	0
Y	0	0	200	200
Z	0	0	250	300

with Dim

Create a coordinate system
Datum point
create pnts off a system.
cartesian

Create the datum curve for the lower tube using the datum points. Be careful to arrange the
middle section of the curve to be tangent to the two end sections. HINT: start by making three
separate curves. Project this datum curve onto a **Make Datum** at a height of 350 above the XZ
plane as indicated below.

without
Curve
Through pnts, CARTESIAN
Single pnt

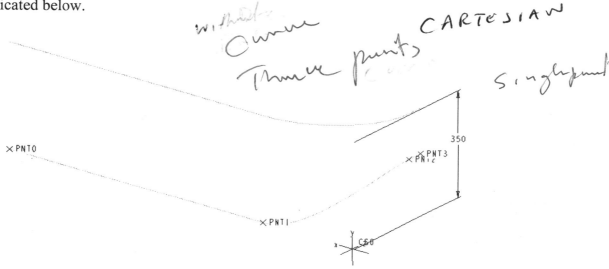

These two datum curves will form the spines or trajectories of the two tubes.

Create the lower tube using a **NormToOrigin** trajectory. The lower datum curve is the origin
trajectory. The upper datum curve is a horizontal reference for the sketch. The section is 25mm
square, centered on the origin trajectory, with a wall thickness of 2.5mm. The horizontal holes in
the tube are created with a pattern table, which is discussed in a later lesson.

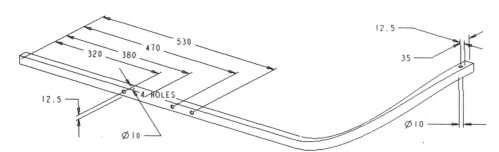

PART: *fram_low_rgt*

Finally, do a **Save A Copy** of the lower tube part to create a part file for the upper frame tube. In this new file, delete the sweep. Use the upper datum curve to create a simple sweep. The vertical holes in the tube are a simple pattern, starting at the left. You can create the horizontal holes for the bracket mount with a pattern table.

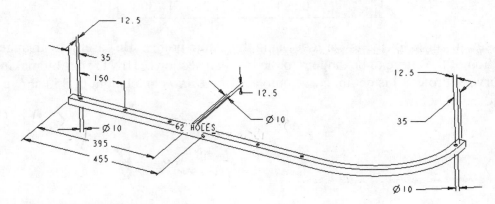

PART: *fram_upp_rgt*

Lesson 3

Advanced Rounds and Tweaks

Synopsis

Simple and advanced rounds (variable radius, thru curve, full round, round sets, round transitions); the Round Tutor; tweaks (drafts, ribs, lips, and ears)

Overview

This lesson will introduce you to a number of "minor" features in Pro/E. The first half will be devoted to the subject of rounds. Rounds are often treated as cosmetic features and are usually added to the model towards the end of the regeneration sequence. Do not confuse "cosmetic" or the "simple" designation for rounds with unnecessary and/or easy. We will see that the round functionality is actually quite powerful, and can create very intricate geometry. In order to do that, the round command set is quite broad and deep. We will not be able to cover all variations here, but should be able to show most of the commands for creating variations of simple rounds, and how to set up and use advanced rounds with round sets and transitions. In the second half of the lesson, we will create a simple part using several of the *Tweak* commands. The most important of these is for the creation of draft surfaces on parts destined for injection molding. Drafts can also become quite complicated so we will restrict our study to the basic principles. Hopefully, at the end of this you will better understand the terminology and be able to expand your knowledge more easily by referring to the on-line documentation.

Rounds

Rounds (or fillets) are usually among the last features added to a model. Most times they are purely cosmetic, but can sometimes be crucial to the geometry. We'll see an example of that in the second half of this lesson. For another example, a sharp concave corner of three edges is impossible to machine so rounding these corners is more than cosmetic. People often have a tendency to add purely cosmetic rounds too early in the regeneration sequence because they significantly improve the visual appearance of the model. Resist this temptation! Unless you have a good reason for doing so, postpone round creation to the end. Cosmetic rounds are usually eliminated from the model (that is, suppressed) for purposes of finite element analysis. Adding rounds too early raises the possibility of setting up undesirable parent/child relations.

There are two major categories of rounds: *Simple* and *Advanced*. Simple rounds are actually not quite so simple, and can come in several varieties (constant radius, variable radius) with a broad range of options. You can often create most rounds in a model as Simple. Occasionally, you will encounter a diabolical case or you might want more control over the round geometry (especially at corners); in this case, you would use an Advanced Round.

Basically, a simple round consists of one of the following:
- a set of edges all with the same round radius
- a single edge that has a variable radius, defined in one of a couple of ways
- a round that removes the surface between two edges (a *Full* round)

For a simple round, the cross section shape is circular. This is often called the "rolling ball" shape obtained as the (hypothetical) ball rolls along in the direction of the edge staying tangent to the adjacent surfaces. For advanced rounds, you can also specify a conic shape.

The order that rounds are created is very important in determining the shape of the intersections. With *Advanced* rounds, we have a bit more control over this shape using optional *Transitions*. With *Advanced* rounds, we can define a number of round sets that are created simultaneously. This lets us put many rounds of different types into the same model feature, simplifying the model tree.

We'll start by creating some *Simple* rounds and then show how to set up an *Advanced* round feature using several round sets. Each round set uses the same commands as the *Simple* round.

To have something to work on, start a new part called **rounds**, and create the simple block shown in Figure 1. We will do most of our exercises on the top front edge of this part.

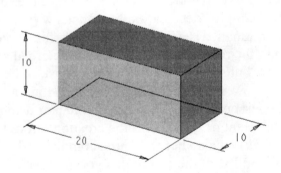

Figure 1 Basic block for round exercises

The Rounds Tutor

There is extensive on-line help for creating rounds. To access this easily, select

> *Help > Tutorials > Rounds Creation Guide*

This is a toggle. The next time we call up the round creation commands, a window will open up providing us context sensitive information on available round commands. To see that,

> *Feature > Create > Solid > Round*

The *Rounds Tutor* window opens up - this may be hidden behind the Pro/E graphics window. The contents of the page we are looking at in the tutor window corresponds to the open menu on the right. The first window describes the two round types (*Simple* and *Advanced*). At the top of the *Round Tutor* window are some navigation buttons for moving through the Tutor. A **Contents** button takes you to a full table of contents. To appreciate how extensive the round command is, click on the **Tutor map** icon. This reveals a table showing the entire command tree for round creation. There is obviously a lot to know here!

If you leave the *Rounds Creation Guide* toggle set under the **Help** pull-down, this window will automatically call up the content for the round command menus on the right. This is an easy way to quickly discover the definitions and meanings of the commands. In addition, the *Guide* contains numerous examples of advanced techniques using rounds, and a number of special cases. We will not be going through the entire set of round creation commands here (that would take an entire book on its own). In any case, the *Guide* is well written and easily used "on the fly" to help you learn some of the more infrequently used commands.

Leave the *Rounds Tutor* window open for now. Feel free to close it at your own convenience.

Simple Rounds

Constant Radius

The simplest round is constant radius along one or more specified edges. In the **ROUND TYPE** menu select

> ***Simple | Done***
> ***Constant | Edge Chain | Done***
> ***One By One***

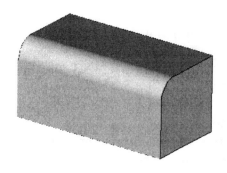

Figure 2 Simple, constant radius round

and pick the front top edge, then ***Done*** in the **CHAIN** menu. Enter a radius of **2.5**. Yellow lines will appear showing the extent of the round. These will be important later when we get to transitions in the advanced round section. To see what the actual round will look like, select ***Preview***. The true edges will show up in red. Spin the model. Select ***OK***. The round looks like Figure 2.

The simple round can also contain multiple edges. To change this round feature definition,

> ***Feature > Redefine***

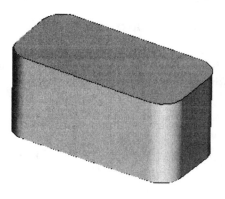

Figure 3 Redefined edges of first round

and click on the round. In the elements window, highlight **References** and select ***Define***. Now, ***Unselect*** the existing edge reference, and select the four vertical corner edges using the ***One By One*** option. In the **CHAIN** menu, select ***Done*** and accept the feature. The part should look like Figure 3.

To see the importance of round creation order, create a simple, constant round along the top edge with a radius of **2** . Since the first round feature modifies the corners, we can now use ***Tangnt Chain*** in the **CHAIN** menu to run a smooth round that yields nice smooth corners due to the previous rounds. See Figure 4.

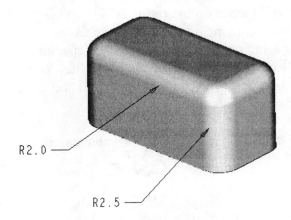

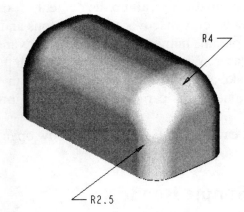

Figure 4 Round created on tangent edge

Figure 5 Top edge round modified. Note corner appearance.

To see some of the difficulties you might get into using simple rounds, ***Modify*** the radius of the top round to **4**. Notice the appearance of the rounds where they join each other at the corners (Figure 5). Up in the message window, you will get a warning about design intent. Select

> ***Info > Geometry Checks***

and select each of the listed items. The radius of the top round is so large that the round is self-intersecting as it goes around the corners. The advice given is to decrease the round radius. This is a common solution when you have round problems. In the advanced rounds section a bit later, we will see some methods that will give you a bit more control over this geometry using transitions. Delete all the rounds.

A little later in this lesson, we will see a couple of shortcuts that will make creation of these simple rounds a snap. For now, let's explore the options for creating simple rounds.

Variable Radius Rounds

There are several ways to create rounds where the radius changes along the edge. Let's start with something simple:

> ***Feature > Create > Solid > Round***
> ***Simple | Done***
> ***Variable | Edge Chain | Done***
> ***One By One***

and pick on the top front edge of the block, then ***Done***. You will see two small red X's on the ends of the edge. We will specify the round radius at these points. We can also create additional radius control points along the edge. Create a new datum point midway along the edge using (the toolbar icon)

> ***Datum Point > Add New > On Curve***
> ***Length Ratio***

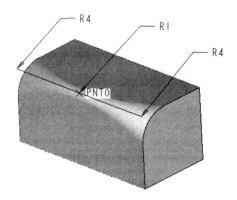

and pick on the edge approximately at the middle, then ***Done Sel***. You are asked to enter the exact position of the new point in a ratio of the length between 0 and 1. Enter *0.5* to place the new point half way along the edge. In **DTM PNT MODE** select ***Done***. Select the new datum point in the middle, then ***Done***. There are now three X's on the edge. Select ***Done***. Pro/E will highlight the various points in green and you can enter the radius values shown in Figure 6. The yellow round edges appear. To have a better look, select ***Preview***. Accept the feature.

Figure 6 A *Variable Radius* round

Open up the Model Tree window, a new feature representing the middle point has been added. Right click on this and select ***Modify***. This will show the location of the point as 0.5 REL along the edge.

Variable radius rounds can be defined along tangent edges. Each vertex at a tangency point can be selected to specify a round value and you can add more points if desired.

Let's look at another way to create a variable radius round. Delete this round and the datum point.

Thru Curve Rounds

If the round is going to have a complex geometry, it may be awkward or inaccurate to create it using a large number of points in a variable radius round as we did previously. There is a better way - using the *Thru Curve* option.

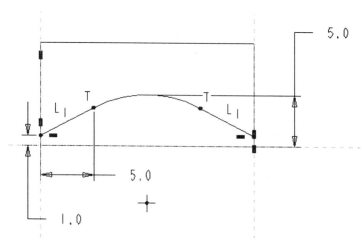

On the top of the block, create a sketched datum curve as shown in Figure 7. Note that this curve is C1 continuous - this a requirement for a *Thru Curve* round.

Figure 7 A *datum curve* to define round extent (must be C1 continuous)

We'll now create a round whose radius along the front edge is determined by the datum curve. The new round will be tangent to the top surface at the location of the datum curve.

Create > Solid > Round
Simple | Done
Thru Curve | Edge Chain | Done

pick the top front edge, then *Done* in **CHAIN** menu. Now (observe the message window), select

Curve Chain

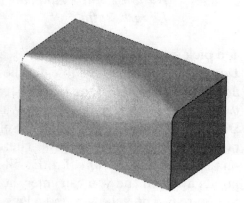

and pick the datum curve. Choose *Select All* in the **CHAIN OPT** menu then *Done*. Preview the round and accept the feature. The round is shown in Figure 8.

The curve reference for a *Thru Curve* round can be any curve, that is, including edges of the part, but as noted above must be composed of tangent edges.

Figure 8 A *Thru Curve* round

Delete this round and the datum curve.

Full Rounds

This is the last variety of simple rounds. Add a cut to the base block to obtain the shape shown in Figure 9. The thin vertical face on the right end is **2.5** wide. Then, select

Create > Solid > Round
Simple | Done
Full Round | Edge Pair | Done

and pick on the two vertical edges on the right (narrow) end of this wedge. The resulting round is shown in Figure 10. The entire right surface has been cut off and replaced by the round going from the front to the back surface.

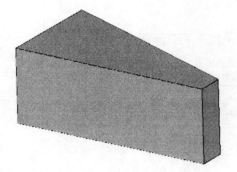

Figure 9 Cut created in base feature

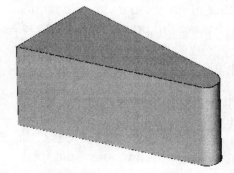

Figure 10 *Full* round on right face

For an *Edge Pair* round, the surface containing the two edges is removed.

Delete the round on the right face, and issue the same
commands to create a full round on the top of the block,
picking the edges on the front and back of the block. Now,
we get a variable radius round between the front and back
surfaces. See Figure 11.

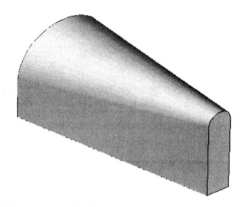

We have seen the major round types available with simple
rounds. Many options have not been investigated here. For
example, we have used *Edge Chain* rounds exclusively
and have not touched on *Surf-Surf* and *Edge-Surf* rounds.
You should spend some time with the *Rounds Tutor* to
learn more about how these options are used. There are
numerous examples there for you to study. You might

Figure 11 *Full* round on top face

also study some of the optional elements (such as terminating surfaces) which are fully discussed
in the Round Tutor.

We have not looked at a number of "diabolical" cases. Quite often, some trial and error will be
required to get exactly the geometry you want. Creating rounds is something of an art. The more
you know about the various alternatives for round creation, the better you will be able to create
your desired geometry. If you have trouble getting a round to create, the most probable cause is
that the radius is too large. Try using a smaller radius and slowly increase it. You will probably
be able to observe what the geometric obstacle is to creating the round with the desired radius.

We will use the base block in the next section, so delete the round and cut and save the part.

Round Creation Shortcuts

There are a couple of shortcut methods for creating simple rounds that you should know about.
These only work for simple, constant radius rounds of a single tangent chain edge. The two
shortcuts involve either a mapkey or a graphics window pop-up menu. The latter method is new
in Pro/E 2001.

Simple Round Mapkey

If you browse around in the *Rounds Tutor* (look in section 1.3), you will find a useful mapkey
definition "mr" for creating a single edge (tangent chain), constant radius round. You can cut-
and-paste this definition to the bottom of your *config.pro* file using a standard text editor. When
you reload your configuration file and **Apply** it, the mapkey will be activated. After launching the
mapkey, all you have to do is pick on the edge you want rounded and enter the radius.

Try out the new mapkey by typing "mr". After you have experimented with this, delete the
rounds.

Object/Action Round Creation

This method of creating rounds is new in Release 2001 and demonstrates the new "object/action"
command structure (as opposed to the previous "action/object" form). It is based on the new

method for picking entities in the graphics window using preselection highlighting. Basically, the idea is to identify the edges on the part first, then tell Pro/E to put rounds on them. We'll try out a couple of variations of this.

In the preselection highlighting group in the top toolbar, make sure the **Select Geometry** button is pressed. Move the cursor over the top, front edge of the block. A small window will appear identifying the edge. Click with the left button; the edge turns blue. Now hold down the right mouse button and select **Round Edges** in the pop-up menu. Two small green drag handles will appear on the tangent edges of the round, and a leader with the radius dimension. You can click on either of the handles to change the round radius, or double click on the dimension value. Enter a value of **2.5**. Then, just middle click and the round automatically regenerates. We have created this feature without ever going into one of the menus on the right.

Delete the round by selecting the **Primary Items** preselection toolbar button. Pick on the round surface, then right click and select **Delete** in the pop-up menu.

Now let's create the rounds on the four vertical edges simultaneously. Once again, to pick edges you must have the **Select Geometry** preselection button pressed. Hold the keyboard Shift key down as you left click on each of the four edges. When all four are highlighted in blue, right click and select **Round Edges** in the pop-up menu. Once again the green drag handles appear on one of the rounds (probably the last one you picked). Drag one of these - all the four rounds change! Double click on the dimension and set the radius to **3**. Middle click to accept the feature.

Let's create one more round. Left click on the top edge, the right click and select **Round Edges**. Set the radius to **2.5** and middle click to accept the round. This automatically uses a Tangent Edge option for round creation.

So, using the new object/action method you can very quickly create simple, constant radius rounds of multiple, tangent edges without ever leaving the graphics window. Pretty easy!

Advanced Rounds

An *Advanced* round is composed of a number of separate rounds organized into *round sets*. Each round set is defined using the same commands as a *Simple* round. For example, in a single *Advanced* round you can have one round set containing several rounds with a constant radius, another set with a specific variable radius round, a third set containing a full round, and so on. This allows you to create several different types of rounds simultaneously, and have all rounds included in the same feature in the model tree. More importantly, the order that the round sets are identified in the *Advanced* round does not matter. We saw above that creation order is important for *Simple* rounds in determining the geometry and appearance of the junction between separate rounds. In *Advanced* rounds, we have explicit controls over the nature of these junctions, called *transitions*. Although default transitions will be used wherever rounds meet, we have numerous options to specify the transition shapes, which are independent of the round set creation order. We will look at some of these transition settings below.

Normally, you can accomplish most of your rounding tasks using *Simple* rounds and it is suggested that you use these as much as possible. However, a number of situations might arise where you will use an *Advanced* round:

- An *Advanced* round can contain many constituent rounds in one feature, thereby cleaning up the model tree a bit.
- Questions of feature creation order are removed in regard to the rounds defined in the round sets.
- A *Simple* round may fail and require you to redefine it as an *Advanced* round.
- You want more control over the transitions.
- You want access to the additional round shape commands available only for advanced rounds (*Conic* and *Normal To Spine*).

Note that a *Simple* round can be promoted to an *Advanced* round (but not vice versa) in order to access these commands. A promoted *Simple* round automatically becomes the first round set of the *Advanced* round. Unfortunately, round sets cannot be transferred or reassigned from one advanced round feature to another.

We will demonstrate the main aspects of the use of *Advanced* rounds (round sets and transitions) using our simple rectangular block, Figure 1. Delete all the other round features created in the previous section in this lesson.

Round Sets

Round sets are created by choosing the *Advanced* option when creating a round feature:

> ***Create > Solid > Round***
> ***Advanced | Done***

The elements window tells us we are creating Round Set 1. In the **RND SET ATTR** menu, we have the familiar commands for defining a simple round. Select

> ***Constant | Edge Chain | Done***

Pick on the front right vertical edge, then ***Done***. Give a radius of **2**. Note that *Preview* is not available for individual round sets, since the geometry depends on all the sets in the feature. Select *OK* in the **Round Set 1** window.

In the **ROUND SETS** menu, select

> ***Add > Constant | Edge Chain | Done > One By One***

and pick on the top front and top right edges of the block. ***Done***. Give them a radius of **2**.

We see the yellow edges that define the extent of these rounds, minus the geometry for the intersection. In the **Round Set 2** window, select *OK*.

Back in the **ROUND SETS** menu again, select

>   *Done Sets*

Now we can *Preview* the rounds. See Figures 12 and 13. Notice the default shape of the corner. Accept the feature.

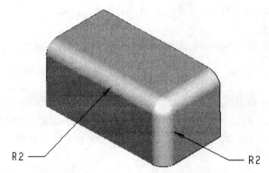

Figure 12 Advanced round #1 (default)

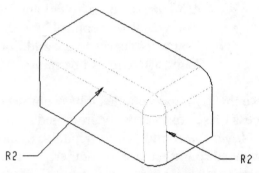

Figure 13 Advanced round #1 (default)

Go to *Feature > Modify* and change the radius of the vertical round to **3**. See Figures 14 and 15. The corner transition has changed. This default transition is determined by the radii of the rounds entering the corner. We will discuss transitions in further detail in the next section.

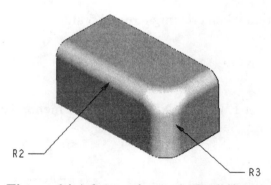

Figure 14 Advanced round #2 (different radii)

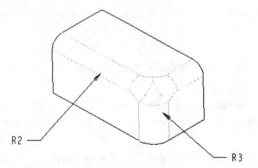

Figure 15 Advanced round #2 (different radii)

Round Transitions

In the two cases above, we saw different corner geometries resulting from the default transitions. We can over-ride this default quite easily.

>   *Feature > Redefine*

and click on any of the rounds. In the elements window, select

Transitions > Define

A number of options are presented for the round transition. Select

Add By Select

and pick on the three green edges of the rounds meeting at the corner, then **Done Sel.** The **TRANS TYPE** menu appears. Select

IntersctSrfs | Done
Done Trans > Preview

Each of the three rounds at the corner are extended until they intersect a surface of the other rounds, see Figures 16 and 17.

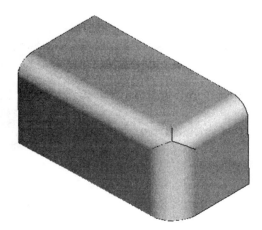

Figure 16 Advanced round #3;
IntersctSrfs transition

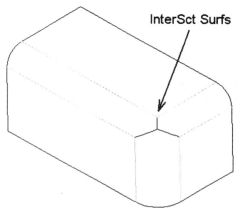

Figure 17 Advanced round #3;
IntersctSrfs transition

Redefine the transition using

Transitions > Define
Redefine > Transition 1
Corner Sphere | Done

If we had not already specified the edge references, we would have to do that now. As it is, these are already known, and we can

Accept | Done.

Note that the *Modify* command here allows us to change the radius of the corner sphere and the locations of the blends between the rounds and the sphere surface. You

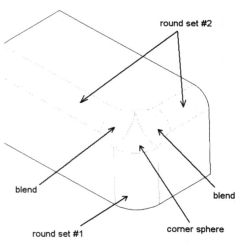

Figure 18 Advanced round #4a;
Corner Sphere transition

might like to come back and try that out. For now, select

> ***Done Trans > Preview***

The geometry just created (Figure 18) is the same as that produced by default, shown in Figures 14 and 15. This may not always be the case - the default transition is determined by the nature of the rounds entering the corner. Accept the feature with ***OK***.

Let's change the radius of the rounds to see what happens to this transition. Use

> ***Feature > Modify***

and click on one of the rounds. Round values for both round sets will appear. Change the radius of the vertical edge (round set #1) to **2**, and the radius of the top edges (round set #2) to **3**. The top surface now has the larger radius rounds. The part appears as shown in Figures 19 and 20.

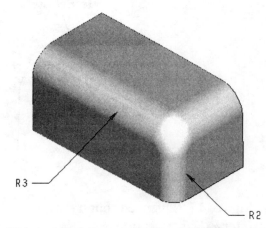

Figure 19 Advanced round #4b; *Corner Sphere* transition, different radii

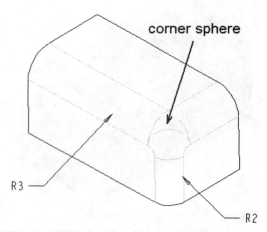

Figure 20 Advanced round #4b; *Corner Sphere* transition, different radii

Remember that we have forced this transition to be a corner sphere. Modify the edges back to their previous values (3 on bottom, 2 on top).

Now redefine to produce a different transition geometry:

> ***Feature > Redefine > {pick on the round}***
> ***Transitions > Define***
> ***Redefine > Transition 1***
> ***Corner Sweep | Done***
> ***Done Trans > Preview***

The new geometry is shown in Figures 21 and 22. The sweep will follow the round with the largest arc. Occasionally, the corner sweep transition may fail, and it is possible to recover by adding an additional curve. See the Round Tutor for more details.

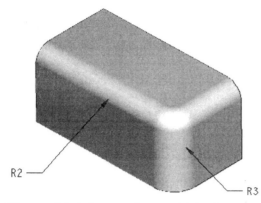

Figure 21 Advanced round #5; *Corner Sweep* transition

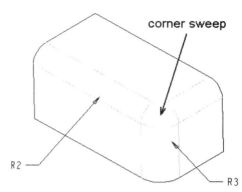

Figure 22 Advanced round #5; *Corner Sweep* transition

Redefine the transition again, this time with a ***Patch***. The round is shown in Figures 23 and 24.

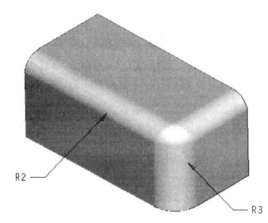

Figure 23 Advanced round #6; *Patch* transition

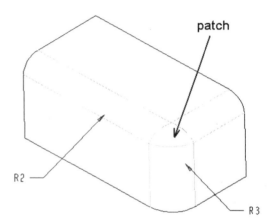

Figure 24 Advanced round #6; *Patch* transition

There are obviously a lot of possibilities for creating *Advanced* rounds. We have looked at a very simple geometry, with only two round sets defined on straight edges. Pro/E's ability to produce rounds on difficult geometry is actually quite astounding. You are encouraged to consult the *Rounds Tutor*, which has considerably more discussion and lots of examples and illustrations of *Advanced* rounds and construction details. There is also considerable discussion of ways to recover from round creation failures.

Ribs and Tweaks

There are a number of special purpose solid features available in Pro/E that construct solid geometry for specific tasks. For example, if you are ever creating a part for molding, you will want to use the draft feature so that the part can be easily removed from the mold. Ribs and lips are features that could be made using standard protrusions and/or sweeps, but the construction demonstrated here is quite a bit quicker. The part we are going to make is shown in Figure 25 which demonstrates several of these specialized features. This part actually contains only 10 features after the default datums. Although it is not immediately obvious from the figure, the part contains no vertical surfaces - these all have draft applied. The treatment of the top sculpted edge is also easily accomplished using the lip feature. And the three spoked features coming off the vertical circular boss are created using ribs.

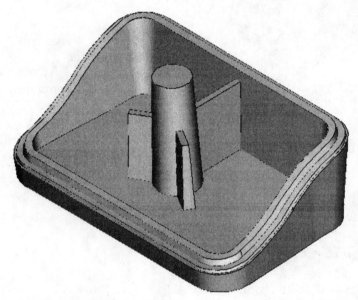

Figure 25 Finished part using ribs, drafts, and lips

We'll start by creating a base feature, adding some rounded corners, shelling it out, and adding the circular boss in the middle. Start a new part called **tweaks**. In the first few steps of this exercise we will produce the geometry shown in Figure 27.

The first feature is a both sides blind protrusion off the SIDE datum plane. The sketch is shown in the figure at the right and the feature depth is **24**.

Next, add some R3 rounds to each vertical corner edge. Note that although rounds are usually added last, in this case we will create them early so that the Shell command will also produce rounded corners on the inside of the part. We are using the rounds more like cuts here.

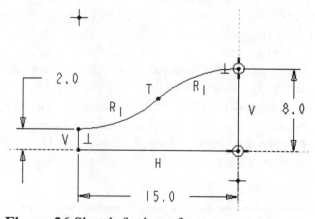

Figure 26 Sketch for base feature

Use the **_Shell_** command to remove the top surface, leaving a thickness of **1.5**.

Finally, create a one-sided solid protrusion of diameter **3** and height **10** coming up from the inside bottom surface in the middle of the part (align the sketch to the SIDE datum). The part should now look like Figure 27. Now would be a good time to save the part.

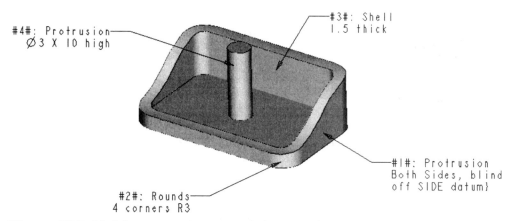

Figure 27 Initial features prior to applying tweaks

Ribs

We will first create the thin vertical feature between the back of the boss and the shell wall.

Create > Solid > Rib

Select the SIDE datum as the sketching plane and the TOP datum as the top reference. For sketching references under Intent Manager use the edge of the boss, the inside back surface and the bottom surface of the shell. To create the rib, we only need to create the single line shown in Figure 28. When the sketch is accepted, you can select which side of the line should be solid. Make sure the direction arrow is pointing down and select *OK*. Enter a rib thickness of **0.5**. The completed rib is shown in Figure 29. Zoom in on the junction of the rib to the cylindrical boss. You will see that the rib end has been merged to the surface. If you tried to create this feature using a both sides protrusion and the same sketch, you would find a small crack between the end of the rib and the boss surface.

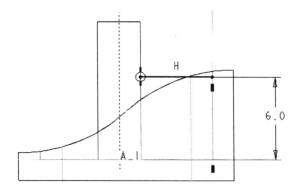

Figure 28 Single line sketch for first rib

Figure 29 Completed first rib

Now add one of the angled ribs on the front of the boss. Sketch this on a Make Datum:

> *Create > Solid > Rib*
> *Make Datum > Through* > {pick the axis through the boss}
> *Angle* > {select the SIDE datum} > *Done*
> *Enter Value*

Observe the green direction arrow. We want the make datum angled at 60° from the SIDE datum. Now pick the TOP datum as the top reference. We spin around to the back of the part to sketch on the yellow side of the make datum. Specify the left edge of the boss, the top of the first rib, and the inner bottom surface of the shell as sketching references. Create the sketch shown in Figure 30. When this is done, enter a rib thickness of **0.5** as before. The rib is complete (Figure 31).

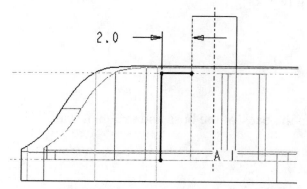

Figure 30 Sketch for angled rib

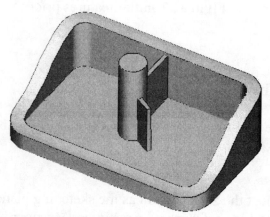

Figure 31 Angled rib completed

Mirror the angled rib through the SIDE datum plane.

Drafts

A draft is a modification to a surface so that the part will be easily removed from molds, as illustrated schematically in Figure 32. Without draft, the part will not leave the mold cleanly and/or may become damaged. Draft features can become quite complex. In addition to the part geometry, application of the draft requires knowledge of where the parting line on the part will be where the mold halves come together, which may also be affected by the location of the gates where material is injected into the mold, and so on. Putting drafts on a part, unless they are fairly obvious, might be a task left to the molding specialist. Consequently, in the following, we will look at only a few of the many options available. If you want additional information, consult the on-line help.

You can think of the draft as a small angular rotation of the surface about a pivot axis. The pivot axis location is determined by either a *Neutral Plane* (Figure 33) or a *Neutral Curve*. By placing the pivot axis in the middle of the surface, you can create a Split Draft with different angles on each side of the pivot. You can also create a Split Draft by projecting a sketch onto the surface that divides the surface into two regions. You can then specify a different pivot and draft angle for different regions of the surface. We will not discuss Split Drafts here - consult the on-line documentation. It is also possible to define a variable draft angle at different points along the pivot. Again, see the on-line documentation for more information.

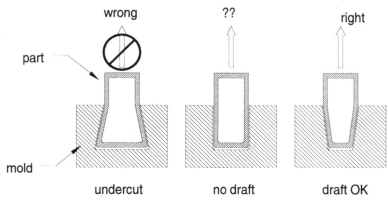

Figure 32 Draft surfaces on molded parts

Like rounds, drafts are usually applied towards the end of the regeneration sequence. However, note that draft must be applied before a round on the edge, and that draft can be applied only to planar and cylindrical surfaces. If you need to put draft on a higher order surface, you may have to use a variable section sweep.

To specify a draft, we basically need to provide three pieces of information: which surface should receive the draft, where the draft angle is measured from (the Neutral Plane, or Neutral Curve) and the draft angle (direction and size). These are illustrated in Figure 33.

First, we'll put some draft on the three ribs. Although we can apply draft to each surface individually, all these vertical surfaces share the same Neutral Plane, so we will create them all at the same time.

Create > Solid > Tweak > Draft
Neutral Pln > Done
No Split | Constant | Done

Select all the vertical faces of the three ribs. As each surface is picked it will highlight in red. There are eight surfaces in total. When all are selected, middle click. The surfaces will turn blue. In **SURF SELECT**, press *Done*. The Neutral Plane is perpendicular to the draft surfaces and defines where the draft surface will pivot. For the ribs, we can select the top surface of any of the ribs. The reference direction determines how the angle is defined and is

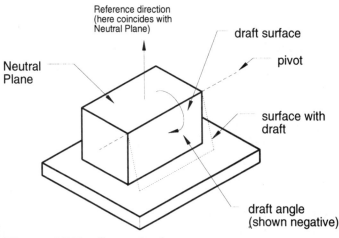

Figure 33 Draft terminology

normal to the plane selected as the reference. In our case, select *Use Neut Pln*. A green rotation arrow and a red highlighted surface will appear. We must now enter the draft angle. Note that the draft angle may have to be negative - observe the direction of the green arrow.

TIP: Draft angles are typically very small, ranging from 0.5 to 2.0 degrees. These are hard to see on the model if you happen to make a mistake. When you first enter a draft angle, you might enter quite a large value, like 4.0, then *Preview* the draft. If the direction is correct, change the magnitude of the angle to the desired value using *Draft Angle > Define* in the elements window.

The magnitude we want here is 2°. A good way to check the draft is to look down on it from the TOP view. This view is shown in Figure 34 which shows the edges at the top and bottom of the rib drafts.

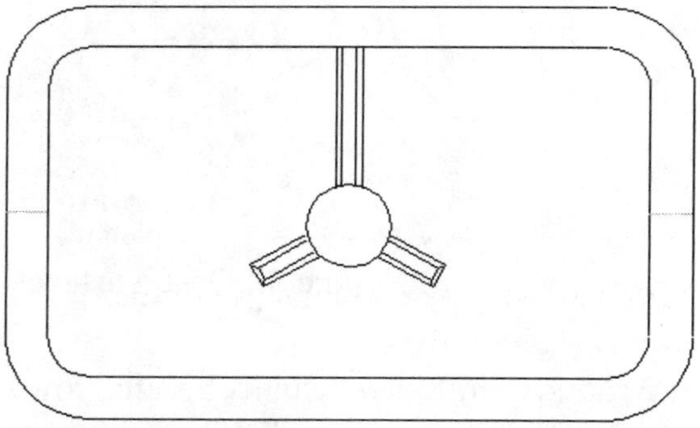

Now we'll add draft to the boss using a slightly quicker way to select surfaces:

Figure 34 Top view showing draft on ribs

>   *Create > Solid > Tweak > Draft*
>   *Neutral Plane | Done*
>   *No Split | Constant | Done*
>   *Loop Surfs*

Pick on the top circular surface of the boss. All surfaces meeting the edge of this face are selected. Middle click. Now select the top surface as the neutral plane, and again for the direction reference. The green direction arrow will appear. Enter a draft angle large enough to see, then modify later. We ultimately want a draft angle of 2°. Go to the Top view to see the draft surface (Figure 35).

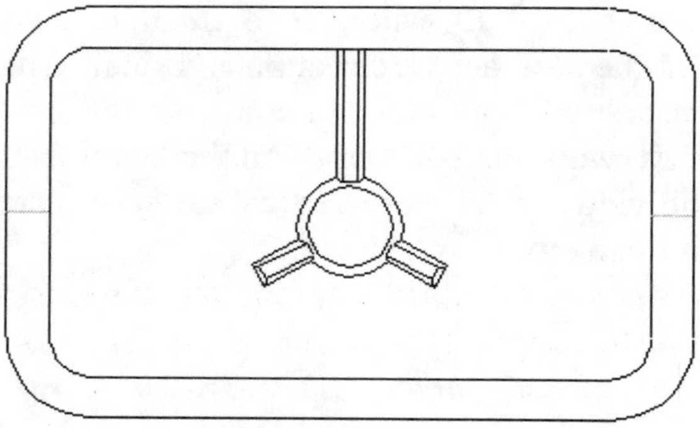

We need some draft on the inner and outer surfaces of the shell, keeping the same curved edges on the top (presuming that they must align with a mating part). The curved edges will be the *Neutral Curves* for these drafts, that is, the draft will "pivot" around the curves.

Figure 35 Top view showing draft on boss

>   *Create > Solid > Tweak > Draft*
>   *Neutral Crv | Done*
>   *No Split | Constant | Done*

Here's a new way to select the surfaces. Spin the part upside down. Then select *Loop Surfs* and pick on the bottom face of the part. Middle click. Now spin the part back upright. To select the neutral curve, select *Tangnt Chain* and pick anywhere on the top outside edge. *Done*. Now specify the reference direction of the draft by selecting the TOP datum plane. The green direction arrow comes up. Set a draft value of 5° (again, this may have to be negative). This is a rather large draft, shown in Figure 36. Notice the effect on the Neutral Curve and shape of the base. Accept the feature.

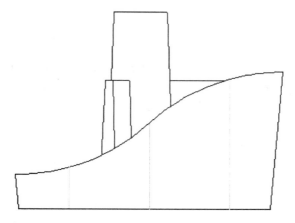

Figure 36 SIDE view showing draft on outer surface of base

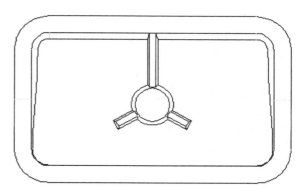

Figure 37 TOP view showing draft on inner surface of base

Put a 5° draft on the inner surface as well:

> ***Create > Solid > Tweak > Draft***
> ***Neutral Crv | Done***
> ***No Split | Constant | Done***

This time select the surfaces individually (there are eight of them). (Why not use Loop Surfs and pick on the bottom inside surface? Would this work?) Use the inner top curve as the Neutral Curve, and the TOP datum as direction reference. The draft should look like Figure 37 from the top view.

What would happen if we put the draft on the outer surface of the base feature before we shelled it and/or applied the corner rounds?

Lips

IMPORTANT: To enable this and the next feature discussed, you must set (and ***Apply***) the *config.pro* option
> **allow_anatomic_features**   **yes**

A lip is a feature that is often added to plastic molded parts, such as an enclosure, where top and bottom parts must mate and lock together. The lip geometry is defined by the five items shown in Figure 38: the lip edge, the surface to be offset, the

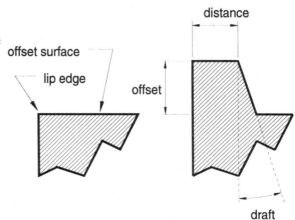

Figure 38 Defining a *lip* feature

offset distance, the distance to the draft, and the draft angle.

Create a lip around the inner top edge:

> ### Create > Solid > Tweak > Lip
> ### Chain

Pick on the top inner edge. It is highlighted. ***Done***. Pick the surface to be offset as the top face of the wall at the back of the part. Enter an offset value of **0.5**. The distance to the draft surface is **0.75**. Select the TOP datum as the drafting reference, and enter a draft angle of **15°**. The lip is now completed. Very simple!

Create another smaller lip on the outside edge that removes material using a negative offset:

> ### Create > Solid > Tweak > Lip
> ### Chain

Pick on the outer top edge. The surface to be offset is the same as before. The offset value is negative : **-0.25**. The distance to the draft surface is **0.25**. The draft reference is the TOP datum and the draft angle is again **15°**. A view of the two lips is shown below.

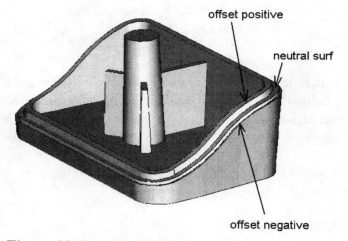

The mating part would use similar lips but with the opposite sign offset to produce a tight connection between the two parts.

This completes all the features we want to add to this part. Save the part.

Ears

Figure 39 Completed *lips* on top edges

This is a really quick way of producing a thin angled tab on the edge of a part, see Figure 41. The sketch of the shape is done in the plane of part surface and the angle of the tab is simply specified. Create a new part called **ear**. The base feature is a one-sided protrusion off the TOP datum, 10 X 20 with a thickness of 5 (see Figure 40). We will add an ear to one edge of this base feature.

> ### Create > Solid > Tweak > Ear
> ### Variable | Done

Pick on the top surface as the sketching plane. The feature creation arrow should be downwards into the block. The right sketching reference is the right face of the block. Create the sketch shown in Figure 40 below. For an ear, the sketch must be open and the sides of the ear must be perpendicular to the part edge where they meet.

When prompted, enter the following: the depth of the ear is **0.5**, the bend radius is **2**, and the bend angle is **30°**. The resulting ear feature is shown in Figure 41.

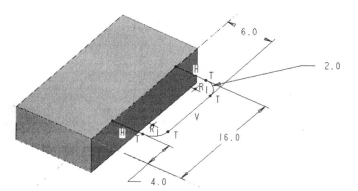

Figure 40 Base feature and sketch for *ear*

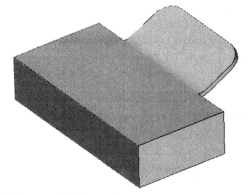

Figure 41 Completed *ear* feature

For the ear feature, check out **Feature > Modify** to experiment with other settings. For example, can the angle be negative?

This lesson has introduced you to methods to create special purpose features. Rounds, and especially advanced rounds, are a study in themselves. The tweak features are not ones you will use a lot, but it is useful to know they are there. The most common tweak feature is a draft, for which there are many options you might look into on your own. For some special cases, the special tweaks like ears may come in very handy.

In the next lesson we will look at modeling database functions: pattern and family tables.

Questions for Review

1. What are the two main categories of rounds?
2. Why are rounds usually created towards the end of the regeneration sequence? When would they be created earlier?
3. What is the name given to the generic shape of a simple round?
4. When using *Simple* rounds, what determines the shape of the corners where several rounds meet?
5. How do you access the *Rounds Tutor*?
6. How many edges can be contained in an individual *Simple* round feature? Can these edges be intersecting?
7. What is the mapkey for creating a simple constant radius round?

8.   How many different ways are there to create a round whose radius changes along its length?
9.   When creating a *Variable Radius* round, does the edge have to be C1 continuous?
10.   How do you create additional points along an edge to specify the round radius in a *Variable Radius* round? Is there a limit on the number of points?
11.   Must a datum curve be used to define a *Thru Curve* round?
12.   What, if any, restrictions are there on the curve used to define the round radius in a *Thru Curve* round?
13.   Is it possible to use a *Full* round to remove an L-shaped surface?
14.   Find out how *Edge-Surf* and *Surf-Surf* rounds are created.
15.   What is the major difference between an *Advanced* and a *Simple* round?
16.   What additional geometry can be controlled using an *Advanced* round?
17.   Does the order of the round sets in an *Advanced* round matter?
18.   A *Simple* round can be promoted to an *Advanced* round. Can it also be added into an existing advanced round?
19.   How many round sets can be included in an *Advanced* round?
20.   Find out from the Round Tutor how Pro/E determines the default transitions.
21.   Name four types of round transitions.
22.   How do you change a particular transition?
23.   What happens if you use a closed sketch to define a rib?
24.   What happens if you try to attach a 2 unit thick rib to a 1 unit diameter boss?
25.   Define the following terms:
             Neutral Plane
             Neutral Curve
             draft surface
             draft reference
             draft angle
             Split Draft
26.   Does the draft reference have to be the same as the *Neutral Plane*?
27.   What happens if the *Neutral Plane* does not intersect the draft surface?
28.   What is an undercut?
29.   What is a lurking danger if you create drafts early in the regeneration sequence? HINT: Think about choosing reference directions for features.
30.   On what type of surfaces can we NOT create draft features?
31.   What are the five items needed to define a lip?
32.   What restrictions apply to the sketch of an ear?

Project Exercises

We will create four more parts for the cart project. Three of these are pretty routine. The fourth one, the cargo bin, has the highest feature count for an individual part and will utilize many of the functions introduced in this lesson. We'll do the easy parts first. The first two parts are fairly routine. On the hubcap, you can use a function in Sketcher to produce sketched text (see **Sketch > Text**). Protrude this through the hubcap and then cut it off using a revolved cut parallel to the upper curved surface.

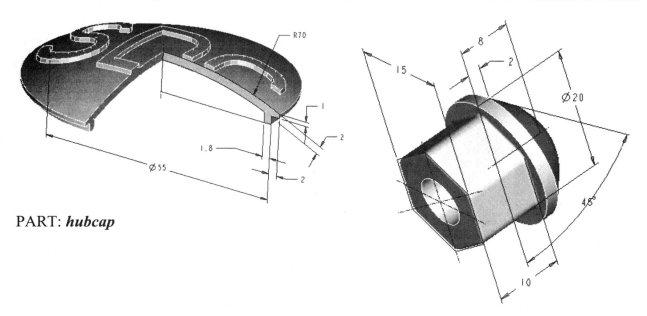

PART: *hubcap*

PART: *lugnut*

The figure below shows the cargo bin and some of its interesting features. Plan your feature creation order carefully for this part! It is basically a solid protrusion that has been shelled out. The side walls have a 2° draft. Before you shell out the base feature, add the rounds to the outside edges using advanced rounds and transitions. The shell thickness is 5mm. There are a couple of sweeps, some patterned holes and ribs, and some simple rounds.

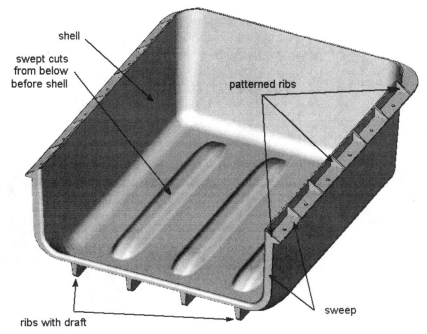

PART: *cargo*

Here are the dimensions for the base feature (a blind, both-sides protrusion) and the corner rounds. This is a case when you would probably put draft on the exterior vertical surfaces of the part prior to forming the rounds and shelling it out.

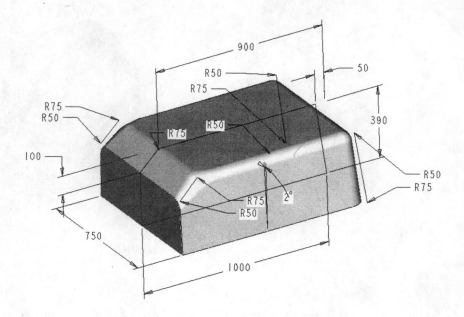

Here are the dimensions for the top sweep and the hole patterns for the cargo bin. For the ribs along the side of the bin, create the pattern leader using an offset **Make Datum** from the end of the bin, say 10mm. The ribs are 5mm thick. Then pattern the ribs (7 ribs, increment 150mm) and change the offset of the pattern leader to half the rib thickness (the rib can't hang out over the end!).

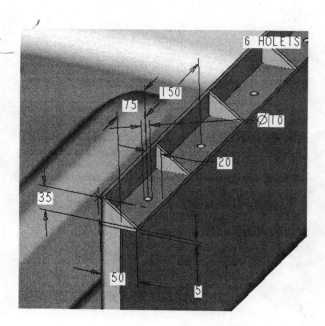

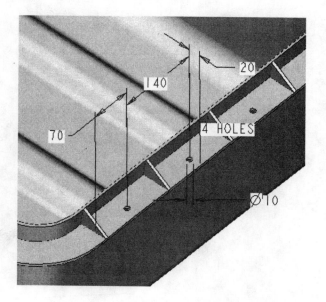

There is also a pattern of ribs on the bottom that look like the figure at the right. These also have draft.

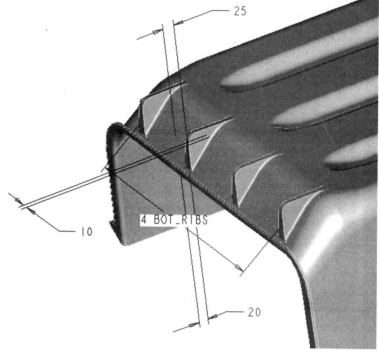

The spring on the side wheels is a simple helical sweep. Some added features at each end are required to attach the spring to the bracket and wheel mount. **IMPORTANT:** For an exercise in Lesson 8, you need to create a relation for this spring that calculates the pitch of the helix based on the number of turns (a fixed number equal to 10) and the profile height, which we are going to make a driven variable later on in the assembly.

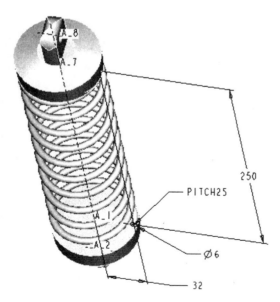

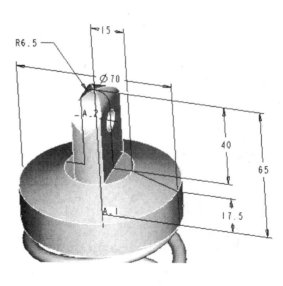

PART: *spring*

Notes:

Lesson 4

Patterns and Family Tables

Synopsis

Patterns of features using values, relations, and tables; *Ref Patterns*; Creating and using family tables for series of related parts

Overview

You will often come across situations where entities must be repeated numerous times in a model or assembly. In a part, the easiest way to create multiple copies of a feature is by using the **Pattern** command. This has a number of options and is very flexible. Once the *pattern leader* has been created, the patterned features, called *instances*, do not have to be identical copies, but can change in size as well. This lesson will examine the major functions involved in creating and using patterns of features.

Family tables are to parts what patterns are to features. That is, if you are producing a series of parts that all contain a central set of base features, then you can control the geometry of each part *instance* using a simple entry in a table defined in the master part, called the *generic*. This can save you a lot of repetitive part creation, not to mention disk space. Furthermore, members of a part family defined by a table can be freely substituted in an assembly. In this lesson, we will look at the basics of creating the generic part, the family table, and some issues that involve parent/child relations in the generic part and its instances.

Advanced Patterns

The creation of patterns of features was introduced in the first Tutorial. In this lesson we will look quite a bit deeper into the options available with patterned features.

To review, a pattern is a multi-copy operation where a feature (the *pattern leader*) is duplicated in a number of *instances* in a prescribed way. Patterns can be created of both placed (holes and datum points, for example) and sketched (protrusions, cuts) features. When creating a *Dim Pattern*, you choose one or more dimensions defined for the pattern leader that you want to increment or modify between instances or copies. Patterns can be unidirectional, bidirectional, or "irregular" (table driven) as illustrated in Figure 1. The variation between instances can be based on constant values or driven by relations. Patterns do not have to be planar. In the exercise below, we will use an angular increment to create the part shown in Figure 3. A *Ref Pattern* is created by referencing a new patterned feature to a previously created pattern.

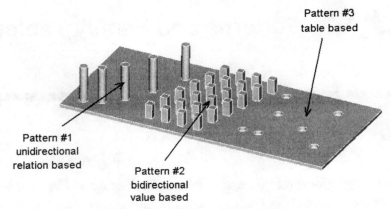

Figure 1 Examples of three types of *Dim Pattern*

It is possible to pattern multiple features at the same time. To do this, the features must be placed in a group (they must be contiguous on the model tree for this), and the special ***Group Pattern*** command must be used. All other details are the same as for creating a pattern of a single feature. This exercise was also performed in the previous Tutorial.

There are three types of patterns: *Identical*, *Varying*, and *General*. The differences between these involve the level of freedom you have over the size, references, and intersection of the instances. Identical patterns have the most restrictions and therefore give the least freedom, but are the quickest to regenerate. At the other extreme, general patterns give you full freedom but take longer to regenerate. The differences are as follows:

 ▸   identical pattern - instances must all be the same size, use the same reference surfaces, and cannot intersect
 ▸   varying pattern - instances can vary in size and use different reference surfaces, but cannot intersect
 ▸   general pattern - instances can vary in size, use different references, and intersect each other

The three types of patterns are created the same way.

The most important thing to remember about patterns is that, when you are creating the pattern leader, you should be planning ahead to figure out how you are going to use the pattern leader's dimensioning scheme to construct the pattern. For example, if you want to create an identical unidirectional pattern across the part, there should be only one single horizontal and/or vertical dimension to be incremented to locate the instances. If you have more than one dimension between the feature and the part in either direction but only increment one of them, the instances will not maintain their shape. See Figure 2 and note the differences in the dimensioning schemes of the pattern leaders. In fact, the pattern on the right in Figure 2 cannot be created as an identical pattern; it would have to be created as a varying pattern.

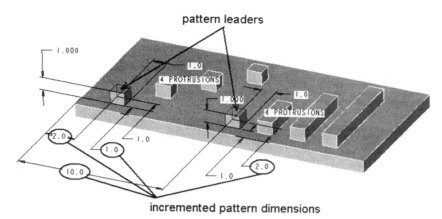

Figure 2 Different dimensioning schemes on pattern leaders can cause unexpected results!

In the following exercises, we will start by trying to create some simple *Identical* patterns. We will discover how Pro/E will respond to errors in the pattern definition. We will then move on to correctly define some uni- and bi-directional *Varying* patterns. We will introduce pattern relations and finish off with an introduction to pattern tables and reference patterns.

The first part we are going to make is shown in Figure 3. This is a thin-walled cylinder with a pattern of cuts distributed around the circumference (we will call this the cylindrical direction) and axially along the cylinder (axial direction). Although not really obvious from the figure, the width of the cuts also increases in the axial direction. This has serious implications, as we will soon see.

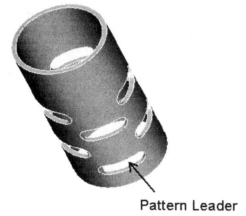

Pattern Leader

Figure 3 Completed part with patterned cuts

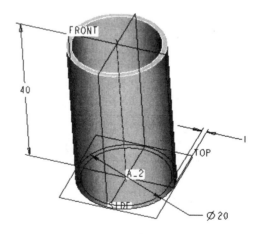

Figure 4 Base feature for *sleeve*

Create a new part called **sleeve**. Start by creating a hollow cylinder as a blind protrusion off the TOP datum plane. The outer diameter is **20** and the wall thickness is **1**. The height is **40**. See Figure 4.

Feature Creation for Revolved Patterns

Now we create the pattern leader. This cut will be sketched on a make datum tangent to the cylinder. In order to pattern this feature in the cylindrical direction, we want to have an angular dimension around the cylinder axis to be associated with the feature. We could do this by creating a number of datum planes, one of which is located by an angle dimension, grouping the associated datums and the cut, and then finally creating a group pattern. This would produce a large number of datum planes in the model. Instead, we will employ a number of make datums. This will embed the angular dimension directly in the cut feature and keep the Model Tree less cluttered.

> *Feature > Create > Solid > Cut*
> *Extrude | Solid | Done*
> *One Side | Done*

We need to create the sketching plane tangent to the cylinder at a certain angle. There are a couple of ways to do this. Here is one, using a series of make datums (see Figure 5). The final make datum we produce will be the sketching plane.

> *Setup New > Make Datum*
> *Through* {select the cylinder axis}
> *Angle* {select the SIDE datum}
> *Done*
> *Enter Value*

and enter a value of **30**. The make datum **DTM1** appears with a feature creation direction arrow. This is NOT the plane we want to use for our sketching plane. In the SETUP SK PLN menu, select

> *Setup New*
> *Make Datum*
> *Tangent* {pick the surface on the front of the cylinder}
> *Normal* {pick on DTM1}
> *Done*

Now we have a tangent make datum **DTM2** at the desired angle. This is our sketching plane. Make sure the creation direction arrow is pointing into the cylinder and select *Okay*. For the sketching reference plane select *Top* and pick on the TOP datum. The resulting planes are shown in the Figure 5.

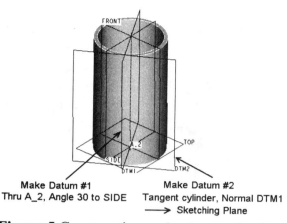

Make Datum #1
Thru A_2, Angle 30 to SIDE

Make Datum #2
Tangent cylinder, Normal DTM1
⟶ Sketching Plane

Figure 5 Constructing make datums for the cut

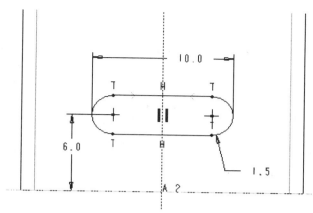

Figure 6 Sketch for the cut

Create the sketch shown in Figure 6. There is a vertical centerline aligned with the vertical datum DTM1, so that a symmetry constraint will be created. Note the dimensioning scheme. The vertical dimension will be used to create the pattern in the axial direction.

Complete the sketch and set a blind feature depth of **3**. Accept the feature. See Figure 7. Notice there is no sign of the make datums to clutter up our view!

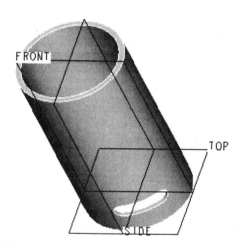

Now we will experiment with the pattern command, starting with simple unidirectional patterns.

Figure 7 Finished cut - the pattern leader

Identical Patterns

Let's try to create a unidirectional pattern along the axis of the cylinder, changing the width of the cut as we go. Can you predict what will happen?

> ***Feature > Pattern*** {click on the cut}
> ***Identical | Done***

All the dimensions appear. Notice the 30° angle dimension that was used in the construction of the make datums for the cut. Later in this exercise, we will use this dimension to create the cylindrical pattern.

For now, click on the height dimension, 6. Read the message window and enter a dimension increment of **5**. Then, click on the radius dimension on the sketch (R1.5) and enter an increment of **0.25**. ***Done***. The number of instances is **4**. Read the message window; there is nothing we want to do in the second direction, so select ***Done***. The pattern creation will abort. Why? The reason is that we have specified an *Identical* pattern, and we are trying to change the size of the feature. Changing the size of the feature is not allowed for *Identical* patterns.

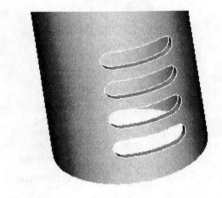

Create this pattern again, but without incrementing the radius dimension. This time the pattern will be created, as shown in Figure 8.

Let's have another look at how an *Identical* pattern can fail. In the FEAT menu select

> ***Del Pattern***

and click on any of the cuts, then ***Done***. The pattern leader is all that's left.

Figure 8 Unidirectional pattern of *Identical* cuts

Let's try to create a cylindrical pattern, making sure to keep the same size. Can we use an *Identical* pattern?

> ***Pattern*** {click the cut}
> ***Identical | Done***

Click on the 30° angular dimension, and specify an increment of **120**. ***Done***. Enter **3** instances. ***Done***. Once again, pattern creation is aborted, even though all the cuts are the same size. What happened this time? The answer is subtle: The outer surface of the cylinder, used to create the tangent make datum, is actually composed of two surfaces, one on the front and one on the back of the part. When trying to create the pattern instance on the back of the cylinder, Pro/E does not recognize the second surface is the one needed to create the tangent make datum, and so the instance cannot be created. What do we do now? Read on...

Varying Patterns

Recall that the second "level" of patterns is *Varying*. This allows instances to move across surfaces, as well as changing size. The instances can still not intersect.

> ***Pattern*** {click on the cut}
> ***Varying | Done***

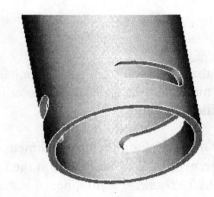

click on the 30° angle and enter an increment of **120**. ***Done***. Number of instances is **3**. ***Done***. Now we get the three cuts around the bottom circumference of the cylinder. See Figure 9.

Now we add a second direction to our pattern along the axis of the cylinder.

Open up the Model Tree, and delete the existing pattern

Figure 9 Successful *Varying* pattern

by holding down the right mouse button on the pattern entry and select *Delete Pattern*. Now create a new one:

> ***Pattern*** {click on the cut}
> ***Varying | Done***

In PAT DIM INCR, leave *Value* selected. For the first direction (cylindrical) click on the 30° angle dimension, enter increment **120**. *Done*. Enter **3** instances. For the second direction, click on the height (6) and enter an increment **6**, the angle (30°) and enter an increment **30**, and finally the radius (1.5) and enter an increment **0.15**. *Done*. The number of instances is **4**. The part regenerates as shown in Figure 10.

Figure 10 Completed pattern

Pattern Relations

As part of our design intent, we usually want to make our models as flexible as possible, with the minimum amount of labor required to make design changes. For patterns, it is often the case that we must modify the geometry based on the number of instances in the pattern. The best way of doing this is with relations.

Recall in the previous Tutorial that we can set up relations to manipulate the dimensions involved in the pattern. In an exercise there, we created a pattern of holes in a flange (a bolt circle) using relations to set the spacing between instances and location of the leader based on the number of holes. Those relations were defined at the part level.

We can also create relations specifically related to the pattern feature and contained within the feature definition. These are stored at a different place from the part relations, and utilize some new built-in symbols to give added flexibility.

For our sleeve part, we want to set up pattern relations so that the cylindrical spacing will be adjusted if we change the number of instances in that direction. We also want each row to line up with the gaps between the cuts in the row below. This will require two simple relations. Each will involve the symbolic name for the number of instances in the cylindrical direction.

In order to find the symbolic name for the number of instances in each direction of our pattern, we first have to create the pattern with a fixed

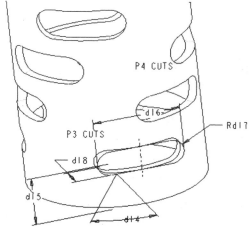

Figure 11 Finding symbolic names

increment and given number of instances. This was done above. To find the symbolic name, select *Feature > Modify*, and click on the pattern leader. The leader dimensions will appear along with the symbols giving the number of cuts in each direction. If necessary, select the *Switch Dims* icon in the top toolbar (or use *Info > Switch Dimensions*) to change from actual to symbolic dimensions. In Figure 11, this appears as P3. (The symbol P4 refers to the number of instances in the axial direction.) Note that the angle dimension to the first make datum is d14. **Your symbolic names will most likely be different from these, so make a note of them.**

Now we can set up our relations. We need to redefine the pattern so that the angle increment is driven by a relation instead of by a fixed value.

> *Feature > Redefine*

click on any of the cuts. In the Elements window scroll down and select

> *Pattern > Define*
> *Pat Incr Type*

In the menus below, *First Dir* is already selected, and the associated dimension d14 is already listed (or whatever your dimension name is). This is the driving dimension for the first direction. Select this dimension, and in the REDEF INCR menu select

> *To Relation > Edit*

The Pro/Table editor will now open up[1]. In the top few lines of this table are listed a number of system symbols that can be used in the pattern relations:

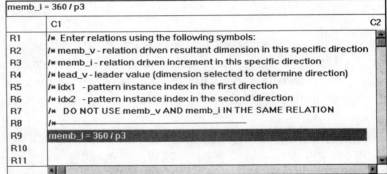

Figure 12 Pro/Table editor for pattern relations

memb_v - dimension of resultant position of pattern instance (this will probably depend on either idx1 or idx2)

memb_i - increment for each instance

lead_v - dimension of the leader

idx1 - index for instance in first direction

idx2 - index for instance in second direction

These definitions are automatically listed at the top of the edit window, so you don't have to memorize them. These symbolic names are not available in relations defined at the part level.

_____

[1] This requires the *config.pro* option
   relation_file_editor   protab
If not, your default system text editor may appear (such as Notepad in Windows).

Some possible uses of these symbols might be:

```
/* a variable spacing for each instance (10, 20, 30, ...)
memb_i = 10 * idx1
/* a sinusoidal variation in instance location
memb_v = lead_v + 10 * sin(idx1 * 180 / p3)
```

The possibilities are endless! Note that memb_v and memb_i cannot be used in the same relation (this wouldn't make sense anyway).

We'll do something simple here. We want to have the instance increment determined by the number of cuts. In the last line of the table, enter

```
memb_i = 360 / p3
```

where p3 is the symbolic name for the number of instances in this (cylindrical) direction, as shown in Figure 11. Leave Pro/Table, saving the relation, using *File > Exit*.

In **MOD PATT REL**, select *Done*.

In the second direction, we want the angular offset for the next row to be half the spacing of the first row. Select

> ***Second Dir***

The three dimensions associated with this direction are listed. Highlight the direction that controls the angle (d14). Select *To Relation > Edit*.

This brings up Pro/Table again. Enter the relation for this direction and increment as (remember to use your own symbolic name for the number of instances, p3)

```
memb_i = 180 / p3
```

Close the editor (*File > Exit*).

Back out of all the menus using *Done* and *Done/Return*, and accept the redefined feature. The sleeve should look like Figure 13.

Try out the new relations using *Feature > Modify* and changing the number of cuts in each direction. For the cylindrical direction, try 2 or 4. What happens if you try to create too many cuts in the cylindrical direction? in the axial direction? What happens if you increase the length of the cuts from 10 to 15 with 4 cuts around the circumference? Can you predict and/or explain what troubles might arise before you try these changes?

Figure 13 Pattern driven by relations

An easy way to edit the pattern relations is the following:

Part > Relations > Pattern Rel

and click on one of the instances. All the dimensions show up. You can select either ***First Dir*** or ***Second Dir***. The associated pattern dimensions that have relations defined are listed. In our case, for both directions only the single angle dimension (d14) appears. Selecting d14 brings up a menu that lets you add, edit, show, etc., all the pattern relations. For example, select ***Show Rel***. Close this window and select ***Edit Rel***. The Pro/Table editor will open to allow you to modify the relation for this dimension for the chosen direction.

We are finished with this part, so save it and then remove it from the session. So far, we have created patterns of regularly spaced features. In the next section, we will explore a powerful way of creating a pattern of arbitrarily spaced or located features.

Pattern Tables

Patterns controlled by values result in regularly spaced instances. Relations allow you to locate instances using formulas or expressions. For example, with appropriate relations you could pattern holes around an elliptical opening. For a pattern of features that have truly irregular locations, we need a new tool - a pattern table.

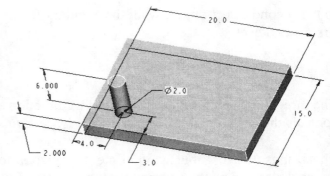

Figure 14 Base feature and pattern leader

Start by creating a new part **bosses**. Create a base plate (20 X 15 X 2 thick) and single circular protrusion (diameter 2, located as shown in Figure 14). Since we are going to pattern the protrusion, make sure it has dimensions as shown giving its location from the left and front faces of the base plate.

Modifying Dimension Symbols

For what we are about to do next, it is very handy to have symbolic names for dimensions. Select

> ***Feature > Modify***
> ***Dim Cosmetics > Symbol***
> *{Click on the boss}*

and click on the horizontal dimension to the center of the boss. Enter a new name "boss_x". Then click on the dimension that gives the vertical location, and call it "boss_y." You may have to select the *Switch Dims* icon

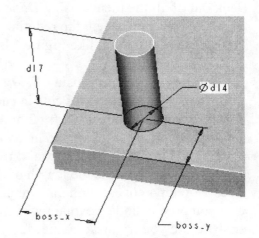

Figure 15 Symbolic names

in the toolbar to see these. These names for the dimensions will appear in the pattern table, and are much more meaningful there than d17 and d18, or whatever.

Creating the Pattern Table

Now we're ready to set up a pattern table.

> *Feature > Pattern*
> {click on the boss}
> *Identical | Done*
> *Table*

Read the message window. Click on the horizontal dimension (boss_x or 4) and the vertical dimension (boss_y or 3), then *Done*. In the PATT TABLE menu, select *Add* and enter a name for the table like "bosses". Now we are in the Pro/Table editor. In this table we can enter values for the chosen dimensions for each instance in the pattern. Each row in the table corresponds to one instance and contains the following columns:

> idx - the instance number, starting from 1. This does not include the pattern leader, which
> is automatically created with the table.
> boss_x - the horizontal location
> boss_y - the vertical position

The pattern leader is shown in row 9 in Figure 16, with its corresponding dimensions in parentheses. The formatting and alignment of these columns is not great. For any row below this, if you want to use the pattern leader's dimension for that column, just enter an asterisk, "*". Enter the data shown in Figure 16, and then select *File > Exit > Done*.

R7	!	Table name BOSSES.	
R8	!		
R9	! idx	boss_x(4.0)	boss_y(3.0)
R10	1	16 *	
R11	2	10	7.5
R12	3 *		12
R13	4	16	12
R14			

Figure 16 Pattern table for *bosses*

We now have the 5 bosses shown in Figure 17 according to the (x,y) positions specified in the table. Note that although the four corner bosses could have been created with an incremental ("value") pattern, we would not be able to create the 5th boss in the center that way.

A common use of pattern tables is to create irregular patterns, for example of mounting holes in a plate.

Figure 17 Pattern created using table

How can we change the locations of the bosses? Try this:

Feature > Modify

click on one of the bosses in the pattern, say the back right boss (number 4 in the pattern table). Change its height (6) to **10**, and its horizontal position (16) to **12**. Regenerate the part. Notice that the height dimension is the same for all bosses, since it was not included in the pattern table. The horizontal location has changed because it is unique to that instance.

For another way to change the locations, select

Modify > Pattern Table

A new window ("Tables") opens up. Highlight the table entry "bosses" in the tree; be careful not to select the part "bosses" at the top. In the icons at the bottom of the window, find the one (third from left) that will "Edit the Selected Table". Observe that the boss_x value for instance idx=4 has changed. Change the horizontal position of the last boss back to 16 in the table. What is the difference between *OK* and *Apply* in this window? Go back to the Part menu and *Modify* the height to 6. *Regenerate* the part.

So, we have two ways to modify entries in the pattern table.

Reference Patterns

A reference pattern involves a second pattern laid on top of a first pattern. The second pattern will "copy" any references used in creating the first pattern.

Create a small solid protrusion at the location of the pattern leader, as shown in Figure 19. We'll call this a fin. It is crucial that this new feature reference only the geometry of the pattern leader. To do that, using Intent Manager you can select just the axis of the boss as a reference. Then create vertical and horizontal centerlines. This will allow a symmetry constraint to be set up for the rectangular sketch, shown in Figure 18. Create the protrusion with a blind height of **4**.

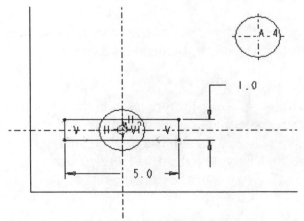

Figure 18 Sketch of the fin

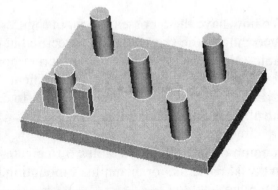

Figure 19 Fin added to pattern leader

Now we want to put a copy of each fin on the other members of the boss pattern.

> ***Pattern***

and select the fin on the pattern leader.

In the **PRO PAT TYPE** menu, select

> ***Ref Pattern > Done***

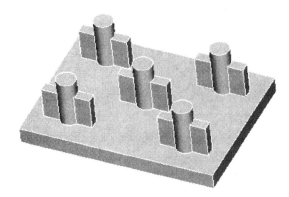

That's all there is to it! The fin duplicates itself onto all the instances in the reference pattern. See Figure 20.

Open up the model tree to see how these two patterns appear there. How is this different from if we had created a group (boss+fin) and patterned the group? What would be the functional difference of this arrangement?

Figure 20 Fins created using reference pattern

Let's edit the pattern table:

> ***Modify > Pattern Table***

Select the table "bosses" and the edit icon. Select the first element in the last row in the table and remove it using ***Edit > Delete***. Exit from the editor and ***Regenerate*** the part.

The important thing to remember here is that the leader in the second pattern should reference only the pattern leader in the reference pattern.

To see the effect of the "*" entries in the pattern table, use

> ***Modify > Value***

to change the horizontal dimension (boss_x) of the pattern leader to **6**, and the vertical dimension (boss_y) to **8**. ***Regenerate*** the part. Notice that, since the pattern is a general type, the fin features can intersect.

Before we leave patterns, note that there is a considerable amount of information in the on-line documentation on the use and manipulation of patterns, in particular pattern relations and creating patterns on surfaces of revolution. For example, once a pattern has been created, you can break the dependence of the instances on the pattern leader with the ***Make Indep*** command in the ***Modify*** menu. This allows you to modify an instance without affecting the rest of the patterned features.

Save the part and erase it from the session.

Family Tables

As mentioned in the overview to this lesson, family tables are to parts what pattern tables are to features. Typical uses for family tables are to construct series of similar-shaped parts like bolts, fittings, housings, gears, and so on. To create a family of parts you do the following:

> ► create a *generic* part (in a pattern this would be called the pattern leader),
> ► create a table to specify which dimensions, features, and/or parameters will vary among the *instances* or individual copies of the part,
> ► edit the table to create new instances by specifying an instance name and associated values for the selected dimensions, features, and/or parameters

In this lesson, we will create a family table that describes some of the parts shown in Figure 21. These elbow fittings have variable diameter, variable angle, variable wall thickness, and can have one of several different end conditions (flange, hose, pipe). All of these variations are contained in a single generic part.

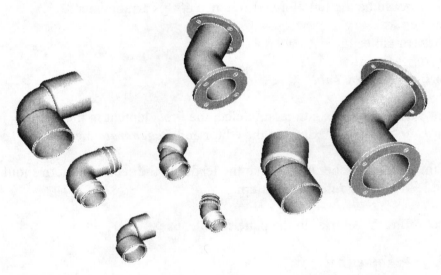

Figure 21 Instances of a part created using a family table

Creating the Generic Part

We will construct the generic part using a sweep to create the base feature. Start a new part called **elbowg**. First, construct a sketched datum curve to serve as the trajectory for the sweep. Sketch this in the TOP datum plane. The sketch is shown in Figure 22.

Use the datum curve as a trajectory to construct a simple sweep whose section is a circle of diameter **50**. Then use the *Shell* command to remove the end faces, leaving a thickness of **2.5**. At this point, your part should look like Figure 23.

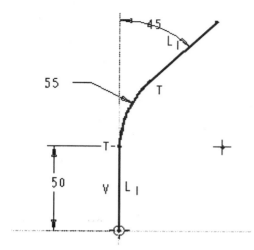

Figure 22 Datum curve sketch

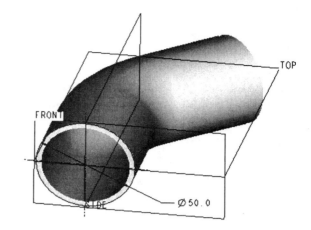

Figure 23 Elbow base feature (sweep along datum curve) plus shell

In the family table, we will enter the angle and the diameter as dimensions to control the instances. Also, so that these dimensions will control other dimensions in the part, we will set up some relations for the length of the straight section and the radius of the elbow. For both these operations, it will be handy to change the symbols for the angle and diameter.

Go to

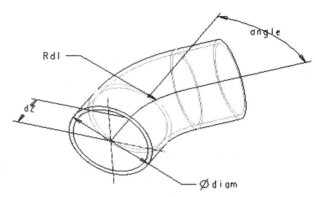

Figure 24 Named dimensions for use in family table

> ***Feature > Modify***
> ***Dim Cosmetics > Symbol***
> *{click on the datum curve}*
> *{click on the sweep and select **Section**}*
> *{click on the shell surface}*

Click on the angle dimension, see the message window, and enter a new name "**angle**". Click on the diameter dimension and enter a new name "**diam**". See Figure 24. Change the symbolic name of the shell thickness dimension to "**thick**".

Now we want to enter some relations. A quick way to do this is

> ***Modify > Value***

Click on the datum curve radius dimension (55) and enter "**1.1*diam / 2**". Pro/E asks if you want this added as a relation to the part; select ***Yes***. This makes the radius of the elbow slightly larger than the radius of the pipe. Why do we want to do this? The answer is so that the sweep will always regenerate for any value of the elbow diameter. If we don't modify the trajectory radius this way and enter a very large pipe diameter, the sweep would fail.

Click on the length dimension for the datum curve (50) and enter "**diam / 2**" and add this as a relation. Now the straight ends of the elbow will change their length depending on the pipe diameter.

Try out the new relations. First, regenerate the part to see the shape governed by the relations. Then *Modify* the angle dimension to **30** and the section diameter dimension to **20**. *Regenerate*. Try an angle of **90** and a diameter of **60**. When you are satisfied that the relations are working correctly, proceed. Otherwise, use *Part > Relations > Edit* to make necessary corrections.

For the following, change the dimensions back to angle **30** and diameter **20**.

Creating the Family Table

In the PART menu, select

> *Family Tab*

This brings up the Family Table editor, Figure 25. To use it, basically follow the instructions in the window. The family table operates the same as a pattern table: each column contains entries for a selected parameter, and each row will yield an instance of the part. Unlike a pattern table, where instances are numbered, the second column in a family table contains an instance name. The icons across the top are your main controls for manipulating the data in the table.

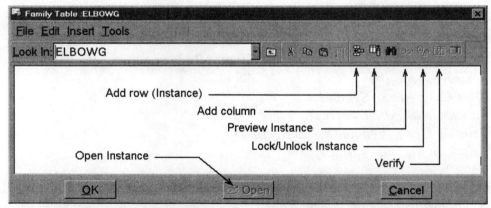

Figure 25 The Family Table editor window (interior text removed)

Click the *Add Column* icon. This opens another window (Family Items) shown in Figure 26. Some choices are grayed out at this time. With the *Dimension* radio button selected in the *Add Item* area at the bottom, pick the datum curve, and select the angle dimension. Pick the sweep section and select the diameter dimension. Finally, pick the shell and select the thickness dimension. As each dimension is picked, it will be added into the item list. Select *OK* when all three are listed.

Back in the Family Table editor, the name of the generic part is indicated along with the generic part dimensions. Each row below the generic is used to create an instance of the part. In the second column of the table, under *Name*, we will enter unique part names for all the instances we want to define. In the third and subsequent columns are the identified dimensions we will vary among instances. To use any of the generic part's dimensions in an instance, use the "*" symbol.

In the pull-down menu, select

Insert > Instance Row

or use the ***Add Row*** icon, or select any cell in the first row and hit the ***Enter*** key. In the new row, enter **E-60-40-3** as a new instance name in the second column. In the angle column, enter **60**. In the diameter and thickness columns enter **40** and **3**, respectively.

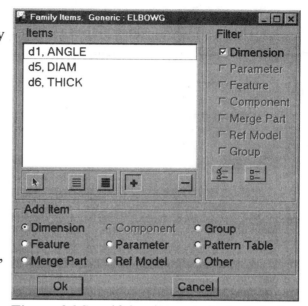

Figure 26 Specifying items to include in the family table

Enter another part instance **E-30-20-2**. In the dimension columns enter angle **30** (or use "*"), diameter **20** (or "*"), and thickness **2**. Using the "*" symbol is handy to get the value from the generic. Beware of using the "*" - this will have ramifications discussed a bit later. The completed family table is shown in Figure 27.

Type	Instance Name	d1 ANGLE	d5 DIAM	d6 THICK
	ELBOWG	30.000000	20.000000	2.500000
	E-60-40-3	60	40	3
	E-30-20-2	*	*	2

Figure 27 Completed Family Table

Verifying the Family Table

Near the right end of the icons, select the ***Verify*** icon. This will validate all the instances in the current family table. A small window will open and allow you to choose which instance(s) to check. Highlight both the instances and select ***Verify***. If all has gone according to plan, you should see the entries "Success" beside each one.   A failure would obviously require us to go back to the generic part to debug the model. If you have a very large model and/or family table, the verify could take some time. ***Close*** the verify window.

A summary of the verification results is written to a file, in this case **elbowg.tst,** in the current working directory. Open this file with your system editor. It contains the name of each instance and the regeneration result (Success or Failure).

Examining Instances

On the screen, we still have the generic part. To view the geometry of an instance, highlight the instance name and select the toolbar icon

> ***Preview***

This opens another small window which displays the instance. Close this window.

Another way to look at an instance (or if you want to do additional work on it, like add more features) is to highlight the instance name and select ***Open*** (bottom center of family table window). For example, do this with the instance *E-60-40-3*. Note that in the lower right corner of the screen you are notified that the part being displayed is an instance, and the name is given. This window is now active, meaning that you could further modify the instance by adding features and so on. We will discuss modifying the instances a bit later. Find out what happens if you try to save an instance of the part[2]. For now, close its window with (from the pull-down menu) ***Window > Close*** and then activate the generic part window (either with ***Window > Activate***, or the short-cut key ***Ctrl-A***). Bring up the other instance of the part. The two instances are shown in Figures 28 and 29. Remember to close the instance window and activate the generic window when you are done. Save the generic part.

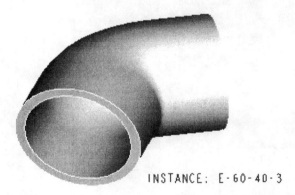

INSTANCE: E-60-40-3

Figure 28 An instance in the family table

INSTANCE: E-30-20-2

Figure 29 .. Another instance

---

[2] **HINT**: Set your *config.pro* file with the following option:
      display_full_object_path   **yes**
and observe the title area at the top of the Pro/E window when you have an opened instance. Also, have a look at the idx file in your working directory.

Adding Features to the Family Table

So far, all we have included in the family table are the variable dimensions for the instances. We can also specify optional features in the generic part which can be included in the instances. These features must be regenerated in the generic, and we have the option of keeping them or suppressing them in each of the instances. We will use this capability to create alternative end conditions for the elbow.

This can get complicated due to parent/child relations. In the family table, we identify single features for presence/absence in the instance. If these features have children in the generic, then we are also implicitly controlling these children in the instances, because if the parent is suppressed, all its children will be suppressed as well.

Furthermore, all the optional features must be able to independently coexist in the generic part. If the regeneration or suppression of one feature in the family table interferes with the references of another, then these references will have to be redefined.

We will create two alternative ends for the elbow - a flange and some ribs for a hose fitting.

First, we'll create the ribs for the hose fitting (Figure 31). The ribs are created using a 360° revolved protrusion, sketched on the SIDE datum. The sketch is shown in Figure 30 and the completed ribs are shown in Figure 31.

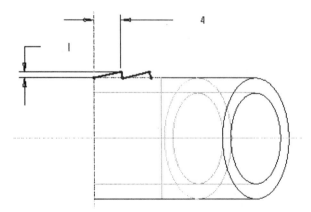

Figure 30 Sketch for the hose fitting
(Sketcher constraints not shown)

Figure 31 Hose fitting on generic part

Now we'll create the flange as a 360° revolved protrusion. But first, we want to make sure that the flange does not reference the ribs in any way by suppressing the ribs. For the flange, use the SIDE datum as sketching plane, and create the sketch shown in Figure 32. Use the FRONT datum as a sketching reference. See Figure 33 for the completed flange.

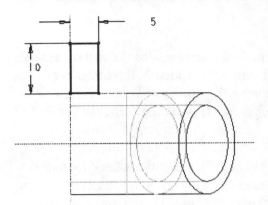

Figure 32 Sketch for the flange

Figure 33 Flange on generic part

Resume the ribs into the generic part, so that both the flange and the ribs are available[3]. You might reposition your screen so that both features are visible. Note that the flange completely covers the rib closest to the end of the elbow. Using *Part > Set Up > Name*, rename the flange and rib features to "**flange**" and "**hose**". This will make entries in the family table a little easier to follow (just like renaming dimensions).

Now, in the PART menu, select

> *Family Tab > Add Column > Feature*
> *Sel By Menu > Feature | Name | FLANGE | Select*

Repeat the *Sel By Menu* command and pick on the **HOSE** feature. Middle click twice, then *OK*.

We have added a couple of columns[4]. In the generic part, both features are present ("**Y**"). Edit the two instances as shown in Figure 34. Note that we are also changing the name of each instance. In the last two columns, the Y and N entries control the presence of that feature in the instance. For the flanged elbow, we want to suppress the ribs, and vice versa. Use *Verify* to check the definitions of the two instances, then *Preview* them. Leave the table editor.

Type	Instance Name	d1 ANGLE	d5 DIAM	d6 THICK	F84 FLANGE	F140 HOSE
	ELBOWG	30.00000000	20.00000000	2.50000000	Y	Y
	E-60-40-3-F	60.00000000	40.00000000	3.00000000	Y	N
	E-30-20-2-H	*	*	2.00000000	N	Y

Figure 34 Features added to Family Table

---

[3] This may be tricky. If the geometry is not what you expected, check the sketching references in the flange when the ribs have been resumed.

[4] You can change column widths by dragging on the column separators.

Child Features in the Generic Part

We want to duplicate the flange/rib fittings at the other end of the elbow. We could make these independently, but this would require additional columns in the family table. A more elegant way is to create these as children of the flange/rib features created above. There are a number of ways of doing this. Several of these require the presence of a datum plane created *Through* the datum curve and *Normal* to the TOP datum at the back of the elbow. You might like to enter **Insert Mode** and create this feature immediately after the datum curve. This datum plane might also come in handy when we get to assembly mode, since we will have similar datum planes at both ends of the elbow.

To create the duplicated end fitting features, some possibilities are the following:

▸   create a *Copy > Move > Rotate*, and set up a relation for the rotation angle
▸   create a *Copy > New Refs | Dependent*
▸   create a new feature, being careful in Intent Manager to reference the existing previous fitting to establish the parent/child relation

Choose whichever method makes the most sense to you (or try all three!). As you are creating each feature, you may want to suppress some features to avoid inadvertently setting up a parent/child relation you don't want. Name these two features **hose_copy** and **flange_copy**.

The completed generic part with both features on both ends of the elbow is shown in Figure 35. Now would be a good time to check on the parent/child relations in the part. You can do this by calling up the Model Tree and holding down the right mouse button on the desired feature in the Tree, and selecting *Info > Parent Child Info*. This will let you browse through all the parent and child relations in the part.

With our new features added to the generic, go to **Family Tab > Verify** to validate the table. With the *Preview* command, call up each of the instances we have created. If everything is correct, you should get the parts shown in Figures 36 and 37.

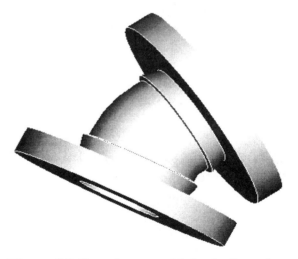

Figure 35 Generic part with both rib and flange features regenerated

INSTANCE: E-60-40-3-F

Figure 36 An instance in the family table

INSTANCE: E-30-20-2-H

Figure 37 Another instance in the family table

We are now essentially completed the creation of the generic part. Save it.

Go to the system (eg in Windows, use Explorer), and bring up a directory listing of the working directory. The only entry for the elbow family in the directory is the generic part, **elbowg.prt**. The instances are not saved separately. You will also notice another file with the same root name as your working directory and the extension *idx*. This is the instance index file for this directory. Open this up in your system editor. It contains a listing of all instances defined for any generic part in the current directory that has a family table defined. The idx file is updated whenever you save the generic part. There are additional functions that reference the idx file. See the command ***File > Instance Operations*** in the pull-down menus. For further information, see the on-line documentation.

With the generic part saved, close Pro/Engineer. We want to see what will happen when we open the generic into an empty session.

Manipulating Parts Containing Family Tables

Start up Pro/E again, then select ***File > Open*** or choose the icon on the toolbar. Although the instances do not exist in the working directory, you will see an entry in the File Open dialog window for each instance. As part of the instance name, you will see the generic part, as in *<elbowg>*. This information was obtained from the index file.

In the File Open dialog window, select one of the instances, say *E-30-20-2-H*. When the part is brought in, you will see the INSTANCE label on the screen. Try the ***Family Table*** command. This does not show us the same data as before. In fact, we could now create another family table with the hose elbow treated as the generic. Nested tables! This is something to experiment with later on your own. For now, close the family table window.

Change the thickness of the shell in this instance. *Modify* the shell thickness to **1**. See Figure 38. Note the message window. You are notified that the shell thickness is table driven, and you can confirm modification to the family table entry. *Regenerate* the instance.

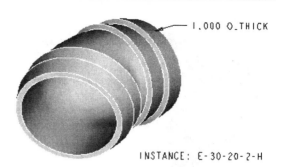

What do you think will happen if you modify a table driven dimension in the instance, that is indicated by "*" in the family table in the generic part?

Figure 38 Modifying a table-driven dimension in an instance

Open the generic part. If you select *File > Open* and select the generic part *elbowg.prt*, you will see the window shown in Figure 39. Examine the contents under the two tabs. Highlight "The generic" in the *By Name* tab and select *Open*. Then select *Family Tab*. The table is shown in Figure 40. Note that the thickness value that we changed manually for the second instance has been modified in the table.

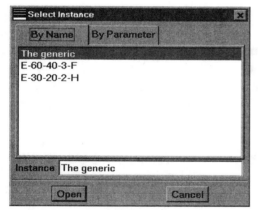

Type	Instance Name	d1 ANGLE	d5 DIAM	d6 THICK	F84 FLANGE	F140 HOSE
	ELBOWG	30.000000	20.000000	2.50000	Y	Y
	E-60-40-3-F	60.000000	40.000000	3.00000	Y	N
	E-30-20-2-H	*	*	1.00000	N	Y

Figure 40 Modified table in generic part due to modified value in instance (Figure 38)

Figure 39 The *File > Open* dialog for a part containing a family table

What happens if you modify a dimension in an instance that is not in the family table? Open up the other instance, *E-60-40-3-F*. *Modify* the flange thickness to **2**. *Regenerate* the instance. See Figure 41. Go to the window containing the generic part (use *Window* in the pull-down menus to select the generic part). The dimension in the generic part has changed as shown in Figure 42. Note that the rib closest to the end of the elbow is now slightly visible in the generic part.

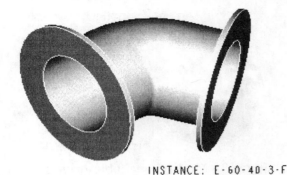

INSTANCE: E-60-40-3-F

Figure 41 Modified flange dimension in instance (not table driven)

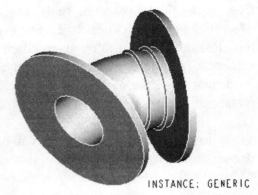

INSTANCE: GENERIC

Figure 42 Modified dimension in generic (not table driven)

Thus, we have the following things to note:

▸   Modifying a table-driven dimension in the instance changes the table entry in the generic part for that instance only

▸   Modifying a non-table driven dimension in the instance changes the generic part (and therefore all other instances using that feature)

If you want to modify a non-table driven dimension in an instance without affecting the generic part, you must do a ***Save A Copy*** when the instance is active. Select and make active the window containing the instance *E-30-20-2-H*. Save this, providing a unique name for the new file, say **E3020TEST**. See the message window. Open the system directory again and you should see this as a new (independent) part file. Back in Pro/E, open this new file. It will appear without the INSTANCE label on the screen. Open the model tree - there are no suppressed features in this part. Change the shell thickness to **3**. Open the windows for the previous instance *E-30-20-2-H* and the generic *elbowg*. Neither of these has been affected by the change in the independent part file E3020TEST.

Locked Instances

When a family table is created, to prevent inadvertent changes to the table driven dimensions (like the shell thickness above), you can put a "lock" in the first column of the family table. Do that now in the generic part using the ***Lock/Unlock*** icon for the instance *E-30-20-2-H*. Switch to the instance, and try to modify the thickness of the shell. Pro/E will inform you that the dimension is locked. If a number of people are using the same generic parts (like bolts, for example), this prevents them from making changes to the table definition that could affect the other users.

Adding Features to an Instance

Let's add a pattern of holes to the front flange on instance E-60-40-3-F. Bring in the instance, and create the first hole using a diameter dimension scheme. Make a straight hole with a diameter of **5**, and select a ***Thru Next*** depth specification. Place the hole on the front flange at an angle of 45° from the TOP datum. In the data entry box for the placement diameter dimension, enter "**diam+10**". This will make sure the holes are outside the diameter of the pipe. Create a pattern of 4 holes using an increment of **90°**. See Figure 43.

Switch to the generic part. The hole pattern is not there. Switch back to the instance and select *Save*. The instance will still not show up in the directory listing as a separate part.

Erase all objects in your session. You must first erase all the instances, then erase the generic.

Open the instance *E-60-40-3-F*. The holes are there! How does Pro/E know how to make them (that is, where is the hole data stored)?

INSTANCE: E-60-40-3-F

Figure 43 Bolt hole pattern created in instance.

This concludes our discussion of family tables for now. We will return to the use of family table-driven parts in a later lesson, to see how these can be used efficiently in an assembly.

This lesson has introduced you to methods to create table-driven features using patterns, and series of similar parts using family tables. As usual, we have introduced the main ideas for these topics and there is considerably more to learn by browsing through the on-line documentation and experimenting on your own. For example, it is possible to include a pattern table within a family table. This might be useful to specify a bolt hole pattern that will vary from one part instance to another. You can also construct families of families. As usual with Pro/E, careful planning up front is required to efficiently use these advanced functions.

In the next lesson we will return to examining some of the functions in Pro/E to create single features and feature groups using User Defined Features (UDF's).

Questions for Review

1. The first feature in a pattern on which all the others are based is called the _____.
2. What are the three main types of patterns? What are the main differences between these?
3. What is a common cause of the failure of an Identical pattern? How would you attempt to fix it?
4. What happens to the pattern leader when you select *Del Pattern*?
5. Can you create an Identical pattern on a cylindrical surface that goes more than 180° around the axis of the cylinder? If not, why not?
6. What is your only option if you are going to create a pattern of features that will intersect each other?
7. In a bi-directional pattern, does the second direction always result in a pattern at 90° to the first direction?
8. What are the built-in symbols that we can use in creating pattern relations? How are these defined? Give an example of the use of each symbol.
9. Do the following relations result in the same pattern?
    ```
    memb_v = 10*(idx - 1)
    memb_i = lead_v + idx*10
    ```
10. In a value-driven pattern, what happens if the increment is negative?
11. From the part level, what is the shortest command sequence you can use to find out the relations that have been used in creating a pattern?
12. What command will toggle the display of dimensions/symbols?
13. Why can there be multiple definitions of memb_i in a single part?
14. How can you rename the dimension symbols in a part?
15. What is the difference between symbols idx1, idx2, ipx, and idx?
16. What are two ways to modify the values in a pattern table?
17. What happens if you modify a feature dimension that is not included in the pattern table?
18. What is the primary restriction for using a reference pattern?
19. What are the three main steps required to create a family table?
20. What command do you use to validate the entries in the family table?
21. What is the main complication when including features in the family table?
22. Why should you rename features to be used in a family table? What happens if you do not?
23. Can you rename a feature after it has been included in the family table? What entry occurs in the family table in that case?
24. What is contained in the instance index file? How is it identified? Where is it stored? Can you have more than one?
25. How can you change a dimension in an instance without affecting the generic part?
26. How can you prevent accidental changes to table-driven dimensions in the generic part?

Project Exercises

The project parts in this lesson involve patterns, pattern tables, and family tables.

Start by adding the horizontal holes to the lower side frame. Create the pattern leader 320mm from the end and then a pattern table, where the pattern contains the dimension of the hole from the end of the frame. The pattern table is shown in the figure at the right.

!	Table name HOLE_LOCNS.	
!		
! idx	d27(320.0)	
1		380.0
2		470.0
3		530.0

The next part to make is the main side wheel. The base feature is a revolved protrusion with the key dimensions shown in the figure. Add additional features such as a hub and a pattern of cuts to make the spokes. The 4 holes in the center are a simple radial pattern. Estimate the location now, and you can modify the pattern diameter later to match the axle we will build in the next lesson. Note that the bolt holes have a 45° chamfer. This will mate with the conical surface of the lug nuts made in Lesson 3. Try using a **Ref Pattern** for the chamfer.

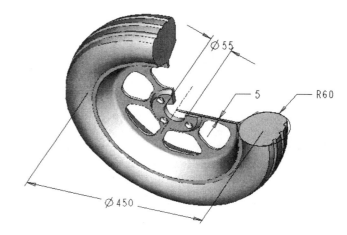

PART: *wheel*

We'll now make two parts that involve family tables. The first is the square tubing to be used in the frame. This is shown in the figure on the left. The family table is shown at the right.

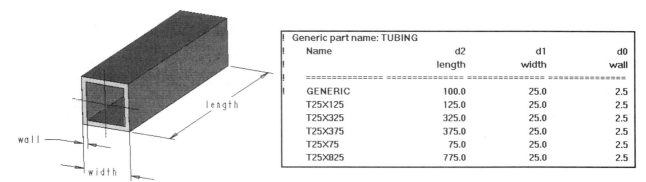

! Generic part name: TUBING			
! Name	d2	d1	d0
!	length	width	wall
! ===============	===============	===============	===============
! GENERIC	100.0	25.0	2.5
T25X125	125.0	25.0	2.5
T25X325	325.0	25.0	2.5
T25X375	375.0	25.0	2.5
T25X75	75.0	25.0	2.5
T25X825	775.0	25.0	2.5

PART: *tubing*

The last part this lesson is a hex-head shoulder bolt. We won't bother with the threads on this. However, notice the lip feature on the top surface. The length is set in the family table.

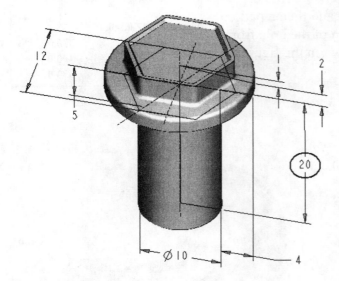

! Generic part name: HEX_BOLT	
! Name	d3
!	length
! ================ ================	
! GENERIC	20.0
H20	20.0
H30	30.0
H40	40.0
H50	50.0

PART: *hex_bolt*

Lesson 5

User Defined Features (UDF's)

Synopsis

Creating and using User Defined Features; *Standalone* and *Subordinate* modes; *Independent* and *UDF Driven*; using family tables; dimension display modes; patterns of UDF's

Overview

Since the beginnings of CAD a few decades ago, a fundamental tenet has been to never reinvent the wheel! Any time a reasonably complicated or common model (or parts of one) is produced, it makes sense to reuse it in another job rather than to recreate it each time. Furthermore, in a corporate environment, there may be particular standards and practices in modeling which are desired. This is the essence of User Defined Features (UDF's). In the former case, UDF's are feature definitions that are stored in separate files and can be brought into any part (and most times assemblies as well). The UDF can be used over and over, thus reducing the need for repetitive modeling activity. In the second case, a library of UDF's can be maintained such that anyone working at a particular site can access and use the same geometric elements. This promotes good practice and standardization and more productive modeling.

This lesson will introduce the main aspects of creating and using UDF's. We will go through three exercises, starting from something very simple, to illustrate the main options and principles. The first exercise contains a UDF composed of a single feature. The second exercise is considerably more complex and involves several features and a family table that is contained within the UDF. The third exercise shows how a single UDF definition file can be used to control the geometry in many other parts simultaneously, even after the UDF has been placed in these other parts. Finally, we will have a look at the UDF's included in the Pro/E Basic Library.

Introduction to User Defined Features

One of the more confusing aspects of UDF's, at least initially, is the meaning of terms. So, a good place to start is some definitions. For the most part, these are consistent terms with the Pro/E on-line documentation so after you finish this lesson you can comprehend the documentation a bit better. The important terms are given below. Other terms relate to options that will be presented as we create and use the UDF's in the exercises below. We will discuss them as they arise.

Definitions

For the graphically inclined, these definitions are illustrated schematically in Figures 1 and 2.

Original model - This is the model where the UDF is created. One or more features in the model are identified as belonging to the UDF. The original model can be the source for several UDF's, depending on how the features are chosen. The model can be an actual part (or assembly) under construction, or, more usually, it is a simple base feature to which only the features for a single UDF are added. Depending on how the UDF is created, the original model may have to be present at all times when the UDF is used (see Exercise #3 below). At other times, a copy of the original model will be created (see *reference model* below) from the original. A third possibility is that once the UDF is created, with certain options, the original model can be deleted.

New model - This is the model where the UDF is used. The UDF definition is read from a file and the features are reconstructed in the new model by specifying references, assigning values to variable dimensions, and so on. Note that in the new model, the UDF appears in the Model Tree as a group, even if composed of a single feature, with the same name as the UDF.

***Standalone* UDF** - If a UDF is created so that it's connection to the original model is broken, then it is classed as *Standalone*. See Figure 1. The original model is not required in order to use the UDF and changes in the original model will not affect it.

Reference model - When a standalone UDF is created, you have the option of creating a copy of the original model along with the UDF. This copy is called the reference model (Figure 1). The purpose of having a reference model is so that, when the UDF is being placed, you can view the reference model in a second graphics window. This makes it easier to determine or visualize the references, dimensions, orientation, shape, and so on, of the UDF before it is placed. In order to keep the size of the reference model small, the original model will usually contain only a base feature and the necessary references to define the UDF.

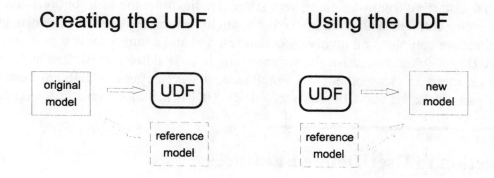

Figure 1 Creating and Using a *Standalone* UDF

***Subordinate* UDF** - This form requires the presence of the original model whenever the UDF is used. See Figure 2. When the UDF is brought into the new model, the original model is consulted for dimension values and other information required to create the UDF. This essentially takes the place of the reference model defined above, and can result in reduced disk space requirements. It also makes it very easy to update the UDF by simply modifying the original model. Whenever a new model is retrieved that uses the UDF, the current definition of the UDF in the original model is used.

Figure 2 Creating and Using a *Subordinate* UDF

There are some other combinations of options during creation and use of UDF's. However, the two modeling scenarios shown in Figures 1 and 2 illustrate the common operating modes of UDF's.

Now, on to some exercises...

UDF Exercises

As mentioned above, we are going to do three exercises using UDF's, of gradually increasing complexity. These will illustrate both *Standalone* and *Subordinate* operation, as well as some variations and options in the UDF definitions.

Exercise #1: Standalone, Independent

The first example will introduce you to the major steps involved in creating and using a UDF. This will be a simple example so that you can see an overview of the process. The part we want to make is an oval shaped cover plate with six "pins" that mate in sockets in another part. The cover plate and a closeup view of one pin are shown in Figures 3 and 4. The reason we want to use a UDF for this task is so that the pin geometry can be reused in additional cover plates without going to additional effort in recreating the pin geometry each time.

The pin will be created as a *Shaft* feature[1] so that the only placement reference required is a single datum point in the center of its base. If we used a revolved protrusion, we would have to specify sketching and reference planes. It is a good idea to have the simplest reference scheme possible for the UDF, as there will then be fewer steps involved, less confusion, and fewer chances for errors later on when the UDF is used.

---

[1] You will need the *config.pro* option
  allow_anatomic_features   yes
to be able to create this feature.

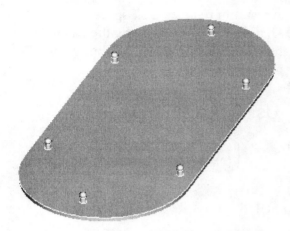

Figure 3 Cover plate with six UDF pins

Figure 4 Pin created as *SHAFT* feature (reference part)

Creating the Original Model

Start a new part called **udf_pin_org**. Using *Part > Set Up*, set the part units to millimeters (unless that is in your default template). Create the protrusion shown in Figure 5, a 20 X 15 X 2 block. Place a datum point on the center of the top surface. The dimensioning scheme for the datum point will not affect the UDF. The pin is created as a *Shaft* feature using the *On Point* placement option. The sketch for the shaft is shown in Figure 6 (remember that the *Shaft* feature requires a closed sketch). The completed original model with the pin is shown in Figure 4.

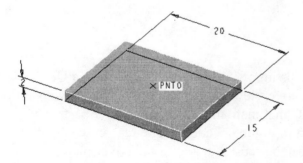

Figure 5 Base feature of original model

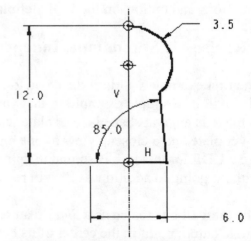

Figure 6 Sketch of *SHAFT* feature

Creating the UDF

To create a UDF of the pin, in the FEAT menu select

      UDF Library > Create

You are prompted for the name of the UDF, enter "**cover_pin**". Select the option

> ***Standalone > Done***

You are now asked if you want to include the reference part. Select *YES*.

The UDF element definition window appears as shown in Figure 7. At the top of the window are shown the name and type of the UDF. The first thing to do is to select features to be contained in the UDF. The UDF FEATS menu should be automatically brought up with the following defaults highlighted

> ***Add > Select > Pick***

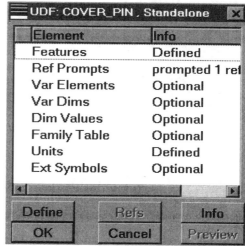

Figure 7 UDF creation elements

Pick on the shaft. It highlights in red. Middle click and select *Done/Return*.

The next item in the elements window involves the reference prompts. What are these? In this case, the only placement reference for the UDF is the datum point. When we use the UDF in a new part, Pro/E will prompt in the message window for this reference location on the new part. We can specify the text to be used in the prompt. Keep the text simple but clear. When using the UDF in the new part with the reference model displayed, Pro/E will show the reference graphically in the reference model. However, since the display of the reference model is optional when the UDF is used, you will want to have a clear prompt here.

Enter the text "*pin placement datum point*". You can come back later to modify the text if desired. In the SET PROMPT menu, select *Done/Return*.

This completes the definition of the required elements for a UDF. We have not specified any of the optional elements. In particular, we have not specified any dimensions as being *variable*. All dimensions in this UDF are therefore *invariable*. This means that when the UDF is brought in to a new part, it will contain the original UDF dimensions and not prompt for alternative values in the new part. All users of the pin UDF will then have the same initial values to work with.

In the element window, select *OK*.

Note the contents of the message window. We are informed that the group *cover_pin* has been stored. The file name for the UDF is *cover_pin.gph*. By the way, the *Modify* command in the current (UDF) menu allows us to come back to change any aspect of the UDF definition. At this time, the reference part *cover_pin_gp.prt* is also stored. In the UDF menu, select *Done/Return*. The storage location for the UDF and the reference part is the current working directory. Once you have the UDF finished and completely debugged (that is, after you have tested it out!), you may want to transfer both these files to a UDF library directory. You can set up the option **pro_group_dir** in *config.pro* to tell Pro/E to automatically search this library for UDF's. If the directory is accessible to other users, they can use the UDF too.

We are now finished with the original model, *udf_pin_org*. **Save** the part and then **Erase** it from the session. You can also erase all the non-displayed objects.

Using the UDF

Start a new part *cover_plate*. Set the units to millimeters. Create a base feature as a simple protrusion using the dimensions shown in Figure 8. Create datum points on the upper surface of the cover plate according to the dimensions shown in Figure 9. You might like to use a pattern table for this (remember that dimensions in a pattern table can be negative).

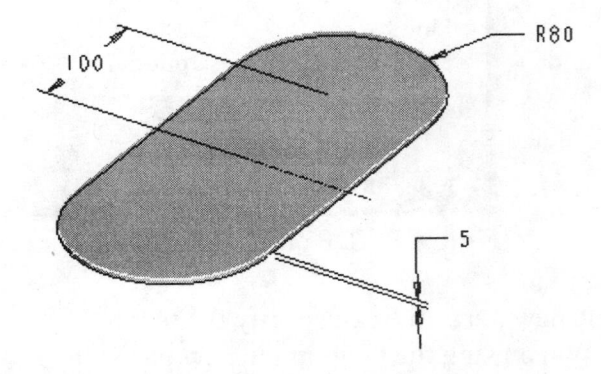

Figure 8 Cover plate base feature

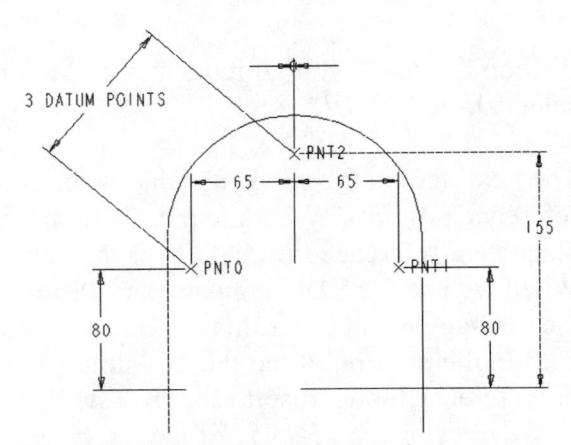

Figure 9 Cover plate datum points

In the FEAT menu, select

> ***Create > User Defined***

The **Open** file dialog window opens up. Depending on how your system is set up, the dialog will either be pointing to your working directory or to a special directory on your system for storing UDF's called the *featurelib*. This may vary according to settings in your *config.pro*[2]. We will have a look at some of the built-in UDF's contained in this library a bit later in this lesson. For now, select the working directory icon in this window (it has a small red check mark). The UDF *cover_pin.gph* should be listed. Highlight this item and select **Open**.

In the message window, you are asked if you want to retrieve the reference part. The default is NO. Depending on how good the UDF prompts are, or how familiar you are with the UDF, you may decide not to bring up and view the reference part. For the first few times that you use a new UDF, it's a good idea to select **Yes** to bring in the reference part. A small window will open

---

[2] The *config.pro* option (Windows NT environment) looks something like (your path may be different)

                    PRO_GROUP_DIR i:\pro_libs\objlib\featurelib

up with the reference part shown. As placement references are required, they will be highlighted on the reference model, in addition to prompts in the message window.

The PLACE OPTS menu is open. Select

> ***Independent > Done***

This option means that after the UDF is placed in the new model, the features will be independent of the UDF definition maintained in the library. The UDF definition *cover_pin.gph* can be changed (or even deleted from the disk), but these changes will not be reflected in the new part. Making the UDF independent increases the portability of the new model (since it no longer requires the presence of the definition file), but increases the file size of the new model. The other option, *UDF Driven*, requires the presence of the UDF definition file whenever the new model is loaded or updated, but allows the "keeper" of the UDF library to enforce standard usage of the UDF among all users. That is, if the UDF definition is modified, these changes will automatically occur in any models using the UDF when they are loaded. There are some complicated issues involved in using the *UDF Driven* option, which we will not get into in great depth here.

The next option is for scaling of the UDF. For now, select

> ***Same Dims > Done***

that is, we want the UDF in the new model to have the same numeric dimension values as in the reference model. Note that if the units (inches and/or mm) of the two models are different, this could cause problems. In that case, you might have to scale the UDF.

Now, using the DISP OPTION menu, we have to set a display option to determine how the dimensions in the UDF will be accessible in the new part. When we created the *cover_pin* UDF, we did not identify any dimensions as being *variable* (we'll do that in the next exercise). Therefore they assume the *invariable* values in the original model. When placing the UDF in a new part, we have three options for dealing with dimensions as follows

▸   ***Normal*** - converts the invariable dimensions to variable, so that we can ***Modify*** them in the new part if desired (this is only available for Independent UDF's)
▸   ***Read Only*** - shows the original UDF dimensions in the new model, but they cannot be modified
▸   ***Blank*** - uses the original dimensions but will not display them in the new model and they cannot be modified.

We are going to try out each of these on our cover plate. For the first UDF in the new part, select

> ***Read Only > Done***.

You are now prompted (in the message window) to select the datum point for placement on the new model. You will recognize the prompt text that we specified when creating the UDF. In the reference model window, the datum point is highlighted. It is possible to *Skip* some UDF references and return to define them later. For now, select the top left datum point on the *cover_plate*, as shown in Figure 10.

In the GRP PLACE menu, we can go back and redefine the model, placement, dimensions (if allowed), and so on. The *Info* command provides information about the UDF. Select *Done* in this menu.

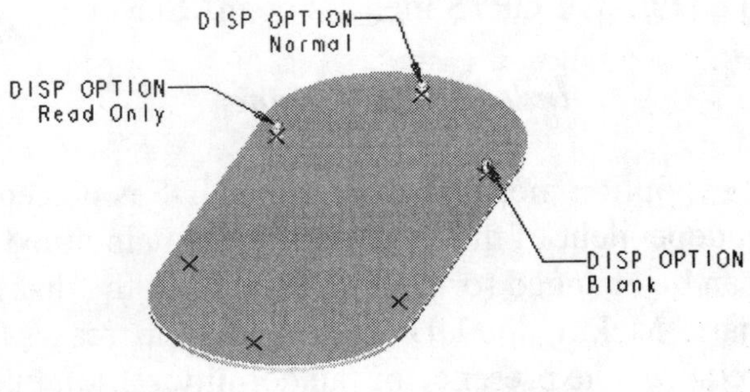

Repeat the above placement procedure two more times, placing the same UDF on two other datum points. For each of these, use a different option in the DISP OPTION menu, as indicated in Figure 10. When you go to select the UDF in the Open dialog window, check out the "In Session" icon (blue and white stripes). The UDF is already in session.

Figure 10 Examining UDF display options

Notice that in the Model Tree, the UDF's appear as Groups, with the name of the UDF.

Zoom in on each pin, and try to *Modify* their dimensions. On the first pin, you will get a message that the values cannot be modified. On the second pin, change the height to 15 and the diameter of the base to 4 and *Regenerate* the part. If you try to *Modify* the third pin, the dimensions will not appear.

Delete the pins. Assuming that you used a pattern table for the datum points, use the UDF to make a pin on the datum point pattern leader. Then it's an easy matter to make a *Ref Pattern* of this first pin. It should now look like Figure 3 at the beginning of this exercise.

This completes our first UDF example. *Save* the part and remove it from the session. Erase the non-displayed objects as well.

Before we leave this example, note that the UDF's do not have to be created on the same surface. In our cover part, we might have created a table pattern of datum points and then a *Ref Pattern* of UDF's. All the pins would have to be in the same plane, and stay the same size. Our UDF is more flexible than this. The part shown in Figure 11 was created using the same *cover_pin* UDF. This is because the *Shaft* feature automatically aligns itself to the surface on which it is placed.

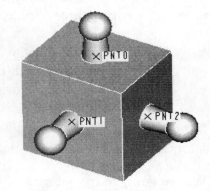

Now, on to something a bit more challenging.

Figure 11 UDF placed on different surfaces

Exercise #2: Multi-feature UDF with Family Table

Now that you have seen the basic procedure for creating and using UDF's, we will proceed with a more complicated example. This uses some of the options that we omitted in the previous example when creating the UDF: variable dimensions and a family table. The UDF will be used to create a pattern of grouped features.

Our goal is to create a UDF that will allow us to easily produce any of the recessed holes shown in the part below (Figure 12). Note that the shape of the recess can be either circular or hexagonal. The diameter of each hole and the size (width or diameter) of the recess will be determined using a family table defined in the UDF. These will be *invariable*. We will create the UDF so that the user can specify the hole placement using a radial dimensioning scheme (distance from an axis and angular placement from a reference plane), and the depth of the recess. Once created, the UDF group can be easily patterned as shown in the next figure, using the angular placement dimension.

Figure 12 Recessed holes created with UDF *combo_hole*

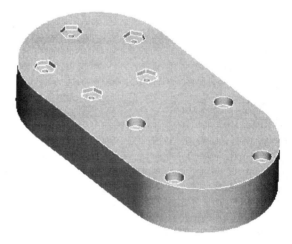

Figure 13 Patterns of UDF *combo_hole*

Creating the Original Model

Start a new part called *udf_recesshole_org*. Set the units to millimeters. Create a solid protrusion as shown in Figure 14. This is a 200 mm square block, 50 mm thick, centered on the vertical datums. Create a datum axis using the **Two Planes** option using the FRONT and SIDE datums. Note the location of the axis label - this defines the "positive" end of the axis and therefore the direction of angular rotations using the right hand rule.

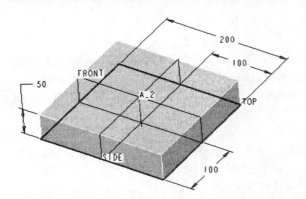

Figure 14 Base feature for original model

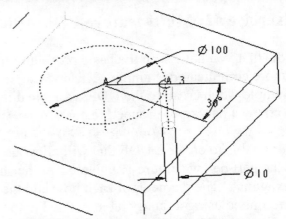

Figure 15 Creating the hole feature

Create a straight *Thru All* hole with a diameter of **10** using a radial placement on the top of the block. See Figure 15. The reference axis for the hole is the datum axis, and the angular (polar) dimensioning reference is the FRONT datum plane. These will be required to place the UDF. Place the hole at an angle of **30°** from the FRONT datum. The DIM TYPE is *Diameter* and the value is **100**.

Now create the circular recess as a *Coaxial* hole. Select the axis of the hole and the top of the block for the placement references, and enter a *Variable* depth of **10** and a diameter of **20**. See Figure 16.

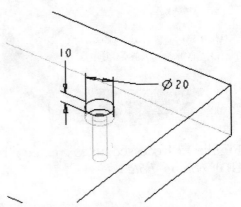

The hexagonal recess will be a bit more tricky because we want to avoid setting up unnecessary references to the part. So far, the only references we have used are the hole axis, the center axis (for the dimension type), the FRONT datum for the angular reference, and the top surface. If we can, we'd like to avoid bringing in additional references since that will complicate the UDF.

Figure 16 Creating the circular recess

Also, we want the hexagonal recess to exist independently from the circular recess. The easiest way to ensure this is to *Suppress* the circular recess. Do that now.

Create the hexagon as a *Blind Cut* feature. Use the top of the block for the sketching plane.

IMPORTANT:
    For the *Top* sketching reference, create a *Make Datum* through the axis of the hole and the central axis. This ensures that all references required for the hexagon are contained within the UDF. In addition, we want the orientation of the hexagon to rotate according to the angular placement of the UDF. This will occur because the Make Datum will rotate with the angle specified for the hole. Otherwise, we could have selected the FRONT datum as the sketching reference since it is already a reference in the UDF. Do not add an

unnecessary reference if you can avoid it.

The hexagon sketch is shown in Figure 17. Using Intent Manager, the only sketching references we need are the axis of the hole and the *Make Datum*. The easiest way to create this sketch is to draw a circle, right click and select Toggle Construction, then draw the lines to create the hexagon. Dimension the sketch as shown in Figure 17. You should be able to fully dimension the sketch with the single dimension shown and some combination of constraints.

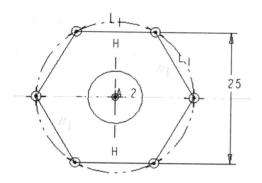

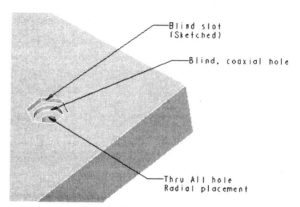

Figure 17 Sketch for hexagonal recess

Figure 18 Three features for UDF

With a successful sketch, set a *Blind* depth of **5**. Remember that the circular recess has a depth of 10, so we will be able to see both features when they are resumed. Accept the feature.

Now resume the circular recess and you should see all three features (hole, circular recess, hexagonal recess) as shown in Figure 18.

Rename the two recess features *CIRC* and *HEX*. These labels will make it easier to locate the features in the model tree.

Creating the UDF

In the PART menu

>   *Feature > UDF Library > Create*

Enter a name for the UDF as *combo_hole*. Make it *Stand Alone* and include the reference part. *Add* the hole and the two recess features. Select the *Info* command (in the UDF FEATS menu) to open a window listing the features included in the UDF. Only the three desired features should be listed. Select *Done/Return*.

You should now be in the **PROMPTS** menu. Read the message window. Some of the references are used by more than one feature in the UDF. We can specify that Pro/E uses the same reference for all, or prompts for each feature individually. For the highlighted axis reference, select *Single* since we want to use the same axis reference for all features. For the prompt, enter "*axis for radial placement*".

For the plane reference (FRONT), enter the prompt "*angle reference plane*".

For the top surface reference, use **Single** and enter the prompt text "*placement surface*". These are all the reference prompts required. You can review these using **Next** in the MOD PRMPT menu. You can modify the prompt text at this time, otherwise select **Done/Return**.

At this time, all the necessary UDF elements are defined. Let's exercise some of the options. We will make several dimensions available for the user to specify when the UDF is brought into the new part: the radial placement dimension (ultimately to be the diameter of the UDF pattern circle), the placement angle (for the pattern leader), and the depth of the recess. The diameter of the hole and the size of the recess will be specified using a family table. The family table will also determine whether to use the circular or hexagonal recess.

Setting *Var Dims*

In the elements window, select **Var Dims > Define**. All the feature dimensions appear. In the VAR DIMS menu select **Add**. The dimensions we want to make variable are (pick on each of these, the order doesn't matter)

> diameter of the placement circle of the hole (100)
> angle placement of the hole from FRONT datum (30°)
> depth of circular recess (10)
> depth of hexagonal recess (5)

After these have been selected (they highlight in red), middle click and **Done/Return** in the VAR DIMS menu.

Now we'll will create text prompts for each of the variable dimensions. Pro/E will highlight the dimension on the screen to identify it. Enter the following prompt text for each highlighted dimension as it shows up:

> "*hole placement angle (note axis direction)*"
> "*hole placement diameter*"
> "*depth (circ)*"
> "*depth (hex)*"

On to the next step...

Creating the Family Table

We will define a family table in the UDF that will specify the recess type (circular or hexagon), the hole diameter, and the recess size (diameter or width). In the UDF elements window, scroll down the elements list and select

Family Table > Define > Add Column > Feature

Pick a surface on the circular recess or the name *CIRC* in the model tree. Then select a surface of the hexagon or pick on the name *HEX* in the model tree.

In the ADD ITEM area, select **Dimension**. Pick the dimension for the diameter of the center hole and enter "*hole_dia*" in the message window prompt. Similarly, pick the diameter dimension of the circular recess and enter "*CIRC_dia*" and the width across the hexagon and enter "*HEX_wid*". Accept the family items list with **OK**.

In the FAMILY TABLE window, enter the data shown in Figure 19 to create the instances for the UDF[3]. What does the symbol in the first column do? What do the "*" entries normally do? What is their effect in this family table? Note that in the generic part, both the circular and hexagonal features are present.

Type	Instance Name	F3 NO_NAME	F6 NO_NAME	d0 HOLE_DIA	d3 CIRC_DIA	d5 HEX_WID
	COMBO_HOLE	Y	Y	10.0	20.0	25.0
🔒	C10-20	Y	N	10.0	20.0	*
🔒	C5-15	Y	N	5.0	15.0	*
🔒	H10-25	N	Y	10.0	*	25.0
🔒	H5-15	N	Y	5.0	*	15.0

Figure 19 Family table to define instances of the UDF

Save the table and close the table editor with **OK**. This completes the UDF definition. In the elements window accept the definition with **OK**. Note that the message window indicates that *combo_hole* has been stored. Leave the UDF menu, **Save** the original part and erase all objects from the session.

Using The UDF with Family Table

Create a new part *combo_test*. Set the units to millimeters. Create a base feature as shown in the figure at the right. Create two datum axes using the **Thru Cyl** option.

Now we'll bring in the UDF and create an instance.

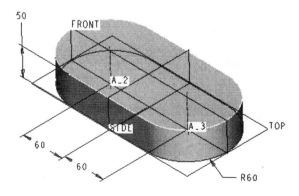

Figure 20 Base feature for *combo_test*

---

[3] In the pre-production version of Pro/E, the feature names CIRC and HEX do not appear in the column headers, as they did in previous versions of Pro/E. Hopefully, this will get fixed by the time you are using the program!

Feature > Create > User Defined

Navigate to the working directory. You should see the UDF's *cover_pin* and *combo_hole*. Select the *combo_hole* and **Open** it. Retrieve the reference part and it will appear in a separate window. Adjust the size and placement of this window so that you can follow the prompts in the main window message area. Since the UDF has a family table, the *Select Instance* window opens up as shown in Figure 21.

Highlight the instance **C5-15** and **Open** it.

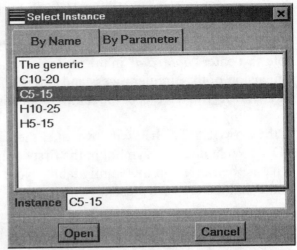

Figure 21 Selecting a UDF instance

Select the following

> *Independent > Done*
> *Same Dims > Done*

At the prompts, enter the following values for the *variable* dimensions (these are the defaults, so you can just hit the Enter key):

hole placement diameter	**100**
hole placement angle	**30**
depth (circ)	**10**

Notice that Pro/E didn't ask for the hexagon depth, since that feature is suppressed in this instance.

Set the display option with **Read Only > Done**.

Figure 22 First UDF - group pattern leader

Now we specify the placement references. The location of the UDF we want is shown in Figure 22. Select the axis at the right end of the new part, the FRONT datum as angle reference, and the top surface as placement surface. The angular displacement is ambiguous, so you will have to pick which side of the FRONT datum for placement. The final position of the UDF may surprise you. Remember that the angle is measured using the right hand rule around the specified axis. Remember also that the axis label appears at the "positive" end of the axis. If the axis is upside down, then the angle may be measured in the opposite direction from what you were expecting. Recall the orientation of the axis in the reference part and compare it to the orientation in the new model. To correct this surprising placement, you could either enter a negative angle when the UDF is being placed, or **Modify** the placement angle after the fact.

Read the message window. In the GRP PLACE menu, select *Done*.

Open the Model Tree to observe that the placed UDF appears as a group. Also, note that the feature HEX is not there (or even supressed). Highlight the group in the model tree, and use the right mouse button to select

> ***Pattern***

Select the angle dimension to increment in the first direction. Enter an increment of **90°** and specify **4** copies. There is nothing to do in the second direction. With the pattern completed, *Modify* the pattern diameter dimension to **75**.

Bring in another instance of *combo_hole*, say the **H5-15** instance. Use *Independent, Same Dims*. Place it at **45°** from the FRONT datum using the axis at the other end of the new part. The placement diameter is **75** and the recess depth is **5**. The display options are *Read Only*.

Finally, create a radial pattern of the hexagonal UDF. Use the angle dimension and increment by **72°**, with **5** copies.

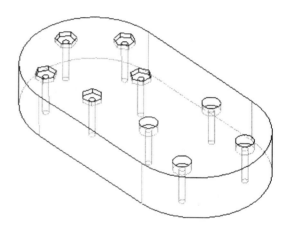

The final part should look like Figure 23. Notice that the hexagons are automatically rotating as the pattern is generated.

See which dimension(s) you can modify on either of these patterns. Can you explain why?

Save the part and remove it from the session.

Figure 23 Final part

Exercise #3: Subordinate UDF

So far, the UDF's we have created and placed have been *Standalone* and *Independent*. When the UDF is in the new model, it has no connection to the original model. There may be cases where you may wish to maintain this connection. For example, consider the following scenario. Suppose you have a complicated group of features in the original model and these are used to create a UDF. The UDF is then used in several new part models. A design revision calls for the modification to one of the features contained in the UDF. You do not want to go through all the independent cases where the UDF was used. Instead, you would like to just change the original model and have the modifications show up in all the new parts. This is what *Subordinate* and *UDF Driven* options can do for you. Not all changes in the original model can be accommodated. Basically, you can change the dimensions of the existing features. If you attempt to change (add or remove) the feature list or references, then Pro/E issues a warning. You might expect problems in any new models containing the UDF if drastic changes are made to its data structure.

Creating the Original Model

We'll demonstrate this using a very simple example.
Create a new part called *udf_csinkhole_org* and set units to
millimeters. Create the protrusion shown in Figure 24 and
place a single datum point on the top center of the block.
Then, create a sketched hole using the *On Point* placement
option. The sketch for the hole is shown in Figure 25.
Place the hole on the datum point on the block.

The final original part model should appear as in Figure
26.

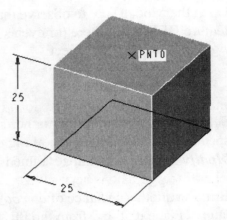

Figure 24 Base feature and
placement point

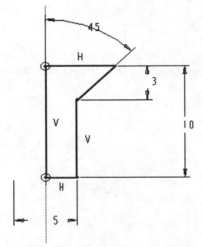

Figure 25 Dimensions for sketched
hole

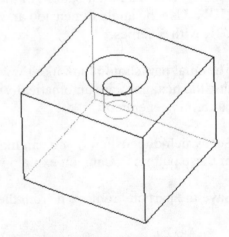

Figure 26 The original model

Creating the UDF

Now create the UDF as follows:

> *Feature > UDF Library > Create*

Enter the name of the UDF as "*csink*". In the UDF OPTIONS menu

> *Subordinate > Done*
> *Add*

Click on the surface of the countersunk hole. In the UDF FEATS menu, select *Done/Return*.

The prompt for the datum point reference is *"hole placement point"*. In the SET PROMPT menu select *Done/Return*.

Let's set the depth of the hole as variable. In the UDF elements window select

Var Dims > Define

and click on the depth dimension (10) then *Done/Return* in the VAR DIMS menu. Enter the prompt *"hole depth"*.

We have finished defining the UDF. In the elements window select *OK*. The message window tells us that *csink* has been saved. Also, note that the part *udf_csinkhole_org* has been saved automatically. For *Subordinate* UDF's, the original model takes the place of the reference model (there is no part file *csink_gp.prt*), and is always saved with the UDF.

Erase all objects from the session.

Using the UDF

Start a new part called *csink_test*. Make a solid protrusion with a couple of datum points as shown in Figure 27.

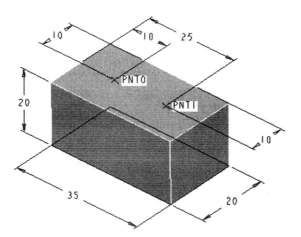

Figure 27 Base feature and datum points for test model

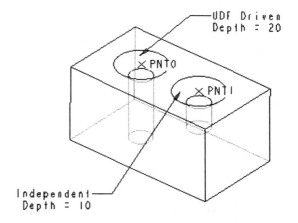

Figure 28 Two UDF's in test model

Now bring in the *csink* UDF. We will do this a couple of times to try out a couple of options.

Feature > Create > User Defined

Go to the working directory and open **csink.gph**. The original model comes up in a small window automatically (recall that with a *Standalone* UDF this is optional).

Select

> *UDF Driven > Done*
> *Same Dims > Done*

and enter a hole depth of **20** when prompted. Notice that the *Normal* display option is not available for *UDF Driven* since all invariable dimensions come from the original model and cannot be changed. Choose ***Read Only*** as the display option here. Select the datum point on the left of the block for the placement reference.

Bring in another copy of the **csink.gph** UDF and place it on the right datum point. Make this one ***Independent***, ***Same Dims***, ***Normal*** and set the hole depth to **10**. The two *csink* holes are shown in Figure 28.

Exploring the Model

To demonstrate how the UDF is linked to the original model, open the original model file *udf_csinkhole_org* and ***Modify*** the depth of the countersink to **5** (see Figure 29). ***Regenerate*** the part. Using the pull-down ***Window*** command, switch to the *csink_test* window and activate it.

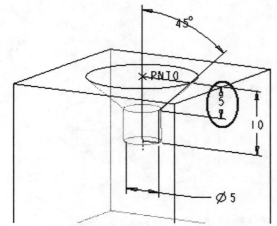

Figure 29 Modifying the depth of the countersink in the original model

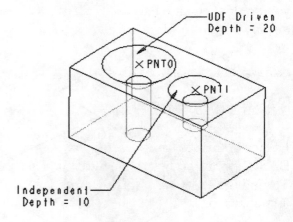

Figure 30 UDF Driven hole modifies with original model after ***Update***

Nothing has changed yet in *csink_test*. We have to do two things for that to happen. Select

> *Feature > Group > Update*

the message window tells us that 1 UDF group has been updated. (Why only 1?) Now ***Regenerate*** the model. Voilà! The UDF Driven *csink* on the left has been changed as shown in Figure 30. Why didn't the one on the right change too?

To further demonstrate the link with the original model, save all your files and leave Pro/E. Go to your system and open your working directory. Notice the files *udf_csinkhole_org.prt* (the original model), *csink.gph* (the UDF definition), and *csink_test.prt* (our test part). Unlike *Standalone* UDF's there is no need for a reference part (like *csink_gp.gph*). **Delete** all but the highest numbered versions of these parts and then rename the original model file to something like *Xudf_csinkhole_org.prt*. Renaming it means that Pro/E won't be able to find it, and allows us to bring it back later.

Now bring up Pro/E and open the file *csink_test*. Both holes will appear, but the message window tells us there is a missing group. Try to **Redefine** the two holes. One hole will allow this but the other won't. Try to **Modify** the dimensions of the two holes. What happens and why? The moral is that if a UDF is created as *Subordinate* and then used as *UDF Driven*, don't lose the original model or you won't be able to do anything with the associated UDF.

Delete the *Independent* hole, and try to bring in the *csink* UDF again. You can't because the original model is not available (we renamed it).

Disassociating a UDF

Suppose you have brought in a UDF using *UDF Driven*, and you want to break the connection to the original model. You can do this with the **Disassociate** command in the GROUP menu. If you do this, you are basically making the UDF *Independent*. You also have your choice of display options (*Normal*, *Read Only*, or *Blank*) for the UDF.

The Pro/E UDF Library

Earlier in this lesson we mentioned that there were a number of UDF's contained in the Pro/E BASIC library. These can be found in the directory such as `pro_libs/objlib/featurelib`. To find the exact location on your installation you may have to consult your system administrator.

You can set up an option in your *config.pro* to automatically bring up this UDF library when you launch **Feature > Create > User Defined**. The setting would be something like:

```
pro_group_dir i:/pro_libs/objlib/featurelib
```

The library contains dozens of UDF's for features commonly used in part modeling (cuts and protrusions of common sections like circles, hexagons, ellipses and so on), machine design, mold design, sheet metal, and piping design. Many of the UDF's produce ANSI standard geometries (for example, for threads) in both standard (ie inch) and metric forms. A directory tree for the feature library is shown in the following listing.

```
featurelib
    design_udf
        design_udf_m
                cntrsnk_scr_hole_m
                hexhead_scr_hole_m
                ret_ring_groove_m
                        hole_groove
                        shaft_groove
                socket_scr_hole_m
                thread_hole_m
                        coarse_pitch
                        fine_pitch
        design_udf_st
                cntrsnk_scr_hole_st
                hexhead_scr_hole_st
                socket_scr_hole_st
                thread_hole_st
                        unc_thread
                        unf_thread
    geometry_udf
        cut_udf
        protrusion_udf
    mold_udf
        gates
        runners
    piping_udf
        beaded
        expanded
        flared
        flattened
        necked
    stm_udf
        beads
        louvers
        offsets
```

As of this writing, the new Pro/E Help pages do not contain references to the BASIC library. In a previous release, these pages (which may still be on your system) were located at

    `PROHELP/html/usascii/libs/basic/basictoc.htm`.

Check this location with your system administrator.

This lesson has introduced you to some methods to create and use User Defined Features. With careful planning and implementation, these can save you and others you work with a lot of time in model creation. They will also promote standardization among parts and assemblies where they are used.

We have, of necessity, only scratched the surface of using UDF's here. For example, we have not discussed creating or using UDF's in assemblies. Most of the steps and details are the same, however there are some important differences. There are some features that cannot be included in a UDF used in an assembly (rounds, for instance). You are encouraged to explore the online help for further information.

In the next lesson we will look at some more tools for automating the geometry creation of a part using a program. We will also look at how layers can be used to simplify the on-screen display of parts and assemblies.

Questions for Review

1. What are the two primary motivations for using UDF's?
2. How many features can be contained in a UDF?
3. How many UDF's can be created from the original model?
4. What is the relation of the original model to the reference model?
5. Is a reference model always produced? Is it always required?
6. How does a UDF appear in the Model Tree?
7. What is the difference between a *Standalone* UDF and a *Subordinate* UDF?
8. Describe the purpose of the reference prompts.
9. What is the minimum set of information required to create a UDF?
10. For a standalone UDF called *trinket*, what are the complete names of the files stored for the UDF and its reference part?
11. What setting is used so that after the UDF is placed in a new model it no longer requires the UDF definition file?
12. What are the dimension settings available when a UDF is being placed in a new part? How do they differ in function?
13. Why would we like to define a UDF with as few references as possible?
14. What are *variable* and *invariable* dimensions? Where are these determined?
15. When you are creating features for a multi-feature UDF, what is the easiest way to make sure that optional features don't interfere with each other?
16. For a UDF involving a family table, is the table created before, during, or after we have identified the features involved in the UDF?
17. At what point in the creation of the family table can you specify names for the symbolic dimensions to appear as family table column headings?
18. What is the name of the UDF element that can be defined so that the user is prompted to enter values for dimensions when the UDF is being brought in to the new part?
19. How do you set up a UDF so that its geometry is always controlled by the original model? Why might you want to do this?
20. Is it possible to change the *invariable* dimensions if the UDF is **Independent**?
21. Is it possible to change the *invariable* dimensions if the UDF is a **UDF Driven**?
22. What does the **Update** command do? Does this command alone bring the new model up to the current geometry?
23. What happens when a part containing several **UDF Driven** groups is loaded?
24. What happens if the original model and UDF definition file are not in the current working directory (a) when the UDF is first added to a part, and (b) when the part is retrieved?
25. When a UDF has been used as **UDF Driven**, how do you break its association with the original model?
26. In what directory can you find the Pro/E Basic library UDF's on your system?
27. How do you set your *config.pro* so that the feature library is automatically consulted when you want it?
28. Try out some of the library UDF's for cuts, protrusions, threads and others.

Project Exercises

We'll create three parts this lesson. One will use two kinds of sweeps to let you review that material. The second is a pretty straight forward modeling exercise. The third will make use of a UDF that you will create.

The first part is the cart handle. The base feature is a simple constant section sweep. The handle is a variable section sweep using two elliptical sketches, one for the trajectory and one to define the radius of the section. You can invent your own dimensions for these.

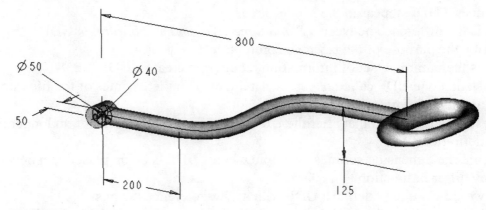

PART: *handle*

The second part is the main mounting plate for the wheel axle. Its construction should be straight forward. See the figures on the next page for the dimensions.

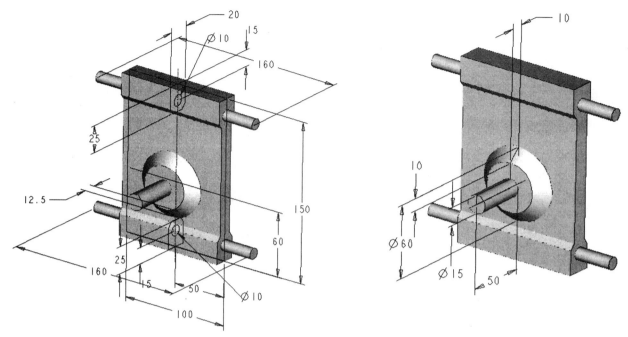

PART: *mount*

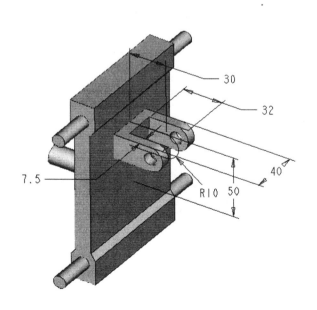

The final part is the wheel axle for the side wheels. This has four stud bolts arranged in a radial pattern. Create a UDF for this stud bolt using a revolved protrusion on a rotated *Make Datum*. Set up the UDF with a variable bolt length and radius to the center of the pattern. Then use the UDF in the creation of the part. The axle part has four studs.

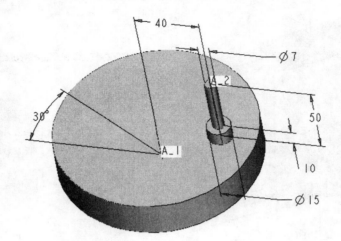

UDF: *stud*

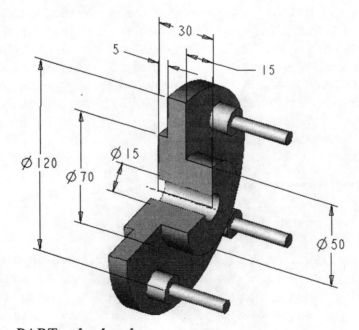

PART: *wheel_axle*

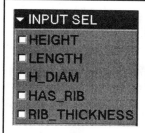

Lesson 6

Pro/PROGRAM and Layers

Synopsis

Using Pro/PROGRAM to create and run a part design file; input variables and conditionals; creating a family table using **Instantiate**; setting up and using Layers; default layers; adding items; controlling the layer display; layer settings in *config.pro*

Overview

This lesson is directed at a couple of very useful utility functions in Pro/E. The first of these, Pro/PROGRAM, allows you to create a script to control what happens during the regeneration of a part. This includes prompting the user for variables that can be used to assign dimensions, or to control the execution of the script. Pro/PROGRAM offers a convenient method to create or add new instances to family tables. The second major utility function concerns the topic of layers. These are used to organize features into logical groupings. Layers can be used to control the display or the selection process for other feature manipulations such as suppression. The assignment of features to layers can be done manually or automatically using settings created only for a single session or universally using entries in the configuration file *config.pro*.

Each of these utility functions will be demonstrated and explored using fairly simple parts.

Pro/PROGRAM

Pro/PROGRAM is a utility that lets you specify input variables (used for dimensions), set up relations, and modify or control the regeneration process for parts and assemblies. PROGRAM is based on a textual description of the part or assembly called the *program* or *design*. Using syntax and logical structure similar to a programming language, you can specify names and values of variables, perform arithmetic operations and logical branching, and other functions that will affect the regeneration sequence. The design file can be as simple or elaborate as you like. PROGRAM lets you and users of your models very quickly create alternative part models. It is very easy for the user to set values for variables and determine whether or not to include features in parts or components in assemblies. The model can also react to these changes by substituting alternate features or components. PROGRAM is also a very convenient way to set up a family table. All this can be done without requiring the user to have in-depth and comprehensive knowledge of the model.

PROGRAM Elements

Every part or assembly has a default program or design embedded in it that is created automatically. A very simple part, such as the cylinder in Figure 1, illustrates the basic structure of this design file, shown in Figure 2. Note that most sections of this default program are empty. In the following, this listing will be referred to as the *program* or the *design*. At times, the listing will be saved to disk, where it becomes the *design file*.

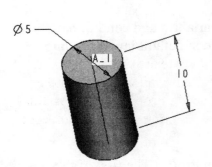

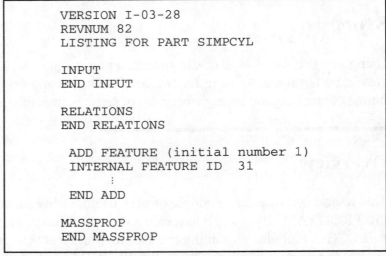

```
VERSION I-03-28
REVNUM 82
LISTING FOR PART SIMPCYL

INPUT
END INPUT

RELATIONS
END RELATIONS

 ADD FEATURE (initial number 1)
 INTERNAL FEATURE ID   31
          ⋮
 END ADD

MASSPROP
END MASSPROP
```

Figure 1 A single feature part

Figure 2 The (abbreviated) design file for the simple cylinder of Figure 1

The program or design contains five areas. At the top are the software version and the model's name. Then come two areas (initially empty as shown in Figure 2) where we can define program *Inputs* and part *Relations*. The biggest area of the file contains sets of *ADD ... END ADD* statements, each set enclosing a single feature. In an assembly design this area is used to *ADD* components to the assembly. At the end is a section where mass properties functions can be placed.

Syntax of PROGRAM Statements

In the space available here, we cannot go into all the variations of syntax or built-in functions available with Pro/PROGRAM. All of this material can be found in the on-line help. There is enough here, however, to be quite useful and to give you a good idea of what PROGRAM can do. We will go deep enough into its operation so that you can implement more advanced functions described in the on-line help on your own.

The *INPUT* Syntax

The INPUT section of the design file is where we indicate the names and types of variables that will be used in the design, part, or assembly. Variable names are alphanumeric and must begin with a letter. There are three types of variables allowed: *Number*, *Yes_No*, and *String*. Along with each variable we can specify a text prompt string that will appear in the message window at the appropriate time (when PROGRAM requires input). Some examples of the format of the input definitions are shown below:

```
INPUT
    plate_thickness number
    "Enter the plate thickness"

    include_flange Yes_No
    "Do you want to include the flange in the part?"

    material string
    "Enter the part material (ABS, PVC, or POLY)"

END INPUT
```

Note that the prompts occur immediately after the variable name and type are defined, and are enclosed in double quotes. Although the text is shown here in lower case, all characters except those included between double quotes will be converted to upper case in Pro/E. String variables can be names of part or assembly files. In some cases, when used as a string variable, names of parts and/or assemblies must have the *prt* or *asm* extensions.

The *RELATIONS* Syntax

The RELATIONS section of the design contains any relations defined for the part or assembly. As such, the syntax of relations is the same as in other areas of Pro/E. They can be created with the *Relations* command, or within the Pro/PROGRAM editor.

The *IF...ENDIF* Syntax

Pro/PROGRAM also allows logical branching using boolean variables. This takes the form

```
IF {boolean expression}
    {do this}
ELSE
    {do that}
ENDIF
```

The boolean expression can involve any of the input variables, part parameters or dimensions, or string variables. This form of branching can occur almost anywhere within the design file. IF statements can also be nested to provide very deep logical branching.

Some examples of the syntax are as follows (required syntax elements in upper case):

```
IF num_holes > 10
    hole_diam = 12
    hole_space = 60
ENDIF

IF material == "ABS"
    wall_thickness = 5.0
```

```
ELSE
    wall_thickness = 8
ENDIF
```

In the second example, note the difference between the "==" sign used in the boolean expression to test for equality and the "=" sign used for assignment of a value. We will see a couple of examples of this later in this lesson.

Pro/PROGRAM contains several other syntax elements and built-in functions. For example, it is possible in an assembly to ADD an instance from a part family table by searching for an instance with prescribed properties. See the on-line documentation for detailed discussion of these functions.

Example: A simple bracket with optional rib

We will create a simple part to demonstrate the basic principles of PROGRAM. We will control the regeneration of a part using the syntax elements presented above. We will not do anything very complicated here. The design will include several *Input* variables and an optional feature (a rib). We will see how to create a Family Table for the part using the *Instantiate* command.

Creating the Part

Start a new part called **bracket**. Create an L-shaped base feature as a both-sides solid protrusion off the SIDE datum. The bracket rests on the TOP datum and the dimensions are shown in Figure 3. Add the two holes (linear placement, one sided, Thru All) shown in Figure 4, noting that the holes are aligned with the SIDE datum on the center plane of the part.

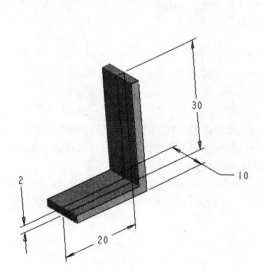

Figure 3 *Bracket* base feature

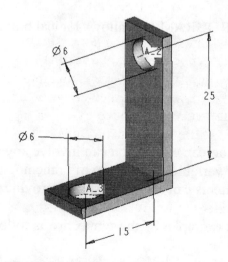

Figure 4 Adding holes to base feature

Round off the ends of the legs of the bracket using cuts (Figure 5). Each cut is coaxial with the holes.

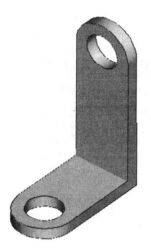

Figure 5 Rounded ends using *Cut*

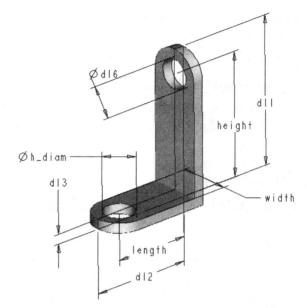

Figure 6 Dimensions named using *Dim Cosmetics > Symbol*

To prepare for using PROGRAM, we will rename some of the symbolic dimensions. Use

Modify > Dim Cosmetics > Symbol

Click on each feature to display the dimensions. Then change the names of the dimensions as shown in Figure 6. These are the vertical height to the hole on the back leg (25), the length along the base leg to the front hole (15), the width of the bracket (10), and the hole diameter (6). Click on each dimension in turn and enter the new symbols shown in Figure 6. Note your symbolic dimension names for the dimensions d11, d12, and d16 in the Figure - we'll need these below.

We are going to set up some relations for this part. These will work together with the part program to determine the geometry during regeneration. We want to set the width of the bracket and the length of each leg based on the hole locations and to maintain a clearance of 2 around the holes. In the PART menu, select

Relations > Add

and enter the following (Note that your dimension symbols *dxx* may be slightly different from those shown in Figure 6):

```
/* top hole diameter
d16 = h_diam
/* height of back leg maintains clearance around hole
d11 = height + h_diam / 2 + 2
/* length of front leg maintains clearance around hole
d12 = length + h_diam / 2 + 2
/* width of bracket to maintain clearance
```

```
width = h_diam + 4
```

As usual, after you have set up some relations, check them out to make sure they are working correctly. Try to modify the vertical leg height - you can't since it is driven by a relation. Try other dimensions to see if they can be modified. Do both hole diameters become equal? Is our intent of maintaining the clearance around the hole implemented properly? If you find any errors in the dimensions, fix them now using **Relations > Edit**. Return all values to the starting values when you are finished (height = 25, length = 15, hole diameter = 6).

We are now ready to set up the part program.

Creating *Input* Variables

In the PART menu, select

Program

The program menu comes up to give you options for dealing with the current design. To see the format of the "default" design (that is, the unmodified part program), select

Show Design

An information window will open containing all the sections of the part program. The major sections were described above (*Input*, *Relations*, *Features*, *Mass Properties*). Notice that the relations we created above are listed in the design. Close this window and in the PROGRAM menu, select

Edit Design

Depending on how your system is set up, this will bring up either the Pro/TABLE editor or a system text editor. Notice that the design file name is *bracket.pls*. In an assembly, the design file extension is *als*.

Add the lines shown in Figure 7 between the INPUT ... END INPUT lines to declare the names, types, and prompts for the input variables. We recognize these as the symbolic names for the bracket dimensions (*height, length, h_diam*). If you enter characters in lower case, they will automatically be converted to upper case when the program is saved.

```
LISTING FOR PART BRACKET

INPUT
 HEIGHT NUMBER
 "Enter height of back leg to hole:"
 LENGTH NUMBER
 "Enter the length of base leg to hole:"
 H_DIAM NUMBER
 "Enter the hole diameter:"
END INPUT
```

Figure 7 Creating input variables

Save the file and exit your editor.

Incorporating the Design

When you leave the design text editor, you are asked if you want to *incorporate* the changed program in the model. Here is what happens next:

- If you select *Yes*: The program is added to or embedded in the model, the part geometry will be updated (regenerated), and the *pls* file is removed from your working directory. The next time you call up the *Edit Design* command, there is only one source for the design file, that is, the one embedded in the model.

- If you select *No*, then the new design is NOT embedded in the model (and thus not changing the current geometry). Furthermore, the *pls* file will remain on the hard disk. The next time you call up the *Edit Design* command, you would be prompted to select which design file to work on: the one contained within the model (*From Model*) or the one on the disk (*From File*). These could be different. There are several reasons why you might have a different copy of the design on the disk without incorporating it: you may have been editing the design file and realized you had to quit the editor and make other modifications to the part in order to make the design work when it is incorporated, or you may be trying out several different ideas in different design files. In the latter case, you will have to be careful about naming the "active" design file; it must always be of the form *<partname>.pls*. If multiple *pls* files exist for the same part, they will be incrementally numbered. *From File* reads the highest numbered file. Also, remember that once the design is incorporated into the model, the *pls* file is deleted.

For now, select *Yes*.

The GET INPUT window opens, a signal that the program is running (see the message window). The first thing that happens is the processing of the INPUT statements. Pro/E wants to know where to obtain values for these variables. For now, select *Current Vals* and check the message window again.

Now select *Show Design*. This time, the information window also shows us the values assigned to the variables in the INPUT section. Close the information window and select *Done/Return*.

We now have a program defined for the part.

Running the Program

The program will execute whenever the part is regenerated (including when it is first retrieved). Do that now:

   Regenerate

The GET INPUT window opens again. This time, select

>**Enter**

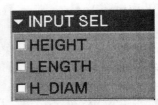

A small menu (INPUT SEL) appears as shown in Figure 8 listing the variables defined in the INPUT section of the program. You can check any or all of the boxes, then **Done Sel**. You will be prompted in the message window to enter new values for the selected variables. Note the current value is always the default and can be accepted by just pressing the Enter key (or middle mouse click). When all selected variables have been set, the part will regenerate. Try this out for different combinations of variables by selecting **Regenerate** over again each time. Before you proceed, return the values to the original ones (height = 25, length = 15, hole diameter = 6).

Figure 8 Selecting *Input* variables

Modifying the Part

Add the *Rib* feature shown in Figure 9 to the part. This is sketched on the SIDE datum plane. The top and front edge of the rib are 1 unit from the edge of the holes. The rib thickness is also 1.

When the rib has been created, rename the thickness dimension symbol to *rib_thickness*.

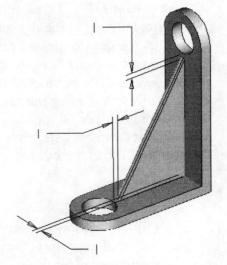

Figure 9 Adding the optional rib

Conditionals

Conditionals (IF statements) can be added at many places in the design file to control the regeneration of the part. In the bracket, we will set up a variable to allow for the optional creation of the rib feature. If the rib is to be included, we will prompt for its thickness. Select

>**Program > Edit Design**

If you have been following the sequence here precisely, then the design editor should come up immediately. If you have to make a choice, use **From Model**.

In the INPUT area of the design file, add the variables *has_rib* (of type *yes_no*) and *rib_thickness* (of type *number*). See the listing in Figure 10. Each variable has a prompt. Note that in the INPUT section, if the user sets the value of *has_rib* to **YES**, then Pro/E will prompt for the value for the rib thickness. To control the regeneration of the rib, add the IF..ENDIF statements to the design file to bracket the ADD..END ADD statements for the rib feature (near the end of the design file) as shown in Figure 11. Thus, if we set the variable *has_rib* to **NO**, then the ADD FEATURE statements for the rib will be skipped. The rib is not deleted from the part, just suppressed.

```
LISTING FOR PART BRACKET

INPUT
 HEIGHT NUMBER
 "Enter height of back leg to hole:"
 LENGTH NUMBER
 "Enter the length of base leg to hole:"
 H_DIAM NUMBER
 "Enter the hole diameter:"

has_rib yes_no
"Does the bracket have a rib?"
if has_rib == yes
rib_thickness number
"Enter thickness of the rib:"
endif

END INPUT
```

Figure 10 Program with conditionals (partial listing 1 of 2) to control input of variables

```
if has_rib == yes
 ADD FEATURE (initial number 10)
 INTERNAL FEATURE ID  232
 PARENTS = 107(#5) 137(#6) 158(#7) 34(#1) 36(#2)
 TYPE = RIB
 FORM = EXTRUDED
 SECTION NAME = S2D0004
 OPEN SECTION
 DEPTH = BLIND

    FEATURE IS IN LAYER(S) :
       7_ALL_FEATURES - OPERATION = SHOWN

 FEATURE'S DIMENSIONS:
 rib_thickness = 1
 d20 = 1
 d21 = 1
 END ADD
endif
```

Figure 11 Program with conditionals (partial listing 2 of 2) to control regeneration of feature

To see how Pro/E responds to a program error, leave out the ENDIF shown in Figure 10. Save the file and exit the text editor. The error is immediately detected, and you can either abort the program change or select **Edit** to re-enter the program editor. Do that now and you should find that an error message

```
!*** ERR: file contains more IF's than ENDIF's
```

is placed at the end of the INPUT section. This is close enough for us to locate the error. Fix it now, save the file, and exit the editor.

Incorporate these changes into the model. When the GET INPUT menu opens, select **Enter**. The new INPUT SEL menu opens (Figure 12) showing the new variables we have added. Check the *has_rib* and *rib_thickness* variables, then **Done Sel**. Set the rib to **NO**. The prompt for rib thickness will be skipped and the part should regenerate without the rib.

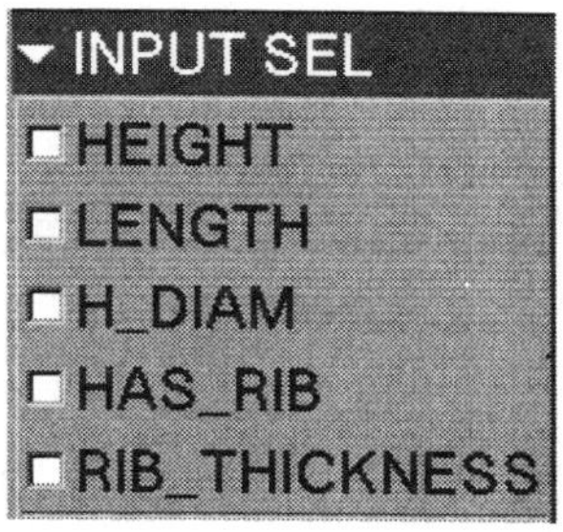

Figure 12 Selecting *Input* variables for Regeneration

Select **Regenerate** and change the setting for *has_rib* and *rib_thickness*.

This illustrates the basic operation of the program and how the user can easily modify values in the design.

Try this: select **Modify**, click on the rib, and enter a new value for the rib thickness (say **2**) by clicking on its displayed dimension. Now select *Regenerate*. Once again you see the GET INPUT menu. Choose *Current Vals*. The part regenerates with the new value for rib thickness. Thus, there are two ways to change the values of variables contained in the INPUT section of the design file, that is using

> *Regenerate > Enter*

or by   *Modify > Regenerate > Current Vals*

Instantiating to a Family Table

One useful function available with PROGRAM is the automatic creation of a family table for the part. A new instance using the current geometry is created if we select (do this now)

> *Program > Instantiate*

Enter the name "bracket". If this is the first instance, the family table will be automatically created, using the INPUT variables as column headings. The current part becomes the first row (and hence the generic) in the table. If there are previous instances, a new entry is made to the family table.

Create another geometry by selecting *Regenerate* and setting the variable values shown in the second line in Figure 13. Then use *Program > Instantiate* again, entering the name given in the table (**B3020-6-R1**) as shown in Figure 13.

Type	Instance Name	d8 HEIGHT	d6 LENGTH	d4 H_DIAM	HAS_RIB	d10 RIB_THICK...
	BRACKET	10.0	8.0	3.0	NO	1.0
	B3020-6-R1	30.0	20.0	6.0	YES	1.0
	B1008-3	10.0	8.0	3.0	NO	1.0

Figure 13 Family table created with Pro/PROGRAM

Regenerate the part using the values shown in the third line, and instantiate the part.

Now open up the family table for the part using

> *Family Tab*

Notice that the family table automatically contains our symbolic names in the column headings. The generic part (**bracket**, in this case) always contains the values of the variables present in the model when it was most recently instantiated by Pro/PROGRAM. The use of the "*" symbol in this table is therefore quite dangerous, and Pro/E will not use one if it generates the instance for you. Create some more instances for this family table. Then, try to modify any of the values driven by the family table. There are several ways to do this:

> *Modify > Regenerate > Current Vals > Program > Instantiate*

OR

       Regenerate > Enter > Program > Instantiate

OR

       Family Tab {edit one or more cells}

What happens to the part and the family table in each case? Do the instances automatically appear as new parts on disk?

Reading Values from a File

Another useful function to investigate is reading variables from a file. For example, using your system text editor, create a file **bracket.txt** containing the following:

```
h_diam = 5
length = 15
height = 30
has_rib = yes
rib_thickness = 2
```

Save this as a simple text file (ASCII). Then in Pro/E, select

       Regenerate > Read File > [bracket.txt]

Now use **Program > Instantiate** to add this to the family table. Pretty slick! The interpretation of this text file is as follows:

- variable names in the file that are not used (for example if we had set **has_rib** to **no** we would not need **rib_thickness**) are ignored
- variable names required by PROGRAM but not included in the file use the current model values
- variable names that are mis-spelled (or have a typo) are ignored

We have finished with the bracket part, so save it and erase it from your session.

Where to go from here?

This concludes our quick introduction to Pro/PROGRAM and hopefully you have caught an idea of how it might be used. There is lots more you can do with this function. For example, you can select UDF's conditionally, or substitute different UDF's depending on variable values. In assembly mode, you can control the presence or absence of components, interchange components or family table instances, pass variables from an assembly down to its sub-components and control execution of programs there. See the on-line documentation for further details. Look in the index for Pro/PROGRAM.

If you have access to it, there is a very interesting model included in the Human Factors Library. This is an assembly of human body "parts" (torso, multi-segment arms and legs, hands, head, etc). Pro/PROGRAM is used to position the mannequin in the desired position by specifying joint angles. This model would be used for ergonomic studies of vehicle cabins or operator workstations.

Layers

The concept of layers has been around in CAD packages for many years. In 2D drawing packages, layers are used to organized related entities on a separate transparent "sheet" of the drawing. The sheets are stacked in "layers" to produce the drawing. For example, a building layout might have layers corresponding to the structural details, piping, air conditioning, and electrical systems. Each layer typically has independent view control so that, for example, the plumber doesn't have to use a drawing covered with details of the electrical system, whose layer can be turned off.

Layers in a Pro/E model (part or assembly) perform a similar function, although of course we are not dealing with 2D entities. Layers in Pro/E contain features in part mode, or components and assembly features in assembly mode. The primary purpose of layers is to organize the feature/component database to simplify the operation of the program. A side benefit is that layers will speed up the graphics display by helping to remove undesired or unnecessary display elements. In operation, layers are used for the following:

- **Controlling the display of some features**. In part mode, this affects only non-geometric features on the layer (see discussion later on geometric and non-geometric features). Independent control over the display state of each layer is possible. The states are: *Show*, *Blank*, and *Isolate*. The *Show* command is fairly obvious. A layer that is set to *Blank* will not display, although the features still exist in the model (they are not suppressed). *Isolate* is the inverse of *Blank* - all layers except the one set to *Isolate* are blanked. This is useful in an assembly when you want only components on a particular layer to be displayed.

- **Organizing features/components into logical or related groups**. Many operations that require feature/component selection, such as suppressing, can be carried out simultaneously on all members of the selected layer(s). For example, a layer might contain all the rounds in the model, or a set of diverse features all relating to one area of a part. This level of organization can be very convenient if planned properly.

We will demonstrate most of the functionality of layers by creating a simple part and then experimenting with the use of layers.

Creating The Model

The model we are going to create is shown in Figure 14. This is a simplified half model of a human mouth and throat (the esophagus) that has been used to study airflow and the delivery of aerosol medications. Start a new part called **throat** and set units to millimeters. The base feature is a simple protrusion on the TOP datum with the dimensions shown in Figure 15.

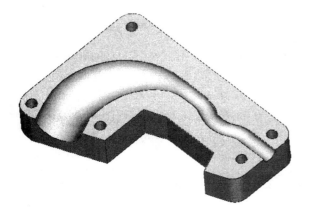

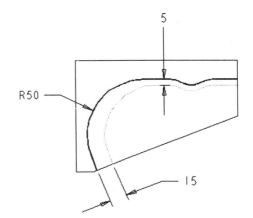

Figure 15 Base feature of *throat* model

Figure 14 Finished *throat* model

The throat passage will be created using a variable section swept cut. To define the origin trajectory of the sweep, sketch a datum curve on the top of the block as shown in Figure 16 (constraint display has been turned off). A second trajectory (Figure 17) will be used to provide a reference that will define the radius of the cut. Note that several portions of the second datum curve were defined with the **Offset Edge** option in Sketcher.

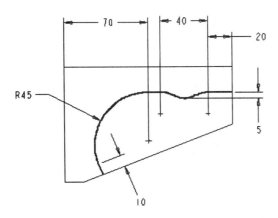

Figure 16 First datum curve (origin traj)

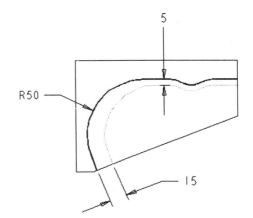

Figure 17 Datum curve for reference trajectory

Now use the datum curves to define a variable section sweep. The first datum curve will be the origin trajectory down the center of the sweep. Use the **Pivot Dir** option with the top surface as the direction reference. The second trajectory will be used to define the radius of the cut. See Figure 18. To refresh your memory of the variable section sweep, here are the commands:

Feature > Create > Solid > Cut
Advanced | Solid | Done
Var Sec Swp | Done
Pivot Dir | Done

Select the top surface as the reference to define the
pivot direction. For the origin trajectory, select

Select Traj > Curve Chain

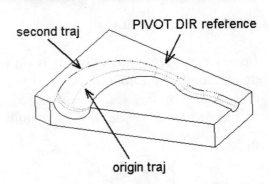

Figure 18 Defining the variable section
sweep

and pick on the first datum curve. A segment of the
curve will highlight. In the CHAIN OPTS menu,
choose *Select All* to get the rest of the curve. Make the
start point on the front (angled) surface of the base block. Use *Select Traj* again to pick the other
datum curve as an additional reference trajectory. Then *Done* (twice). The section sketch is a
180° arc centered on the crosshair at the start of the origin trajectory. The second trajectory can
be used as an endpoint of the arc to define its radius. Remember that the sketch must be closed
(use a straight line along the top of the block). Remove from inside the sketch and accept the
feature.

Now we'll put some holes in the base block. Start by making the first hole in the rear left corner.
This uses a linear placement, with dimensions to the left and back edges. The hole diameter is
7.0mm. This will be used as a pattern leader for a table driven pattern. Prior to making the table,
modify the dimension symbols of the pattern leader as shown in Figure 19. This makes the table
easier to read. Then create the pattern table shown in Figure 20.

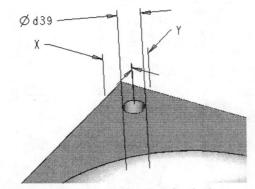

Figure 19 Pattern leader for hole

!	Table name HOLE_PATT.	
!		
! idx	X(10.0)	Y(10.0)
1	130.0	10.0
2	130.0	36.0
3	8.0	92.0
4	50.0	76.0

Figure 20 Pattern table for
holes

Finish off the model to this point by adding some R10 rounds to four of the vertical edges of the block as in Figure 21.

We are now ready to start playing with the layers.

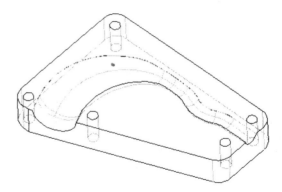

Figure 21 Rounds added to model

Using Layers

Virtually all layer operations are performed from a single dialog and display window. Most commands can be executed directly from the layer tree. In many cases, there are multiple ways to select the same command - something for everyone!

The main entry point into layer operations is

> *View > Layers*

which brings up the **Layers** main dialog window. You can also add a toolbar icon to access this dialog window. If your system has any default layers defined, they will be shown in the window. We will assume that you have no layers defined.

There are usually several methods that can be employed within this window to launch the layer-related commands. We will see these variations several times in this exercise:

- using the pull-down menus
- right-clicking within the main layer tree display panel
- clicking a tool icon at the bottom of the window

Let's see how these work...

Creating Layers

First we need to create some layers to put the features on. The **Layers** window is shown in Figure 22. New layers can be created by selecting any of the indicated three options (pull-down menu, right click in the display panel, or tool icon). Any of these will open the **Layer Properties** dialog shown in Figure 23.

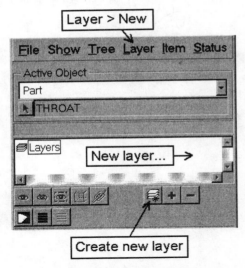

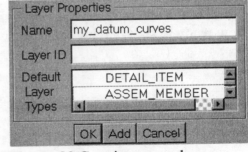

Figure 23 Creating a new layer

Figure 22 Options for creating new
layers

New layers are created by entering a name in the *Layer Properties* window. We will discuss the
other fields in this dialog a little later. For now, type in each of the following into the **Name**
field. When you press the Enter key after each line, the new layer will be added to the layer tree.
You can then type in the next layer name. Add these layers:

```
my_datum_curves
my_protrusions
my_rounds
my_holes
my_cuts
```

The "*my_*" prefix will help us to identify these layer names, and not get confused with feature
types or default layers. After entering these layer names, select *Cancel* in the New Layer window
rather than OK, or you will continue to create layers LAY0001, LAY0002, and so on.

If you make a mistake typing, or create a layer you don't want, the offending layer can be
modified or deleted by selecting it in the Layer tree window and holding down the right mouse
button. This brings up the pop-up menu shown in Figure 24. Select the appropriate command to
either delete the layer or access its properties. The *Layer Properties* command brings up the
dialog in Figure 23 which, among other things, allows you to rename it or correct spelling errors.

Figure 24 Command menu with right click on highlighted layer

Figure 25 Adding items to a layer

Adding Items to a Layer

We will look at a number of options for adding items to the layers. The three ways to launch this function are shown in Figure 25. The same item(s) can be added to several layers at the same time.

First, add the round feature to the MY_ROUNDS layer. Highlight the MY_ROUNDS layer (only) in the layer tree and select one of the options shown in Figure 25 to add an item to the layer. In the LAYER OBJ menu, select

> ***Feature > Select***

Pick on one of the corner rounds. All the rounds are in the same feature. Accept this selection with ***Done/Return*** in the LAYER OBJ menu.

In the pull-down menus in the Layers window select the following:

> ***Show > Layer Items***
> ***Tree > Expand > All***
> ***Tree > Highlight***

The MY_ROUNDS layer should show the feature just added. Click on this feature in the layer tree and it should highlight in green on the model.

Try to **Blank** the MY_ROUNDS layer. Again, there are three ways to do this: using the icon illustrated in Figure 26, right clicking on the layer to get the menu in Figure 24, or using the **Status** pull-down menu at the top. Highlight the layer in the tree and select one of these three methods, then **Repaint** the screen. Although the layer now shows as blanked (red stroke through icon), the rounds are still there. Why? As presented in the introduction to this section, blanking will only affect non-geometric features, that is, ones that do not alter the model geometry (like datums, axes, notes, points, and so on). Thus, the rounds cannot be blanked, although any non-geometric items on the MY_ROUNDS layer would be blanked at this time.

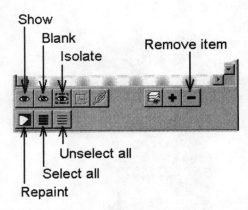

Figure 26 Icon commands in the *Layers* window

To demonstrate the use of the model tree with the layer tree, open up the model tree now. If the Layers window disappears, bring it back with **View > Layers** or the **Layer Display** toolbar icon (if you've set that up).

We'll add the holes to their layer. Highlight the MY_HOLES layer in the Layers dialog window. Again, you have your choice of command locations to find the **Add Item** command. In the LAYER OBJ menu select

Feature > Select

Click on the **Pattern** in the model tree. Only the pattern leader will highlight. Accept the selection and check the contents of the HOLES layer. All we got was the pattern leader. We want to get all the holes, so select **Add Item** again and in the LAYER OBJ menu select

Feature > Feat/Child

Now expand the pattern in the model tree and click on the pattern leader. You would expect all the other holes (the children) to highlight here but they don't. In the LAYER OBJ menu select **Done/Return**. Expand the MY_HOLES layer and you should see all five holes on the layer.

We'll add the datum curves to their layer using another selection option. Make sure the model tree is available. Highlight the MY_DATUM_CURVES layer, right click and select **Add Item**. In LAYER OBJ select

Feature > Range

Note the feature numbers of the two datum curves in the model tree. Enter the first datum curve feature number (should be 5), then the second (should be 6) to define the range. Accept the selected features. The layer is now expandable and you should see the two datum curves there.

Since we now have a layer with some non-geometry items on it, try to **Blank** the MY_DATUM_CURVES layer. Find the three command locations to do this! As expected, when you **Repaint** the screen, the datum curves are no longer visible.

Here is an interesting question: The datum curves are blanked, but these are parent features of the swept cut. So how can the cut regenerate? The answer is that, although the visual result is the same, **blanking is NOT like suppressing**. Features on a blanked layer are still regenerated and are part of the model. The situation is similar to turning the display of datum planes or axes on and off without affecting their children.

A final way to select features to add to a layer is by feature type. Highlight the MY_PROTRUSIONS layer, **Add Item** and select

> **Feature > All of Type**

and check the box beside Protrusions. The entries in this window will vary depending on what features are present in the model. **Done**. Finally, **Done/Return** in the LAYER OBJ menu. Check that the protrusion is in the correct layer.

Removing Items from a Layer

Manipulations of items on layers is very easy. For example, suppose we want to blank only the second datum curve (used as the second trajectory reference in the swept cut) and leave the datum curve down the center of the cut unblanked. We have to remove the center datum curve from the layer. If it is not being displayed, **Show** the MY_DATUM_CURVES layer. Expand the layer tree, highlight and then right click on the first datum curve feature. The menu shown in Figure 27 will open. Select **Remove Item**. Now when you blank the layer, the center datum curve should still be visible. Note that the same result could be obtained by leaving both datum curves on the layer, **Show**ing the layer, then selecting **Hide** from the right mouse pop-up menu for the second curve in the model tree.

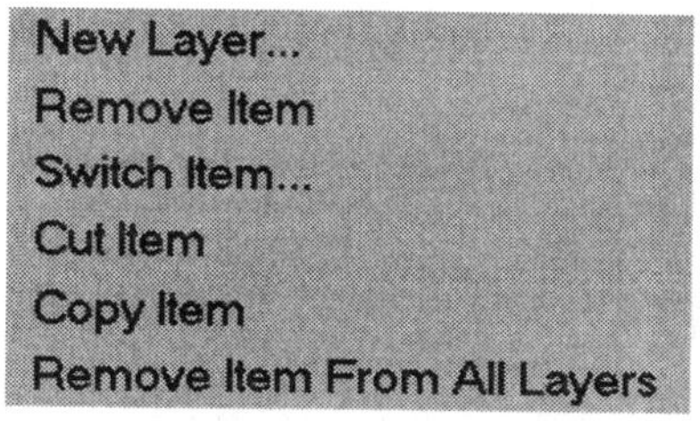

New Layer...
Remove Item
Switch Item...
Cut Item
Copy Item
Remove Item From All Layers

Figure 27 Command menu with right click on feature in layer

Copying and Switching Items

Other manipulations of individual features on layers is easily accomplished using the commands shown in Figure 27. These are fairly obvious in their function. For example, to include the round on the PROTRUSIONS layer (don't know why!), highlight the round feature in the MY_ROUNDS layer, then right click and select **Copy Item**. Highlight the MY_PROTRUSIONS layer and hold down the right mouse button again. Now you can use **Paste Item** to put the round feature into this layer. You might like to experiment with these commands a bit. Remember that features can appear on more than one layer at a time. In the model tree, you can add a column that will show the layer(s) associated with each feature.

Creating Default Layers

Default layers are used so that features are automatically assigned to one or more specified layers as soon as the feature is created. This eliminates the laborious job of assigning them manually.

There are two ways of creating default layers. We will look at the first one here, and deal with the second way in the next section. In the procedure presented here, we create default feature-to-layer assignments using the feature type and the layer name(s). These assignments are "temporary" in that they will not be saved with the model, although they will be valid throughout your current Pro/E session (including any other models you work on). More importantly, the default layers created this way will operate only with features created *after* the assignment is set up. Thus, the default layers should be set up early in the modeling process. The second method of setting up the default layers (using *config.pro*) uses virtually the same syntax and is discussed a bit later.

We'll set up a default for the MY_CUTS layer. Highlight this in the Layers window, right click and select *Layer Properties*. In the scrollable list beside "Default Layer Types", select CUT_FEAT. A green "+" sign appears. Then select *OK*.

Create a similar default layer assignment for the MY_PROTRUSIONS layer. The type is PROTRUSION_FEAT.

REMINDER: the default layers assignments we just created are NOT saved. They will be valid only for the rest of the current session.

To try out the cut assignment, create the cut shown in Figure 28. Open up the layer display to confirm that the *MY_CUTS* layer now has a feature.

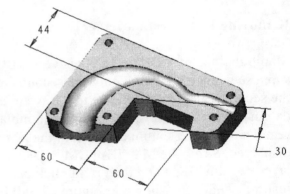

Figure 28 A *cut* added to the model

Default Layer Setup in *config.pro*

Unless you have a need for special layers created only for a single model and session, it makes sense to create a set of default layers that will be used for all your modeling. There may even be company standards for layer definitions that everyone should use all the time. These default assignments are made in your *config.pro* file. To create these, select

Utilities > Options

In the **Option** data field, type in the option name *DEF_LAYER*. In the **Value** field, open the pull-down list and select *LAYER_CURVE*. Now you must manually add the text "curves" to the value setting. Select *Add/Change*. Repeat this procedure to create the entries shown in Figure 29. Remember you have to *Apply* the new settings to activate them (which also automatically saves the config file). What does

```
!=====================================
!== DEFAULT LAYER DEFINITIONS
! DEF_LAYER        LAYER-TYPE       layer_name

DEF_LAYER          LAYER_CURVE curves
DEF_LAYER          LAYER_FEATURE all_features
DEF_LAYER          LAYER_NOGEOM_FEAT nogeometry_feats
DEF_LAYER          LAYER_ROUND_FEAT all_rounds
```

Figure 29 Some default layer assignments in *config.pro*

the blue wand icon mean?

The next time you load Pro/E, these four layers will be created automatically when *config.pro* is loaded.

To see if the default assignments are working, create a single datum curve (say a circle in the FRONT datum). Open up the layer display. You will see that the single feature occurs in all three layers (*all-features*, *curves*, *nogeometry*). **Blank** the layer CURVES and **Repaint**. The datum curve will disappear, even though the other layers it appears on are not blanked. Blanking a layer with non-geometry features will automatically blank those features even if they appear on other layers.

The *nogeometry* layer is a good way of catching any and all items that are "blank-able."

If you have access to it, the *pro_stds* directory on your installation has a *config.pro* which makes a number of default layer assignments. Check it out!

Manipulating Features by Layer

As mentioned at the beginning of the layers discussion, organizing features in layers makes it possible to manipulate them in groups. As a demonstration, select

> **Feature > Suppress > Normal > Layer**
> **MY_HOLES | Done Sel**
> **Done**

Open the layer display and expand the *MY_HOLES* layer. A small symbol ■ indicates the features are suppressed. The **Layer** command is available in may places where features are selected.

As you can see, layers allow you a lot of flexibility in organizing the features in your model. The functionality we have seen here for a part also applies to assemblies. There, we can assign different components to different layers. The layer display works somewhat differently in assemblies, as it interacts with the shading and hiddenline display of components. You might like to experiment with this on your own.

This lesson has introduced you to the operation of Pro/PROGRAM and Layers. The former allows an easy interface for users not familiar with how the model was constructed to create variations on the model geometry by specifying input values for variables and to control the regeneration sequence. Pro/PROGRAM also presents an easy way to create family tables.

The use of Layers will not only give you more control over the screen display of the model, but will assist you in organizing the model so that operations on groups of related features are simplified.

In the next lesson we will look at some advanced techniques used in the creation of drawings.

Questions for Review

1.   What are the five content areas in a design file?
2.   What is the file extension associated with a design for (a) a part and (b) an assembly?
3.   What are the three types of variables that can be used as input to a design?
4.   Give examples for the syntax used for the following elements in a design:
        a.   user input of variables
        b.   a relation
        c.   a conditional branch
5.   In a boolean expression, what is the correct form for an equality test?
6.   What is meant by "incorporating" the design?
7.   What is the difference between reading a design from the model and from a file?
8.   When does a design file execute?
9.   Where can a conditional branch be placed in a design file?
10.   How does Pro/E react if there is a syntax error in the design file?
11.   How do you create the generic part in a family table for a part which includes a design?
12.   Why is it dangerous to use "*" in a family table for a part driven by a program?
13.   What are the two primary functions of layers?
14.   What types of entities can be organized in layers?
15.   Why can a parent feature be blanked without affecting its children?
16.   Describe four ways of selecting items to be added to a layer.
17.   What is meant by a non-geometric feature?
18.   What happens if you blank a layer containing both geometric and non-geometric features?
19.   Describe the purpose of the default layers.
20.   What two pieces of information are required to create a default layer?
21.   Identify and compare the two methods for creating default layers. In particular, describe when the default layer assignment is active.
22.   Can you delete or rename a default layer that is assigned when Pro/E is started up?
23.   What settings are required in the Layers window to
        a.   highlight individual features in green
b.   automatically show all the features assigned to all the layers
24.   How can you create a layer that will blank all non-geometric features at the same time?

Project Exercises

Only three parts to do in this lesson. These are pretty straight forward again - in one case trivial! We will be using Pro/PROGRAM when we get to Lesson 8. The parts are all related to the front wheel of the cart:

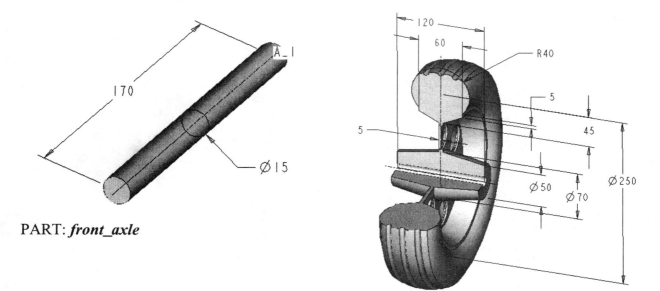

PART: *front_axle*

PART: *front_wheel*

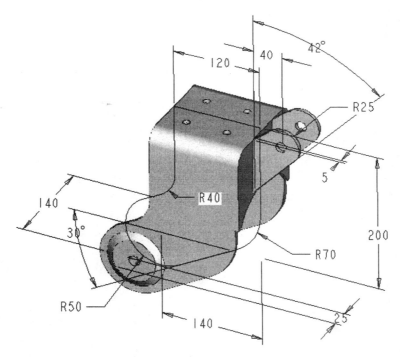

PART: *front_wheel_brack*

Notes:

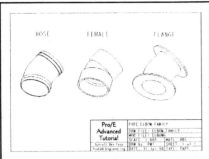

Lesson 7

Advanced Drawing Functions

Synopsis

The drawing setup file; dimension symbols; draft dimensions; tools for creating draft entities; drawing formats and parameters; tables and repeat regions; multi-model drawings; multi-sheet drawings; drawing templates

Overview

In this lesson we will examine a number of advanced features and techniques relating to the creation of drawings. We will concentrate mostly on drawings of parts, but many of the ideas will carry over to assemblies. We will discuss the drawing setup file and how to create a default setup. We then move on to techniques involved in detailing and interpreting the dimension symbols on the drawing. There will be a very brief introduction to the tools that you can use to create draft entities on the drawing. We will spend some time discussing tables, formats, and repeat regions, all of which can make creation of drawings a much more efficient task. We'll look into multi-sheet drawings and creating drawings with more than one model. This topic is particularly relevant to assembly drawings (which we will deal with in the next lesson). Finally,, we'll have a look at the creation of drawing templates.

This is a lot to cover, so let's get going...

Drawing Set-up Files

There are well over a hundred settings that control the appearance and functionality of a drawing. Some of these are contained in *config.pro*. Most are included in a drawing setup file. When a drawing is first created, it has embedded in it the values of the settings in a default setup file. Different drawings, even in the same session, can have different setup files, or variations of a single file. In this part of the lesson, we will look at some of the options for determining the setup file, how to change the settings contained in it and apply it to the drawing, and how to create your own default setup file.

Start Pro/E and create a new drawing:

File > New > Drawing > [tut_drw_test]

Deselect the option "Use default template" and select *OK*. The New Drawing dialog window appears. Leave the Default Model as **none**, check the radio button **Empty**, leave orientation as Landscape, set the size to **A**, and select the *OK* button.

The default drawing settings for your installation could be determined in a number of ways. To see your current settings, select

Advanced > Draw Setup

This brings up the **Options** editor with your system's default drawing setup file, see Figure 1. This dialog window operates in much the same way as the window for dealing with your Pro/E configuration file *config.pro*. The first two columns contain the setting names and the setting values. Unlike *config.pro*, where you only see options that differ from the default, in this drawing setup window you see all the options - there are around 130 settings listed in this file. Browse through them to see some of the options. Notice that the third column shows you a default value. You will find options for text height, text thickness, view options, arrow styles, cutting line styles, dimension appearance options, tolerance display, leaders, axes, and so on. Unless your system is set up differently, the default settings are ANSI standards. All the options are described on-line (go to *Contents > Using Foundation Modules > Using Pro/DETAIL > Drawing Setup File Options*).

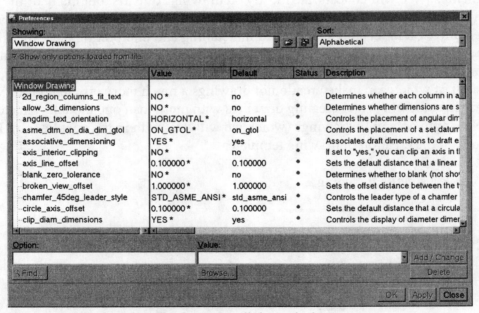

Figure 1 The drawing **Preferences** dialog window

Note that the default Sort method (see the top right corner of the window) is **Alphabetical**. Change this to **By Category**. This is a useful way to organize settings. Note also that the Find button and "Show only options loaded from file" are disabled. This is because the drawing setup file always contains all the settings. A copy of this file is actually embedded in every drawing you do. Thus, you can make many variations of this file, and the one that is loaded when a new drawing is created will be applied to that file (unless settings are changed in the drawing later).

A standard Pro/E installation contains a number of drawing setup files that adhere to various standards. The default file *prodetail.dtl* is for ANSI standards. Standard setup files are available for ISO and DIN. To see some of the other standard setup files, select the ***Open File*** icon. The **Open** dialog window appears, with a list of dtl files in your current working directory (probably none!). Select the pull-down list beside the directory name at the top. In this list, select **Drawing Setup Directory**. This is actually the directory **/ptc/proe2001/text**. Select the *iso.dtl* file, then ***Open***. This is a setup for a metric drawing - browse through the listed settings. Note the text height ("drawing_text_height") is in millimeters and the projection type ("projection_type") is first angle, as is common in Europe.

Once a setup file has been brought into a drawing, it will override any current settings. You will have to ***Apply*** the current values to the drawing to see the changes.

In the **pro_stds** directory under the Pro/E loadpoint (if you have it installed), there are two dtl files: *english.dtl* and *metric.dtl*. This metric setup file uses third angle projection which is the standard in North America.

Retrieve the *prodetail.dtl* setup file from **/ptc/proe2001/text**. Set the sort method to ***As Set***. Change the drawing text height to **0.125**. Then ***Add/Change***. This setting will apply only to the current drawing (when you select ***Apply***). To make this change "permanent" we need to save the new setup file:

> ***Save As***

Select your working directory and enter a name ***def_ansi*** (the extension dtl is added automatically), then ***OK***. The file is now stored in the current working directory. Select ***Close***.

Your default drawing setup file is determined by a setting in *config.pro*. If this setting is omitted, the default is *prodetail.dtl*, which produces ANSI standard (English units) drawings. To change the default setup file to the one we made above, add the following to your *config.pro*:

```
drawing_setup_file          i:/myfiles/proe/def_ansi.dtl
```

Make sure the path to the *dtl* file matches your normal startup working directory. ***Apply*** the change in *config.pro* (remember that this also automatically saves the file). This will ensure that Pro/E is always able to read this file. On a network with several users, this *dtl* file (and any others in common use) can be placed in a directory accessible by all the users. Each user's *config.pro* setting should point to this directory (if different from the default) using the configuration option pro_dtl_setup_dir.

To see if the new *config* setting is working, erase the current drawing and create a new empty drawing. Examine the setup file for this new drawing using ***Advanced > Draw Setup***. You should find it contains the modified text height that we set above.

Erase this drawing from the session.

Detailing: Dimension Symbols and Draft Entities

In this section we will look at some of the commands and functions for detailing on the drawing. As you know, when a drawing is being created from a model, the dimensions in the model can be placed on the drawing using the ***Show and Erase*** command. These are called, appropriately enough, "shown" or "driving" dimensions. These dimensions have *bidirectional associativity* with the model - the numerical value can be changed in either the model or the drawing and the other will update automatically - they "drive" the model.

One of the ramifications of using a constraint-based modeler such as Pro/E is that some of the geometry in the model may have been determined by constraints set up when the various features were created, particularly in Sketcher. These include alignments, equal radii, equal length, perpendicularity, and so on. Thus, there may not be any dimension values available to be shown on the drawing for some features. Although the solid modeler is happy with this (since it knows what the constraints are), the person trying to read the drawing may not be aware of these constraints and therefore would perceive that some dimensions on the drawing are missing. The main subject of this section is to look at how these additional dimensions can be created and manipulated.

We will explore this subject by creating a simple plate model, shown in Figure 2, and then creating a drawing. Start a new part called **dim_plate** using your part template from Lesson #1 or using the built-in **inlbs_part_solid** template. The plate is a simple one-sided protrusion off the FRONT datum plane. The sketch is shown in Figure 3. Note how few dimensions are required in Sketcher due to the constraints that have been used to define the lines along the top of the plate. The plate thickness is **0.5**. That's all there is to this model. Save it.

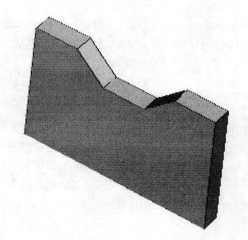

Figure 2 The plate model

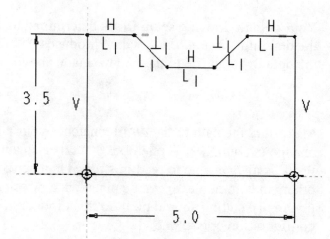

Figure 3 Sketch for plate model

Now, create a drawing using the ***File > New*** command or the ***Create New Object*** toolbar button. The name of the drawing is **dim_plate**. Select the ***Drawing*** radio button, deselect the "Use default template" box, then ***OK***. Set the template to **Empty**, choose Landscape orientation, and specify an **A** size sheet.

Add the front view of the model to the drawing (similar to the sketch):

Views > Add View
General | Full View | No Xsec | No Scale | Done

Click in the center of the screen and orient the view using the datum planes (or select *Saved Views > Front > Set*). Turn off the datum plane display and change the sheet scale to 1.0 with the *Edit > Value* command.

Drawing Dimensions

To apply the shown dimensions, select:

View > Show and Erase

Select the dimensions icon, the *Show by(Part)* option, *With Preview*, *Show All* and confirm. You will see just the two dimensions used in Sketcher. *Accept* these and close the dialog. Use *Tools > Clean Dims* to clean up the spacing. See Figure 4. To see the symbolic names for these dimensions,

Info > Switch Dims

or select the *Switch Dims* toolbar button. The driving dimensions created in Sketcher appear (Figure 5) as *d0* and *d1*. Your symbolic names may be different.

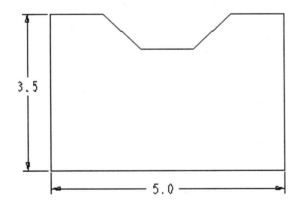

Figure 4 Dimensions created with Show/Erase (driving dimensions)

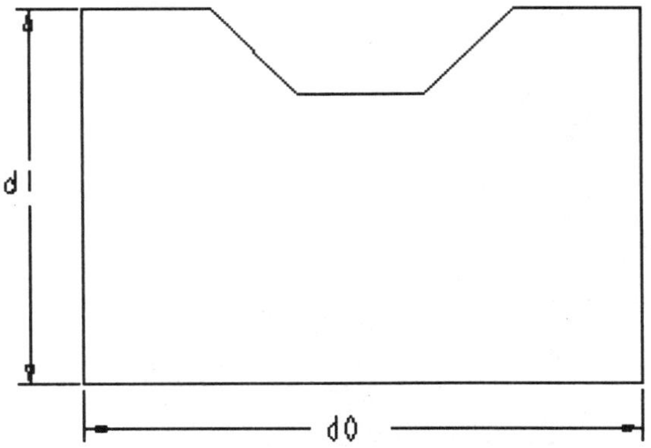

Figure 5 Driving dimension symbols, *d#*

Would you send this drawing down to the shop? Probably not. Clearly, there are insufficient dimensions on this drawing to define the notch along the top edge. We need to put some additional dimensions along the top of the part. The dimensions we are about to add to the drawing are called "created" or "driven" dimensions.

Before we do this, check that the following option is set in your drawing setup file (use *Advanced > Draw Setup* to view and/or edit this file):

```
associative_dimensioning   YES
```

Also, in your *config.pro* file, make sure the following option is set (don't forget to **Apply** the *config* file if you change or add the setting):

```
create_drawing_dims_only   YES
```

These options control where these dimensions will be stored (in the model or in the drawing) and how the new dimensions will relate to the drawing entities.

Switch the dimensions back to their numeric values with **Switch Dims**.

Standard Dimensions using *New Ref*

In the pull-down menus, select

> ***Insert > Dimension > New References > On Entity***

Left click on the top left horizontal line. Middle click to place the dimension above the line. To dimension the depth of the notch, left click on the center horizontal line (bottom of the notch) and on the top right horizontal line and place this dimension with a middle click. Finally, dimension the top right horizontal line. The drawing should look something like Figure 6[1]. Now switch dimensions again (Figure 7). The symbolic names appear as *add#*, which stands for "associative draft dimension". This naming convention is the primary method to determine which dimensions are driving (*d#*) and which are driven (*add#*).

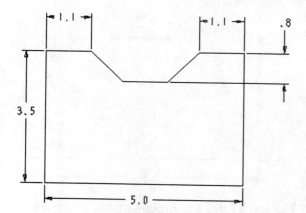

Figure 6 Draft dimensions applied to drawing

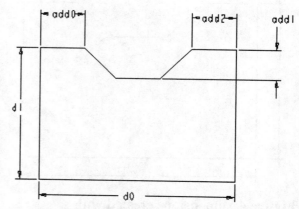

Figure 7 Symbol names for driving and driven dimensions

---

[1] To set the number of decimal places in the dimensions, use Shift-left click to select all the dimensions. Then right click, select **Properties**, and set the desired number.

What happens if the part changes size? Use *Switch Dims* to get the numerical values back. Left click on the width dimension (5). Right click and select *Nominal Val*. Enter a new value of **6**. Of course, we have to regenerate the model. The drawing should now appear as Figure 8. The associative dimensions all change as required - they are truly "driven" by the model. Change the width back to 5 before proceeding.

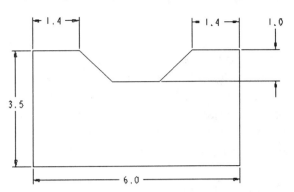

What happens if you try to change the depth of the notch? Why?

Figure 8 Model regenerated with new width

Common Ref Dimensions

Another format for the created dimensions is the following. Erase the two created dimensions across the top by picking them (use shift-click) with the left mouse button (they will highlight in red); then use the keyboard *Delete* key. (Incidentally, can you delete the 5.0 dimension? Why?) Then select

Insert > Dimension > Common Reference > On Entity

Read the message window and click the left vertical edge of the part. This sets the reference line (in magenta) for the following dimensions. See Figure 9.

Intersect

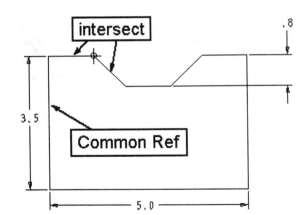

Figure 9 Creating a Common Ref dimension

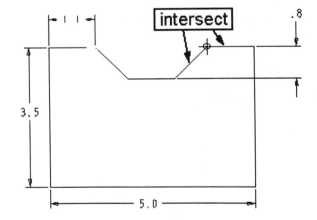

Figure 10 Second Common Ref dimension

In the ATTACH TYPE menu, select *Intersect* and pick the two lines that meet at the right end of the top left edge. A small marker appears at the intersection. Middle click to place the dimension. Select *Intersect* again and pick the two edges that intersect on the other side of the notch. See Figure 10. Middle click to place the dimension.

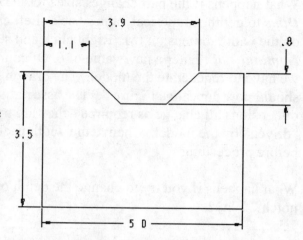

The final *Common Ref* dimensions are shown in Figure 11. If you switch dimensions, you will see that these are associative.

Try to *Modify* any of these associative dimensions. You can't, as stated in the message window.

Figure 11 *Common Ref* dimensions on the top of the part (*add#*)

Foreshadowing what is to come, try moving this view on the drawing sheet. Go to

> *Views > Move View*

click on the view and drag the outline sideways. Left click to drop the view at the new location. All dimensions move with the view. Does this always happen? Before looking into that, we'll conclude this section by reviewing all the dimension types that might appear on a drawing.

Save the drawing.

Dimension Types

For future reference, there are actually six different types of dimensions on a Pro/E drawing. The dimension type depends on how it was made, what it references, and on the settings in the *dtl* and *config.pro* files. It is unlikely that you will come across all these variations often. The most common dimension types, as we saw above, are the *d#* and *add#* types, and will be created with the default settings in the setup and *config* files. All six types are shown in Table 1. Unless otherwise specified in the table, the default settings are assumed to be

```
associative_dimensioning     YES    (in dtl file)
create_drawing_dims_only     YES    (in config.pro)
```

Table 1 Dimension Types and Symbols

Dimension Type	Dimension Symbol	Notes
driving	*d#*	"shown" dimension of a feature created in the model (eg with Sketcher) placed on drawing with **Show and Erase**
driven	*ad#*	dim created in drawing with **Insert > Dimension** *config.pro* set to `create_drawing_dims_only` NO dim stored with model dim is associative
driven	*add#*	dim created with **Insert > Dimension** dim stored with the drawing dim is associative
draft	*dd#*	dim created with **Insert > Dimension** *dtl* file set to `associative_dimensioning` NO dim stored with drawing dim is not associative
draft	*add#*	dim created on draft entities only with **Insert > Dimension** dim stored with the drawing dim is associative
mixed	*add#*	dim created on draft and model entities with **Create > Dimension** dim stored with the drawing dim is associative

Creating Draft Entities

You may occasionally want to add drawing elements (entities) to the drawing in addition to the ones displayed in the views. As an example, suppose that we want to mark an area on our plate for the placement of a small sticker. This placement location is not included in the solid model (although it possibly could be done using datum curves), so we have to add it here. Entities to define the placement location for the sticker can be added using some sketching tools available in the toolbar menu on the right. These sketching commands are very similar to those in Sketcher. Explore the tool buttons and flyouts for a minute. You will also find two new buttons at the top of the toolbar. We will use one of these (Enable Sketching Chain) in a little while.

Look ahead to Figure 12. We want to create a small rectangle on the plate. Left and right edges are lined up with corner vertices on the top edge. Here's how we can do that...

Create a couple of vertical construction lines. On the flyout from the Line toolbar icon, find and select the Construction line icon. The cursor changes to a red cross-hair with a cyan marker at the intersection and a new window opens (it may be partly hidden). This is the Snapping References dialog. These references operate in much the same way as references do in Sketcher. You may select any entity on the screen and it will become "snap-able" for new sketched entities. We want to snap to the two corner vertices, so pick on the existing drawing edges that meet at the vertices. As you pick them, they will turn blue with yellow vertex highlights.

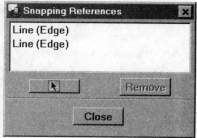

Figure 12 Dialog window for creating snapping references

As each reference is selected, it appears in the Snapping References window (Figure 12). As you move the cursor cross-hair around, it will snap to the designated references.

Note that if you middle click, you will return to drawing mode and the Snapping References are lost. If that happens, just pick a sketching tool again and reselect the references. Picking on a listed reference will make it highlight on the drawing (and the Remove button becomes active).

First, create a couple of construction lines through the existing geometry. With the Construction line icon selected, click on one of the top vertices of the notch. The construction line will snap to vertical. Repeat for the other vertex. Note that the two construction lines are now listed as Snapping References.

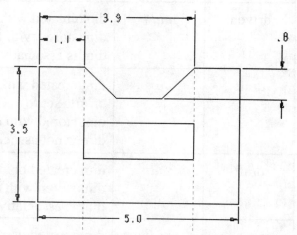

Figure 13 Draft geometry entities

Now choose the **Line** command icon to create the two horizontal edges of the rectangle. These also become snap-able references. Close the two ends of the rectangle, which should now appear as in Figure 13. Middle click to leave sketching mode. The newly sketched lines appear in white and the references disappear.

If the corners of the rectangle don't exactly meet, don't worry about it because we will be trimming these up in a minute or two.

Dimensions of Draft Entities

We want to create a couple of dimensions for the rectangle.

> *Insert > Dimension*
> *New References > On Entity*

pick on the bottom edge of the part and the bottom line in the rectangle. One edge will highlight in red and the other in blue. Middle click to (try to) place the dimension. Pro/E will not let you do this - see the message window. We'll find out why in a minute. Try to dimension the height of the rectangle. This will work, and create an associative draft dimension, Figure 14.

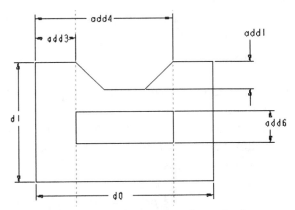

Relating Entities to Views

To illustrate a problem with what we've just done and also why the previous dimension wouldn't appear, try to move the view. In the top DRAWING menu select

Views > Move View

Figure 14 Dimension created on draft entities

or right click on the screen and *Modify Item*. Click on the view and drag it sideways. *Repaint*. The rectangle is no longer in the same place on the part, Figure 15. The view has moved but the draft entities are stuck to the drawing sheet.

We want to move the view back to its original position and have the draft entities revert to their previous position. It is unfortunate that Pro/E does not have an Undo command yet (except in Sketcher!). You will have to delete the draft entities (construction lines through dimension) and create them again - good exercise anyway!

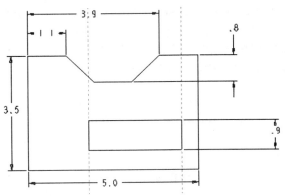

Figure 15 View moved; draft entities left behind (not *related*)

Go ahead and delete these entities now, and move the view back to the center of the sheet. Let's do something a bit different here. Recall that the previous rectangle was drawn one edge at a time. Create the two vertical construction lines as before (through the reference vertices on the top corners). Now middle click to accept them - they will turn gray. Select the *Enable Sketching Chain* icon at the top of the sketching toolbar. Now select the *Create Lines* icon and use the **Snapping References** dialog window to pick the two construction lines as references. Use *Done/Sel* instead of middle click (which takes you out of drawing mode). Now you can create the rectangle with a series of mouse clicks (one at each corner vertex). The end vertex of each line becomes the start vertex of the next, in the style of Sketcher, and each new line rubber-bands from the start vertex. When all four edges are drawn, middle click once to end line creation, then again to accept the drawing entities. Dimension the height of the rectangle as before. Your drawing should once again look like Figure 14.

We need a way to tell Pro/E to keep the draft entities attached to the view. This is called *relating* the entities. In the DRAWING menu, select

Views > Relate View > Add Items

Click on the view - this is what we want to add items to. Then in the GET SELECT menu, se'

Pick Many > Pick Box > Inside Box. Surround the entire view (including the dimensions) with a box. Select *Done Sel*. This will select all draft entities within the box and relate or attach them to the view.

Now try *Views > Move View* again. The rectangle lines move with the view but the two construction lines don't. It is easy to understand why - they weren't selected to be related to the view because they were not completely inside the selection box above. We don't need them any more anyway, so delete them. The original height dimension still appears at its original location. Fix that by selecting

> *View > Update > Drawing View*

and it will move to the correct location.

Create the dimension from the bottom edge of the part to the bottom of the rectangle. This is the one we couldn't do before - it works now because both entities being dimensioned are related (in the same view). Now both dimensions will move with the view for the same reason. Thus, remember the following:

> *Draft entities must be related to the view before they are dimensioned. This also applies to other detail items like leaders, detail text, and so on.*

More Drafting Tools

There is quite a lot you can do with the drafting tools available in drawing mode. You can, in fact, enter this mode directly (without creating a solid model first) and create complete 2D drawings. Although Pro/E is not known for the convenience of doing this, it does have all the necessary tools. With the new drawing interface layout of sketching tools in 2001, it is becoming easier. You will normally require these tools only to "touch-up" an existing drawing. Just so that you have a look at these, some of the tools are described below. While you are doing this, scan down the command menus to see other options. You might come back later and experiment with these on your own.

Moving and Trimming Draft Entities

We want to make the rectangle a bit taller. Can we do that by changing the dimension value? Select *Edit > Value* and pick on the height dimension (or left pick to select the dimension, then right click to select Modify). We cannot make this change. (Why?) Instead, we have to move the rectangle edge.

Click on the bottom edge of the rectangle. Drag it downwards. The vertical dimension values will adjust (remember that they are associative). Drag the upper line upwards. Move the lines until the rectangle height dimension is about **1.5** as shown in Figure 16, and the rectangle is about **0.75** from the bottom of the part. The corners have probably become disconnected. To restore nice corners on the rectangle, select (in the DRAWING menu)

Tools > Trim > Corner

Pick on the lower horizontal line and one of the vertical lines. Repeat for the other four corners of the rectangle.

While you're here, browse through the remaining drafting tools. Between these and the Sketch menu, you can do just about anything for creating 2D drawings.

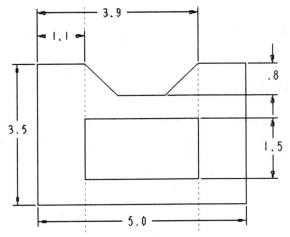

Figure 16 Final rectangle size

Changing the Line Style

We don't want the rectangle to show on the drawing as a visible edge, so let's change the line style. Starting in the pull-down menu select

Format > Line Style > Modify Lines > Pick Many

and draw a box around the rectangle. Middle click. A new dialog window appears. In the Line Font pull-down list, select **CTRLFONT_S_S** and then *Apply*. If you don't like that font, try another one and *Apply* again. You can also set the color of the line. When you're happy with the line style, select *Close*. Select *Done/Return* in the Tools menu.

You can change the line style of any line on the drawing. This is handy if you bring in datum curves (perhaps as the trajectory of a sweep) and want to show them in a centerline font, for example.

Adding a Note and Hatch Pattern

Fill in the rectangle with a hatch pattern by selecting the four sides (Hint: use shift-click to select more than one entity at the same time), then select

Edit > Fill > Hatched

Type in a name like "sticker". In the MOD XHATCH menu select *Retrieve* and bring in the hatch pattern for zinc. If this does not come up on your installation, just use the default hatch. Change the hatch spacing and angle if you want. Then select *Done*.

Finally, let's add a note to the drawing:

> *Insert > Note*
> *Leader | Enter | Horizontal | Standard | Default | Make Note*
> *On Entity | Arrow Head*

Pick on the edge of the rectangle then middle click where you want the note elbow. Enter some text for the note like "PUT STICKER HERE". See Figure 17.

Do you have to relate the hatch pattern and the note to the view? Try to move the view. What happens and why? Save the drawing and part, and erase them from the session.

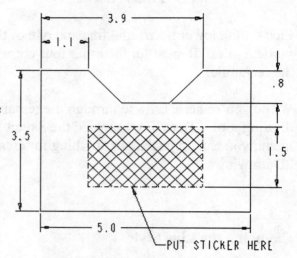

Figure 17 Final drawing of *dim_plate*

Drawing Formats and Tables

A format for a drawing contains such things as the border and title block which you use often in creating your drawings. The format can be applied either when the drawing is created or after the drawing is already underway. Formats can also be removed or replaced on drawings. Formats are defined for specific sheet sizes. You can have multiple formats defined and select the one you want for an individual drawing or sheet.

There is no default format but there are several standard formats available with a normal Pro/E installation containing ANSI standard title blocks for several sheet sizes (*a.frm*, *b.frm*, and so on). If not installed in the default location (`\ptc\proe\formats`), a specific format directory can be identified in *config.pro* using a setting similar to (your path may be different)

```
pro_format_dir          c:\myfiles\proe\formats
```

You may have occasion to create your own format. This section will show you the steps required to not only create the format with a title block, but also to make automatic entries in the title block. This will be accomplished using a table with model and drawing parameters.

Creating a Format

In the Pro/E main window, select

File > New > Format > [tut_format] > OK

In the New Format window use the **Empty** radio button, set the size to **A** (an 8.5 X 11 sheet), and select Landscape, then *OK*.

We will first place a 3/8" border around the page using some drawing tools. In the sketcher toolbar at the right select

> ### *Create Lines*

The cursor will change to a red cross hair. Now right click and select

> ### *Specify Absolute Coords*

Note the XY coordinate system at the bottom left of the sheet. For the first point, enter the absolute coordinates X = **0.375** and Y = **0.375**.

A cyan line will rubber-band out from the first vertex. For the second point, right click again and select

> ### *Specify Absolute Coords*

and enter X = **10.625**, Y = **0.375**.

Now to create the left vertical edge. First, right click to pick the *Select Reference* command, then pick on the horizontal line you just finished. This now becomes a snap-able reference. Start the next line by picking on the left end of the reference line. For the other end, right click and select

> ### *Specify Relative Coords*

and enter the relative coordinates X = **0**, Y = **7.75**.

Create a horizontal line across the top. Make the left vertical line a reference (right click and select Reference, then click on the line). The horizontal line should still be a reference; if not, add it to the reference list as well. Now select Create Lines, and pick on the top of the left edge (snap-able). Move the cursor horizontally to the right. The line should snap to horizontal, and should also snap to match the length of the lower horizontal line.

For the final vertical line on the right side, you should be able to snap to existing vertices. Select Create Lines and just pick on the right ends of the bottom and top lines. We now have a rectangular border 0.375" from the edge of the page.

There were a lot of mouse short-cuts here, and an inadvertent middle click may have bounced you out of drawing mode before you wanted. Just for practice, then, erase these lines and draw the border again.

Now, on to the title block. Rather than create individual lines to produce this, we will use a table. This not only makes the construction easier, but also makes it possible for the title block to fill in automatically when the format is used.

In the DRAFT GEOM menu, select *Return*.

Creating a Table

The title block table will be placed by identifying a starting point and the direction in which to "grow" the table (add rows and columns). Our table will start at the bottom right corner of the border and grow upwards and to the left.

> *Table > Create*
> *Ascending > Leftward > By Length > Vertex*

"By Length" means we will specify column widths and row heights using drawing units. Pick on the lower right hand vertex of the border we just drew and check the message window.

We first enter the column widths. We will have three columns, all of width **2**. After the third width is entered, hit the Enter key again. Now you are prompted for the height of the rows. Create five rows with height **0.25**, and a final row of height **0.5**. Notice the markers that appear as this data is entered. When the final row is identified, the table will be created as shown in Figure 18.

Now we can modify the cells in the table by combining or merging them. Look at Figure 19 to see where we are going. First, combine the top four cells in the first column

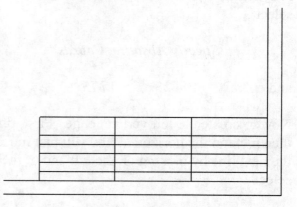

Figure 18 Creation of title block table

> *Modify Table > Merge > Rows*

Click on the top and 4th cell in the first column. This will remove the intermediate row lines. Select

> *Columns*

and click on the elements in the middle and right columns in rows 1, 2, and 3 (down from the top). The final table should look like Figure 19.

On a drawing, notes can be added to the cells in this table, a laborious and repetitive process. We can do a lot better than manual operations here, as described in the next section.

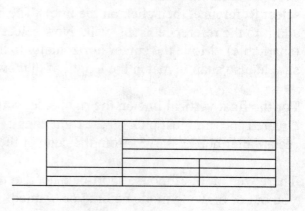

Figure 19 Completed title block table showing merged cells

Using Drawing Parameters

We would like entries in the title block (drawing and model file names, drawing scale, sheet number, title, date, and so on) to be made automatically when the format is used in a drawing. For a preview of the final result, see Figure 20. This is done by entering drawing parameters in various cells in the format table. When the format is added to the drawing, the table contents will automatically display the values of the drawing parameters. There are two types of parameters to consider: system and model parameters. These are discussed below. In our title block, we will use both types of parameters.

System Parameters

System parameters are built in to either the drawing or the model, and can be used wherever you want (with one exception). Parameters you might like to use in a drawing are shown in Table II. Most of these parameters can be used anywhere on the drawing, for example, in a note. The exception is *&todays_date*, which must be used inside a table (or else it just shows up as "&todays_date").

TABLE II System Parameters

Parameter	Definition	Parameter	Definition
&model_name	name of model	&dwg_name	name of drawing file
&scale	drawing scale	&type	model type
&format	format size	&todays_date	date format added to drawing
&linear_tol_0_0	linear tolerance values	&angular_tol_0_0	angular tolerance values
&current_sheet	sheet number of current drawing sheet	&total_sheets	total number of sheets in drawing
&pdmdb	product database of origin	&pdmrev	model revision
&pdmrl	model release level	&pdmrev:d	drawing revision

We will add some of the system parameters shown in Table II to the title block. In the TABLE menu, select

Enter Text

Pick in the second row from the top on the right of the table, and enter the following:

```
DRW FILE: &dwg_name
```

Click in the row below this and enter the following:

```
MOD FILE: &model_name
```

Enter the following parameters in the cells indicated in Figures 19 and 20:

```
SCALE: &scale
SHEET: &current_sheet of &total_sheets
TYPE: &type
DATE: &todays_date
```

Some of the text may overlap adjacent cells - don't worry about this. The final text will fit within the cells when the parameter value is displayed.

Model Parameters

Model parameters are determined by the user, either by creating the parameter in the model or in the drawing. When the format is applied to the drawing any parameters present in the format that are not defined either in the model or drawing will result in a prompt to the user to enter a value.

In the rows indicated in Figure 20, enter the following text and model parameters:

```
&description
DRW by &drawn_by
MATL &material
```

When this is complete, select **Done/Return** in the TABLE menu.

&description	
DRW FILE: &dwg_name	
MOD FILE: &model_name	
SCALE: &scale	MATL: &material
DRW by: &drawn_by	
DATE: &todays_date	

Figure 20 Entering parameters in the format title block

Let's make sure that the text displays nicely in the cells. Select (in the pull-down menu)

Format > Text Style > Pick Many

and click on opposite corners of a selection box bounding the title box. All the text entries should highlight. Middle click. In the Text Style dialog window, set *Justification Vertical* to **Middle**, and *Justifification Horizontal* to **Left**. Click on the *Apply* button and the text should all move within each cell to the requested alignment. Select *OK*.

We are finished creating the format. If you like, you can add additional elements to the title block, like a company logo. This can be drawn with the tools under the Sketch menu or you can import various kinds of graphics files (IGES, DXF, TIFF and so on) and place them in the format. You can use either *Insert > Note* or *Table > Enter Text* to add additional text to the title block table. The text formatting controls will let you center the text within the cells. When you are finished, save the format file and then erase it from the session.

Using a Drawing Format

Let's try out the new format file. We'll use the *bracket* part we made in the last lesson. Open the generic of this part and make sure the units are set to millimeters. The only parameter currently defined in this model should be *has_rib*. All our other symbolic names were dimensions. Check this out with

Setup > Parameters > Part > Info

After confirming the existing parameter, close the information window. To create the required additional parameters you need to specify the parameter type, name, and contents. In the MODEL PARAMS menu select

Create > String > [description] > [CORNER BRACKET]
String > [material] > [STEEL]

Note that the parameter names are lower case - these will be converted to uppercase automatically. The string values are case sensitive (what you type here is exactly what will show up on the drawing later). Check the *Parameters > Info* window again to confirm these parameters are in the data base. Save the part *bracket*.

Now create a drawing:

File > New > Drawing

Call the drawing *lesson7a*. Deselect "Use default template", then *OK*. The default model is **bracket**. Select the radio button for **Empty with format** then retrieve the format *tut_format* in the current working directory. When prompted for the model, open the generic part in **bracket**.

All the parameters currently in the format table are known (they are either system parameters or model parameters that we just created), with the exception of one: the format requires a value for the parameter *drawn_by*. Whenever an unassigned parameter is found, Pro/E will prompt you to enter a value. This is very handy here. Enter your name or initials for the *drawn_by* parameter. The title block should now be filled in as shown in Figure 21.

Pro/E Advanced Tutorial	CORNER BRACKET		
	DRW FILE: LESSON7A		
	MOD FILE: BRACKET		
	SCALE: 1.000	MATL: STEEL	
Schroff Dev Corp	DRW by: RWT	SHEET: 1 of 1	
ProCAD Engineering	DATE: 31-Jul-00	TYPE: PART	

Figure 21 Title block on drawing with values assigned for all parameters

Add a view of the bracket

Views > Add View
General | Full View | No Xsec | No Scale | Done

and pick in the left center of the drawing sheet. To set the orientation, if you have saved views in the model, you can select one of these directly. If you have these named views, select *Saved*

Views and highlight the model view desired (in this case **Left**). The drawing should look like Figure 22.

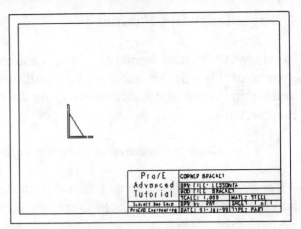

Add an additional view

> ***Add View***
> ***Projection |...| No Scale | Done***

and pick to the right of the existing view. Add another projected view above the first view. Select ***Done/Return*** in the VIEWS menu.

Figure 22 First view placed on drawing

Change the drawing scale by selecting

> ***Edit > Value***

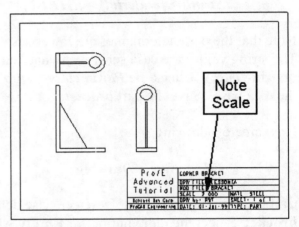

and click on the *Scale* entry at the bottom of the graphics window or in the title block. Enter a new value of **2**. Note that the title block has automatically been changed, Figure 23.

Save the drawing, but don't erase it since we need it in the next section. This use of a drawing format with parameters can save you a lot of time (and also leads to increased consistency) when creating drawings. In the next section, we'll construct

Figure 23 Views added and scale set to 2.0

another table that will automatically display all the members of the bracket family.

Repeat Regions

A repeat region is a portion of a table that will automatically grow and shrink according to the data in the model database. For the bracket part, we will use a repeat region to list the instances in the family table. In a later lesson, we will use a repeat region to construct a BOM (Bill of Materials) that lists (and counts) all the components in an assembly.

To construct a repeat region, we first make a table. Then we identify which cells in the table are to be repeated and what data is to be placed in each cell. As the data changes, the table will expand or shrink accordingly.

We will create a display of the family table instances for the bracket using two variations of the repeat region (*Simple* and *2D*). The first method is a bit more work for the family table display but gives more control over such things as individual column width and formatting within each column. The 2D repeat region requires less work, but is trickier and has somewhat less control over the display.

A Simple Repeat Region

The first repeat region exercise is based on the table shown in Figure 23. To create this, start in the DRAWING menu and select

> ***Table > Create***
> ***Descending | Leftward | By Num Chars | Abs Coords***

and enter X = **10.625**, Y = **8.125** (the top right corner of the drawing). (Why can't we use the *Vertex* option here?) A string of characters streams off to the left from this initial point showing character widths (because we selected ***Num Chars*** in the command). Click between the first 6 and 7 from the right end to set the width of the first column. Do this four more times. The last column is 12 characters wide. To stop creating columns, middle click. You are now prompted for row heights. Pick between the 1 and 2 twice to create two rows. Middle click again. The table now appears as in Figure 24.

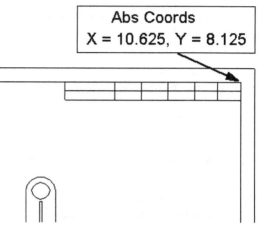

Figure 24 Creating the table for the repeat region

Now add some text to the top row to serve as column headers. Select

> ***Enter Text***

and click in the first cell in the top row (column 1). Enter the text `Part ID`. Enter the following text in the indicated columns (see Figure 25):

column 2	`Height`
column 3	`Length`
column 4	`Hole`
column 5	`Rib?`
column 6	`Thick`

The second row will be used to define six simple repeat regions. We need separate repeat regions for each cell since we are going to apply filters later, which operate over an entire repeat region. We will need separate filters in each column, hence they must be separate repeat regions. In the assembly BOM we'll create in the next lesson, we will define an entire row as the repeat region.

> ***Repeat Region > Add > Simple***

Double click on each of the cells in the second row. This is actually one click to show the starting cell, and one click to show the finishing cell of the repeat region.

Now we need to add some parameters to each cell:

Enter Text > Report Sym

Click in the first column and select the following sequence of menu picks (observe the one-line message below the graphics window):

fam.. > inst.. > name

You should see the characters *fam.inst.name* in the cell.

In each one of the other cells, use the following (it is probably best to work right to left here, since the text will overlap into adjacent cells):

Enter Text > Report Sym
fam..> inst.. > param > value

Now we want to generate the table.

Repeat Region > Update Tables

The table expands (Figure 25) to include all information in the family table. Pro/E does not know yet how to organize the parameter value information into the various columns, so it puts the entire table into each column. Recall that the display parameter for each repeat region is just set to *value* without specifying which parameter, so Pro/E puts them all in there!

Part ID	Height	Length	Hole	Rib?	Thick
B3020-6-RI	30	30	30	30	30
B1006-3	20	20	20	20	20
	6	6	6	6	6
	TRUE	TRUE	TRUE	TRUE	TRUE
	1	1	1	1	1
	10	10	10	10	10
	8	8	8	8	8
	3	3	3	3	3
	FALSE	FALSE	FALSE	FALSE	FALSE
	0	0	0	0	0

Figure 25 Table after first update and before filters

To clean up this table, we need to specify what information to keep in each column, and therefore what to ignore. This is done using *filters*.

Repeat Region Filters

To tell Pro/E how to restrict the data displayed in each repeat region, we use a filter defined for each region in the table (this is why we needed separate repeat regions for each column).

Filters

Pick on the second column (second row or below), then

By Rule > Add

Enter the filter

```
&fam.inst.param.name == height
```

and press the Enter key twice. Note the double-"=" sign for the equality test. That is, we only want to display entries in the repeat region associated with the height parameter. Select **Done >
Done/Return** and the column should shorten to contain data in only the first two rows(or more if you have been experimenting with the family table entries). Repeat this procedure for each of the remaining columns using the following filters:

column 3	`&fam.inst.param.name == length`
column 4	`&fam.inst.param.name == h_diam`
column 5	`&fam.inst.param.name == has_rib`
column 6	`&fam.inst.param.name == rib_thickness`

When the final filter is entered, the table should shrink to just enough rows to show all the current instances in the family.

Go to the pull-down menu and select

Format > Text Style > Pick Many

Draw a box around the table. The text should highlight in red. Middle click and in the Text Style dialog window, set horizontal justification to **Center**, and vertical justification to **Middle**. Click the *Apply* button, and select *OK*. The text should appear as shown in Figure 26.

Part ID	Height	Length	Hole	Rib?	Thick
B3020-6-R1	30	20	6	TRUE	1
B1008-3	10	8	3	FALSE	0

Figure 26 Completed repeat region

You can experiment with the commands (*Mod Rows/Cols*) to change the column widths in this table. You can also set different text styles, alignments, colors, etc, in each column, since the repeat regions are not linked together.

Now that we have seen a Simple repeat region, we're going to do this all over again using a 2D repeat region. In the TABLE menu

Delete

Click on the table and confirm its deletion.

A 2D Repeat Region

This form of repeat region is ideal for displaying family tables (check the message window when we ask for the 2D region). It requires a bit more thought and planning to set up, but requires fewer commands and keystrokes. There is somewhat less control over formatting within the table.

The 2D repeat region for the family is based on a 2 X 2 table. The table will automatically expand in rows and columns depending on the data in the family table. The 2D repeat region is specified using an outer region (the 2 X 2 table) and an inner region (in this case a single table cell). The definition of the repeat region also depends on how the original table is set up, that is in which directions it expands (Ascending or Descending, Leftward or Rightward). In the following, we will set up the table to expand downwards and to the right, as illustrated in Figure 27. Other variations of this are possible. The thing to remember is that not all 2 X 2 tables are created equal, and the definition of the 2D repeat region must be consistent with the expansion directions specified for the table. Another way we could set up the table is shown in Figure 28.

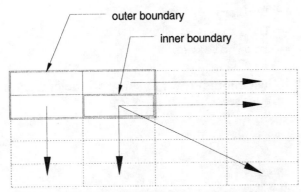

Figure 27 A 2D repeat region expanding down and to the right (Descending Rightward table)

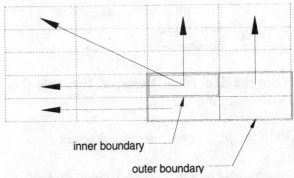

Figure 28 A 2D repeat region expanding up and to the left (Ascending Leftward table)

In the TABLE menu, select

> *Create*
> *Descending | Rightward | By Length | Abs Coords*

and enter X = **5.625**, Y = **8.125** for the top left corner of the table. This location is so that the table will just reach the right border when it expands to its full width (six columns). The first column width is **1.25**. The second column width is **0.75**. Press *Enter* twice. The top row height is **0.25**, the second row height is **0.2**. *Enter* twice. We now have the 2 X 2 table as shown in Figure 29.

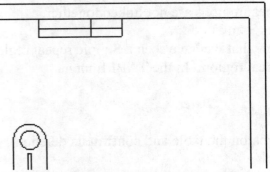

Now we define the repeat region

> *Repeat Region > Add > Two-D*

Figure 29 Table created for 2D repeat region

For the cells defining the outer border, click the top left and lower right cells (see Figure 27. For the inner border, click the lower right cell. All lines will highlight and the message window will indicate that the repeat region has been defined.

We only have to enter three parameters into the table. These are shown below. Compare these entries to the expansion directions of the repeat region shown in Figure 27.

	`&fam.inst.param.name`
`&fam.inst.name`	`&fam.inst.param.value`

Select

> ***Enter Text > Report Sym***

Pick the lower left cell and select

> ***fam.. > inst.. > name***

In the top right cell, enter the following

> ***fam.. > inst.. > param..> name***

and in the lower right cell enter

> ***fam.. > inst.. > param.. > value***

Now go to ***Repeat Region > Update Tables***. The table expands over to the right border and fills in with the data. Note that no additional filters or other adjustments are necessary to create the table. The only problem is that the column heading for the last column is a bit too long to fit within the column.

Select

> ***Format > Text Style > Pick Many***

draw a box around the table and middle click. Set the horizontal and vertical justification to center and middle.

To change the order of the columns to match the order in the family table

> ***Table > Repeat Region > Sort Regions***

and click on the table. Then select the radio button ***No Default*** (see the line below the graphics window). ***Done***. The columns will rearrange to match their order in the family table.

Let's create a new instance of the part. Recall that this part is driven by Pro/PROGRAM. Bring up the generic part *bracket*, and select

> ***Regenerate > Enter***

Check the height, length and rib thickness variables. Enter new values of **25**, **25**, and **2**, respectively for these. The part regenerates with these new values. To put this new part into the family table select

> ***Program > Instantiate***

and enter a new instance name **B2525-6-R2**.

Using the same commands, create another instance, **B1515-5** (smaller hole size and without the rib) and instantiate it. Go to

> ***Family Tab***

to see the new instances in the family table.

Now switch to the drawing window. The table has automatically updated to show the new instances. See Figure 30. You can go into **Sort Regions** to change the order of presentation in the HAS_RIB column.

	height	length	h_diam	HAS_RIB	_thickness
B3020-6-R1	30	20	6	TRUE	1
B2525-6-R2	25	25	6	TRUE	2
B1515-5	15	15	5	FALSE	0
B1008-3	10	8	3	FALSE	0

Figure 30 Family table on drawing updates automatically for new instances

Restore the part to the generic dimensions shown in the top line of the table (for **B3020-6-R1**). Save the part (required to save the new family table entries).

Displaying Symbolic Dimensions

The last thing we want to do for the bracket drawing is to identify the parameters (height, length, and so on) on the drawing views. We want to show the name indicated in the table, and not the actual dimension value. In the VIEW menu, select

> ***Show and Erase***

Select the dimensions option, and **Feat_View**. Click on the holes in the right view and top view in the drawing. Then click on the rib in the right view. Accept these dimensions.

Right click on the graphics window and select **Properties**. Click on the dimension value for the hole height. In the Dimension Properties window, select **Dimension Text**. The numerical value of the dimension is displayed because of the @D specification in the dimension text. Change this to **@S** and accept the dialog. This changes the dimension to show the parameter name as a string. Do the same for the hole diameter, the length dimension, and the rib thickness dimension. The final drawing should look something like Figure 31.

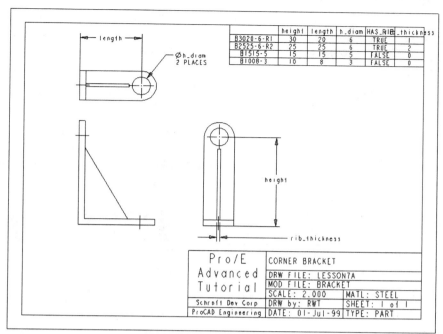

height | length | h_diam | HAS_RIB | rib_thickness

	height	length	h_diam	HAS_RIB	rib_thickness
B3020-6-R1	30	20	6	TRUE	1
B2525-6-R2	25	25	6	TRUE	2
B1515-5	15	15	5	FALSE	0
B1008-3	10	8	3	FALSE	0

Figure 31 Finished drawing of bracket

We are finished with this brief introduction to the use of repeat regions. There is lots more you can do with them (including nesting of repeat regions), and it is left as an exercise for you to experiment with these capabilities. As mentioned above, we will utilize a repeat region a bit later to produce a BOM for an assembly.

Save the drawing and erase it from the session. If you haven't already, also save the bracket part and remove it from the session.

Multi-Model Drawings

It is very easy to set up a drawing to display more than one model on a single sheet. This is particularly useful for drawings of related components, as in an assembly. This will be demonstrated by creating a drawing showing three of the instances in the family of elbow parts we made in an earlier lesson. Note that it is not necessary for the models to be related (as in instances of a family table), but may be independent parts. If you have not completed the elbow part, you can substitute other parts as desired, preferably one with a family table.

Open up the part **elbowg.prt**, being careful to bring in the generic of this part. We must make a few modifications to the model to go with the steps that follow. First, create two parameters (*Setup > Parameters > Part > Create > String*):

```
material            "ABS"
description         "PIPE ELBOW FAMILY"
```

As you recall, these parameters are used in the drawing format we created earlier in this lesson.

Second, add a new end type ("female") using a revolved protrusion and a revolved cut. Add these features to the bottom of the model tree, *being very careful about your feature creation and sketching references*. (Neither the protrusion nor the cut should reference the HOSE or FLANGE features.) Recall that the shell thickness dimension symbol is "thick". We want the diameter of the cut to be the same as the elbow (diameter symbol "diam"); the outer diameter of the revolved protrusion should be set using the relation "diam + 2*thick". Name the revolved protrusion "FEMALE." See Figures 33 and 35 for a rough idea of the geometry. Copy the protrusion and cut to the other end of the elbow. Add the appropriate entries to the family table for the part. Edit the family table to define the three instances shown in Figure 32. Note that the names of the instances have also changed. IMPORTANT: *Verify* the table.

Type	Instance Name	d1 ANGLE	d5 DIAM	d6 THICK	F84 FLANGE	F140 HOSE	F543 FEMALE
	ELBOWG	30.00000	20.00000	2.5000	Y	Y	Y
	E-30-40-3-G	30.00000	40.00000	3.0000	Y	N	N
	E-30-40-1-H	30.00000	40.00000	1.0000	N	Y	N
	E-30-40-2-F	30.00000	40.00000	2.0000	N	N	Y

Figure 32 Family table for generic part *elbowg*

We are going to place section views on the drawing. The sections can be created in drawing mode but it is more convenient to do this in part mode. In the PART menu, select

X-section > Create > Planar | Single | Done

Type in a name for the section "A", and pick the TOP datum to define the section. We can modify the hatching (spacing and angle), but we'll leave that for the drawing. Save the part.

Creating the Drawing

Create a new drawing called **elbow_family**. Turn off the "Use default template" option. Select the default model as **elbowg.prt** and use "Empty with format". Retrieve the format *tut_format.frm* and select **OK**. Select the generic instance. Recall that the string parameter *drawn_by* is required by the format. Enter your name or initials for this.

Observe on the bottom of the window that the type of model is *PART* and the name of the current model is *ELBOWG*.

We are going to bring in the three instances in the *elbowg* family table and place them all on this sheet.

Setting the Active Model

In the DRAWING menu, select

> *Views > Dwg Models > Add Model*

and select *elbowg.prt*, then select the instance **E-30-40-1-H**. Note the name change on the bottom of the graphics window. The model file identified on the format title block is still *elbowg* (this was determined when the format was placed with *elbowg* as the active part). Create a view of this active model:

> *Add View*
> *General | Full View | No Xsec | No Scale | Done*

Pick a point on the left side of the drawing sheet. Accept the default orientation for the view.

Change the active model to the second instance:

> *Dwg Models > Add Model*

Select the generic *elbowg* again, and this time select **E-30-40-2-F**. This name now appears as the active model on the bottom of the window. Add a general view of this in the center of the sheet in the default orientation.

Finally, add the model and create a general view of the third instance **E-30-40-3-G** and place it on the right of the sheet in default orientation.

Rearrange the views for spacing, remove all the hidden lines, and add some notes as shown in Figure 33. You might also change the line style of the datum curve used to define the trajectory for the sweep used in creating the elbow.

A drawing can have any number of models. To see which models are currently loaded,

> *Views > Dwg Models > Set Model*

and all the currently loaded models are listed. To change the currently active model to any of these, either click on the name in the list, or click on the view of the desired model on the sheet. Do that now, selecting the view of the hose end instance on the left. Note the name entry at the bottom of the drawing window, which should indicate that **E-30-40-1-H** is the active model. Set the active model back to **elbowg**.

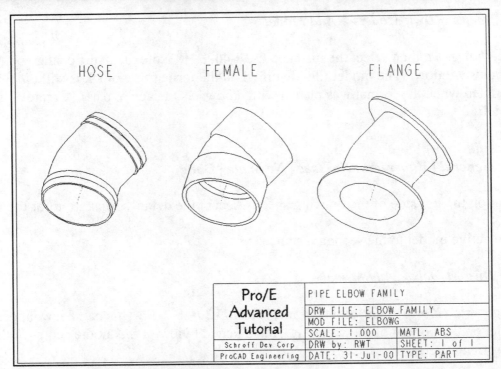

Figure 33 Drawing sheet with three models

Multi-Sheet Drawings

A drawing file may consist of a number of physical drawing sheets. As your parts and assemblies get more complicated, this will be necessary to show all the views you want to generate without requiring a large number of separate drawing files. It is very easy to navigate between sheets, switch views, tables, or draft entities from sheet to sheet, reorder the sheets, and print the sheets individually or all at once.

We will create three more sheets for the elbow family drawing. Each sheet will show a general view and a cross section view of one of the instances. Although we won't do it here, it is permissible to have multiple models shown in each sheet.

For the following, you need to make a change/addition to your *config.pro*. Since we are going to use the same format on multiple sheets and we want the format parameters to carry over between sheets, we must instruct Pro/E to add the format parameters to the model. This is done using the *config.pro* setting:

```
make_parameters_from_fmt_tables  YES
```

If you are starting a new session at this time, load the drawing **elbow_family**, and set the current model to **elbowg**.

Adding a Drawing Sheet

To add a drawing sheet to the drawing, in the DRAWING menu select

> ***Sheets > Add***

You may have to identify the parameter type and enter your name or initials for the parameter **drawn_by**. Observe the title block and the bottom line in the graphics window. The model name indicated in the title block is still *elbowg*. Other parameters have been carried over from the previous sheet due to the *config* setting made above. Set the current the active model to **E-30-40-1-H**. Add a general view of this model to the right side of the sheet, accepting the default view. Now add the section view on the left side of the sheet using the cross-section "A" defined and named in the part:

> ***Add View***
> ***General | Full View | Section | No Scale | Done***
> ***Full | Total Xsec | Done***

Pick a center point for the drawing view on the left half of the sheet. Orient the view so that the TOP datum plane is facing FRONT, and the SIDE datum plane is facing RIGHT. You may have a saved view list, in which case, the view is the TOP view. Accept this orientation.

Select the cross section **A** that we defined in the part. Read the message window - we do not want section direction arrows, so middle click. You might erase the section title and adjust the hatch spacing and angle. Change the scale to 1.5. The screen should look something like Figure 34. There are a few minor differences - can you spot them? We will see in a few minutes how to fix these.

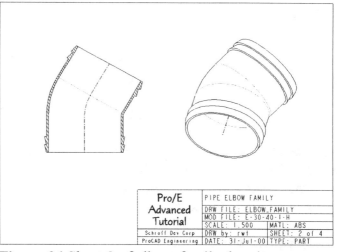

Pro/E	PIPE ELBOW FAMILY	
Advanced	DRW FILE: ELBOW_FAMILY	
Tutorial	MOD FILE: E-30-40-1-H	
	SCALE: 1.500	MATL: ABS
Schroff Dev Corp	DRW by: rwt	SHEET: 2 of 4
ProCAD Engineering	DATE: 31-Jul-00	TYPE: PART

Figure 34 Sheet 2 of elbow family drawing

Now we want to add another sheet showing the next instance. This time, we will first select the new active model, then create the new sheet:

> ***Views > Dwg Models***
> ***Set Model > E-30-40-2-F > Done/Return***
> ***Sheets > Add***

We are now on sheet 3 with a new active model. Note the model name in the title block, and on the bottom of the screen. Create the same two views (general and section) as we did for the previous model. Change the scale as before. See Figure 35.

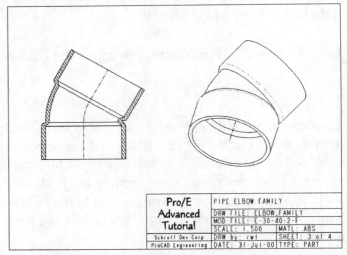

Figure 35 Sheet 3 of elbow family drawing

We are going to add one more sheet for the flanged elbow. To remind you how the format works, we are once again going to add the sheet before we change the active model:

> *Sheets > Add*

We are on the fourth sheet with the model name **E-30-40-2-F**, that is, the model name from the previous sheet. Now change the active model:

> *Views > Dwg Model > Set Model*

and select **E-30-40-3-G**. Observe the bottom line in the window to confirm this is the active model. The entry in the title box is still for the previous instance. This is because the value of the parameter name *&model* was already set when we added the format to this sheet. We will come back in a minute to fix this.

Meanwhile, add the same two views (general and section) for the flanged elbow. Make your cosmetic changes as desired.

To update the title block, we need to replace it (with a new copy of itself!):

> *Sheets > Format*
> *Add/Replace*

and select *tut_format.frm* (either from In Session or your working directory). Note the message window. Since there is a table in the existing format that you may want to keep (like a repeat region or BOM), you must confirm the deletion of the table. Select *Yes*. The format comes in with the now-correct

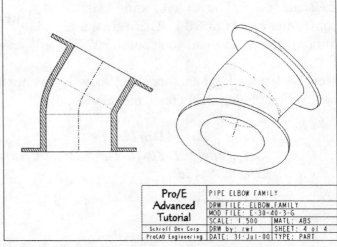

Figure 36 Sheet 4 of elbow family drawing

entry in the title block, Figure 36.

Navigating between the sheets is a simple matter of selecting

> ***Sheets > Previous***
> ***Sheets > Next***
or   ***Sheets > Set Current***

Notice that ***Previous*** and *Next* wrap around - that is if you select *Next* from sheet 4 you end up on sheet 1. You can also reorder sheets and remove them. The command

> ***Sheets > Switch Sheet***

allows you to move views, tables, draft items and so on onto another sheet.

On the DRAWING toolbar, there is also a counter/selector that lets you move between sheets, either by clicking the up or down arrows, or entering the desired sheet number directly. Go back to sheet 2 and replace the format so that the title block displays correctly.

When you go to print out the drawing, you can direct Pro/E to produce hard copy of all sheets associated with the drawing.

Don't forget to save the drawing! Then erase it and all associated objects.

Creating a Drawing Template

As you probably know, a standard Pro/E installation includes a number of drawing templates. These are similar to drawing formats, but with some important additional capability. Templates can contain the following information:

- Basic information required on the drawing that is not included with the model, such as tolerance notes, special symbols, and so on.
- Information for laying out and configuring views: view type (section views), view display (hidden, no hidden, etc.), dimensions and snap lines, balloons, and so on.
- Parametric notes that are driven by model parameters and dimensions.

Like part templates (but unlike formats), a drawing template must be chosen when a new drawing is created. In this section, we will create a new drawing template and then make a simple part to try it out. Also like part templates, a drawing template is used to control the initial creation of a new drawing. Once the drawing (or part) is created, all aspects of it can be modified however you want - you are not permanently stuck with the template layout. You can, for example, delete an unnecessary view.

We start the creation of a new template by creating an empty drawing using

> *File > New*

Select the **Drawing** button, enter a name **tut_template**, deselect the "Use default template" button, and *OK*. Leave the default model area blank (**none**), select **Empty**, Landscape, and size A. A new blank drawing is created. Now in the pull-down menus, select

> *Applications > Template*

We can create a border and title block exactly the same way we did previously for the format exercise. See if you can do that without referring back to those instructions (remember that "practice makes perfect!") Create the table and enter the parameters as we did before[2]. Adjust the text alignment, font, spacing and so on. Add a note that specifies the default tolerances for the drawing. When you are finished, the template should look something like Figure 37.

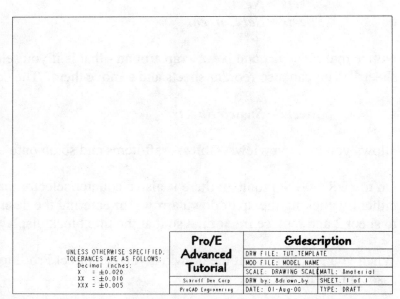

UNLESS OTHERWISE SPECIFIED.
TOLERANCES ARE AS FOLLOWS:
Decimal inches:
X   : ±0.020
XX : ±0.010
XXX : ±0.005

Pro/E Advanced Tutorial	&description	
	DRW FILE: TUT_TEMPLATE	
	MOD FILE: MODEL NAME	
	SCALE: DRAWING SCALE	MATL: &material
Schroff Dev Corp	DRW by: &drawn_by	SHEET: 1 of 1
ProCAD Engineering	DATE: 01-Aug-00	TYPE: DRAFT

Figure 37 Template under construction - border and title block complete

Now we will add the information for laying out and configuring the views to appear on the drawing. In the TMPLT DWG menu, select

> *Views > Add Template*

A new window opens (Figure 38), the contents of which will change as we proceed with the options described below. The view name will default to VIEW_TEMPLATE_1. The Orientation will be **General**, using the saved view name **FRONT** (as stored in the model). In the View Options area, select the following options and settings:

> *Model Display*   *Hidden Line*
> *Tan Edge Display*   *No Disp Tan*

---

[2] If you are in a real hurry, then use *Sheets > Format > Add/Replace* and select the format **tut_format** we made earlier.

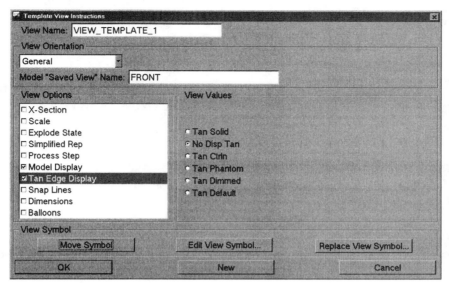

Figure 38 The Template View Instructions dialog window

You may want to move the dialog window over to the side a bit. Select the **Place View** button at the bottom. Drag the red view symbol and click on the left-center of the drawing sheet (see Figure 39). This will be the location of our primary (front) view.

Let's add another view. At the bottom of the Template View Instructions window, select

> *New*

The View Name will be **VIEW_TEMPLATE_2**. This will be the right view, which we want to show as a dimensioned, full section. (Note that section views in templates can only be full cross sections). The View Orientation we want is **Projection** (in the pull-down list). The view will be a projection from the previous **VIEW_TEMPLATE_1**. In **View Options**, select

X-Section	*Name: A* (we'll set this up in the part)
	Arrow Placement: VIEW_TEMPLATE_1
Model Display	*No Hidden*
Tan Edge Display	*No Disp Tangent*
Snap Lines	*Number: 3*
	Increment: 0.375
	Initial: 0.5
Dimensions	*Create Snap Lines*
	Increment: 0.375
	Initial: 0.5

Now select **Place View**, and put the view symbol to the right of VIEW_TEMPLATE_1. We have asked for a projection from the front view. We do not have to be precise about the placement of the symbol, since if we are "close enough" Pro/E will know what to do. If we place the symbol too far away (vertically) from a true horizontal projection, Pro/E will complain via an error window when the template is used (and create a file **template.err** in your working directory).

Now add a top view to the drawing. Select

>   *New*

The view name will be **VIEW_TEMPLATE_3**. The View Orientation we want is **Projection** (in the pull-down list). The view will also be a projection from **VIEW_TEMPLATE_1**. In **View Options**, select

(Turn off X-Section)	
Model Display	*Hidden Line*
Tan Edge Display	*No Disp Tangent*
Snap Lines	*Number: 1*
	Increment: 0.375
	Initial: 0.5
Dimensions	*Create Snap Lines*
	Increment: 0.375
	Initial: 0.5

A new button, *Set Display Priorities*, appears. This lets us choose the priority list for where Pro/E should place the dimensions on the drawing (ie which views). Leave VIEW_TEMPLATE_2 at the top of the list. Now select *Place View*, and place the view symbol at the top of the sheet. Select *OK* and back out to the TMPLT DWG menu. Your drawing should look like Figure 39. If you want to move any of the views, right click on the screen, select *Modify Item*, then drag and drop the view symbol to the position you want.

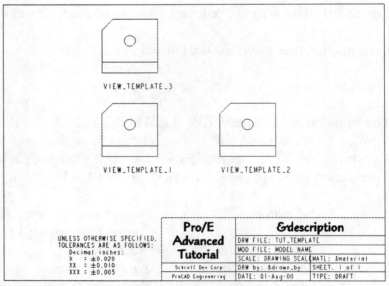

Figure 39 Completed template *tut_template.drw*

Save the template in your working directory.

We need a simple part to try out this new template. Create the part **small_tank** as shown at the right. Use the **inlbs_part_solid** part template. The part is basically a revolved protrusion that has been shelled out (thickness **0.25**). Then a flange is added using another revolved protrusion. Because we want these dimension to appear in the right view, make the sketches for these solid features on the SIDE (RIGHT) datum. Finally, create a planar cross section (named "A") on the SIDE (RIGHT) datum. Also, make sure we have parameters *description*, *material*, and *modeled_by* defined and specified in the part. Save the part.

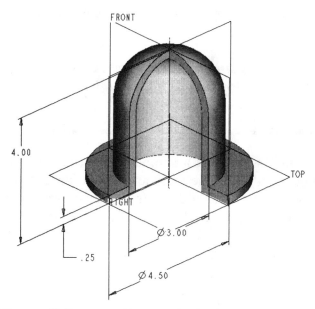

Figure 40 Part **small_tank** (units inches)

Now for the fun part! Create a new drawing called **small_tank**. Deselect the "Use default template" option, then *OK*. The default model should be **small_tank**. Select the "Use template" option, and use the ***Browse*** button to find the **tut_template.drw** file in your working directory. Then select *OK*. Sit back and watch your drawing appear as specified: three views, including a section view and arrows, view display as desired, dimensions and snap lines, and a completed title block. Pretty simple! You will probably still want to do some cosmetic clean-up on this drawing. Are all the usual tools available? For example, you may want to move some dimensions to a different view, change the placement of some dimensions, move views, add center lines and axes, and so on. However, we have basically automated most of the production of this drawing.

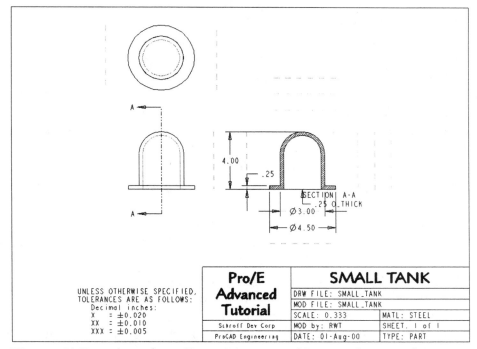

Figure 41 Drawing of **small_tank** as created by template *tut_format*

For further information on drawing templates, consult the on-line help by going to the **Contents** area and selecting

> *Using Foundation Modules > Using Pro/DETAIL*
> *Drawing Fundamentals > Customizable Drawing Templates*

In this lesson, quite a number of topics relating to creation of drawings have been introduced. You should become familiar with setting and modifying the options in the drawing setup file. Draft entities may be required to touch-up or place additional information on a drawing. In Pro/E, you have all the tools of a 2D drawing package to do this. Tables were introduced as a way to organize information on the drawing. This was applied to the creation of a format with title block and a repeat region to display family instances. A quick look at multi-model and multi-sheet drawings has introduced you to some useful methods and functions to create more comprehensive drawing sets. Finally, we looked at the creation of drawing templates.

In the next lesson we will look at functions relating to assemblies. We will finally start putting the cart together! There are three more parts to be made at the end of this lesson, though.

Questions for Review

1. Where is the default drawing setup file located on your system?
2. Where are the additional setup files stored on your system?
3. How do you identify drawing setup files (that is, what is the file extension)?
4. How do you point your system to a specific drawing setup file to be the default?
5. What commands do you issue to edit a setup file?
6. Can you create a metric drawing on a sheet whose format was created using English units?
7. What is the difference between first angle and third angle projection?
8. How do you apply a new setup file to a previously created drawing?
9. In regards to dimension types, explain the terms (and the relations between them): "shown", "driven", "driving", and "created".
10. How can some features appear on a drawing with no dimensions even if you select *Part > Show All*?
11. What is a "reference dimension" and how do you create it?
12. What determines whether created dimensions are stored with the model or with the drawing?
13. How do you find out the symbolic names for dimensions?
14. Explain the difference between *d#* and *add#* dimensions. What does the "*a*" stand for?
15. What is meant by **Common Ref** dimension scheme?
16. What happens if you delete a *d#* dimension? (Trick question!)
17. Where are the drawing commands for creating draft entities?
18. Where are the commands for editing draft entities?
19. Suppose you have just created a drafted construction circle on a view of the part. Can you dimension the location of the circle relative to an edge of the part? Why?
20. Is it possible to delete a line on the drawing that is a part edge in a view?

21. Can you change the line style of a line representing a physical edge of the part?
22. When can you specify the format for a drawing?
23. How many formats can be included in a multi-sheet drawing?
24. Where are format files stored on your system?
25. Where are the standard formats containing the ANSI title blocks stored?
26. When specifying absolute coordinates of a point on the sheet is the origin at the corner of the sheet, or the corner of the border?
27. What options are available to set the width and height of the cells in a table?
28. How do you set the directions for growing a table?
29. How can you add columns or rows to a table after it has been created? What determines their width/height?
30. How can you remove columns or rows from a table after it has been created?
31. Can you remove a table row from a repeat region driven by a family table?
32. Suppose you want to put some text into a table. What is the difference between *Table > Enter Text* and *Detail > Create > Note*?
33. Explain the difference between a system parameter and a model parameter.
34. What happens if a format containing model parameters is applied to the drawing of a part that does not have those parameters defined?
35. How do you assign the parameters to a cell in a repeat region?
36. What happens in a repeat region for a family table if a parameter value in the table is "*"?
37. How can you sort a repeat region? What options are available?
38. What happens if a repeat region grows off the edge of the drawing sheet?
39. How do you modify a dimension so that it shows the symbolic name?
40. What does the dimension text "@O" do? This is a capital O not a 0 (zero).
41. Is it possible to have a model added to a drawing without showing it in any views?
42. How do you determine which model in a drawing is currently active?
43. How many models can be brought into a drawing?
44. If you remove a sheet that contains the only view of a model in a drawing, is the model removed as well?
45. Can you place a projected view of a model on a different sheet from the original view?
46. List some of the advantages and disadvantages of using drawing templates, including some of the various options.

Project Exercises

Here are the last three parts for the cart. Pretty routine stuff!

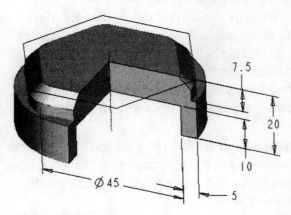

PART: *pillar_cap*

In the part below, make sure you use a pattern to create the four mounting holes - we will need that in the next lesson.

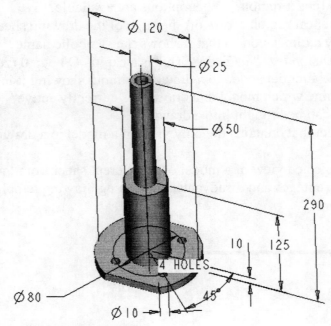

PART: *front_pillar*

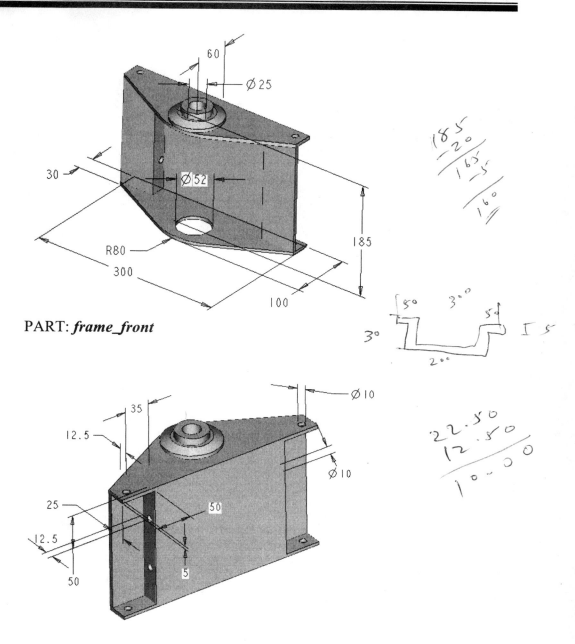

PART: *frame_front*

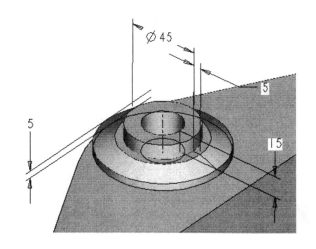

NOTES:

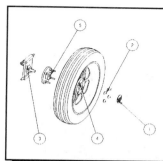

Lesson 8

Working with Assemblies

Synopsis

Creating parts using *Merge* and *Mirror*; advanced component assembly techniques (*Repeat*, *Pattern*, *Ref Pattern*); creating parts in the assembly; using evaluate features; using Pro/PROGRAM in an assembly; creating a drawing with BOM and balloons

Overview

In this final lesson, we are going to assemble all the components in the cart. The various parts have been described in the project exercises at the end of the previous lessons. First, we will examine the assembly plan to determine a strategy for assembly. The cart assembly makes extensive use of subassemblies to help organize the work. We will utilize some useful functions to create new parts by merging (like welding them together) and mirroring. Then we will begin putting together the subassemblies. This will involve some advanced component placement functions for duplicated components, like repeating and patterning. We will employ a new feature called an *evaluate feature* to automatically determine some assembly dimensions and then use relations and Pro/PROGRAM to make the cart assembly automatically adjust to changes in the wheel suspension geometry. Finally, we will create a couple of assembly drawings which will include a bill of materials and balloons.

Creating the Assembly

We are finally going to put together all the cart components. Along the way, we will explore a number of functions available in assembly mode. These functions allow you to do a lot more than just constraining the components. We will also create some new parts, set up relations, and make a program to control some aspects of the geometry of the assembly and individual components.

Before we start any of that, since the cart is a pretty complicated system, it is necessary to develop a plan of attack - the assembly plan.

The Assembly Plan

Before you start creating an individual part, you (should) probably have a pretty good idea how you are going to select various features and the regeneration sequence. The same planning process is required before starting an assembly. How will we organize the various components into subassemblies? In what order should we put the components and subassemblies into the main assembly? How will be set up and manage the placement constraints and the parent/child references created? What additional assembly features like datums will be required, and where and when should these be created? Answering these questions before you start putting the assembly together will allow you to organize your efforts and prevent back-tracking later on. The end result is that you will be more efficient in your work and you will have a cleaner and more flexible model.

The main difference between an assembly plan and a part plan is the use of subassemblies. There is no (direct) analog to subassemblies in part creation (although UDF's come close). We will make extensive use of subassemblies in the cart. The total assembly can be thought of as a tree structure, as shown in Figure 1. The major branches of the total assembly are subassemblies. This does not show individual components added to the assembly at the top level (like all the bolts!) nor the individual components used to connect the

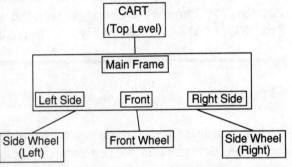

Figure 1 The cart assembly tree structure

subassemblies (like the wheel suspension arms). The physical configuration of these subassemblies is shown in Figure 2.

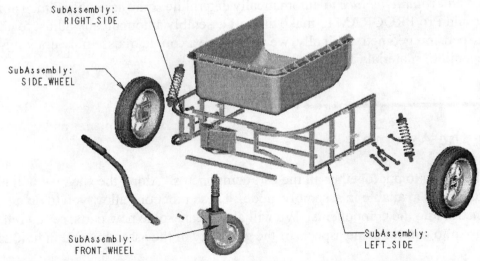

Figure 2 The major subassemblies in the cart model, plus single parts

Each of the subassemblies, of course, could contain additional subassemblies at a lower level. Once a subassembly is created, it is treated as a component in the parent. This nesting of subassemblies can go many levels deep. Once the assembly plan has been developed, we can start at the bottom of the tree to create the lowest level subassemblies.

Before we actually start putting things together, recall some basic aspects of working in assembly mode:

♦ **Assembly Constraints**. Components are located in the assembly using constraints (*Mate*, *Align*, *Orient*, etc) to existing components and assembly features. A fully constrained component involves all six degrees of freedom of location and orientation. When you are placing a component (particularly involving alignment of axes) sometimes Pro/E reports that the component is fully constrained, yet it still has a rotational degree of freedom. This is often all right (for example when placing the bolts) but sometimes not (for example when adding the hubcap). If this occurs, you can just add an additional constraint.

♦ *Separate Window* vs *In Assembly*. When a new component is being assembled, you can view it either in a window by itself or in the same window as the assembly. This is a matter of personal preference. If the component and the assembly are very different in size, it is probably easier to use the separate window.

♦ *Place* vs *Move*. Pro/E will allow you to move a component around in the assembly by translating and rotating relative to picked entities like planes and edges. This is useful if you have the existing assembly and the new component in the same window. Pro/E will let you leave the component at the moved position, but remember that this is not constraining the component in any way. New components cannot be constrained to a component that is itself not fully constrained. If the component is constrained in any way, then the movement allowed with *Move* will automatically maintain the existing constraints.

Let's get started...

The Side Frames

We'll start by putting together the tubing to make the side frames. You will note that we did not create any components for the frame on the left side of the cart. We will do that here using mirror. Also, we presume that the side frame will be welded together to form a single piece. So, we will create an assembly of the right side frame and then weld it together using a special merge procedure.

Using the start assembly and mapkey you created as an exercise in Lesson #1, create an assembly called *frame_right*. The assembly should have named default datum planes and named views for TOP, FRONT, RIGHT, and so on.

Assemble the lower right side tube, *fram_low_rgt.prt*. Constrain this to the assembly default datums using *Align*.

Retrieving a Family Instance Component

The next component to place is one of the 4 vertical tubes along the side of the cart. The tube we want is one of the instances in the family table of *tubing.prt*. Bring this into the assembly with

> *Component > Assemble*
> *tubing.prt*
> *T25X325*

We are going to make a pattern of this component therefore we need a dimension to be incremented between instances of the pattern. We will use an *Align Offset* for this (with a small negative offset, like -15). Assemble the tube as shown in Figure 3.

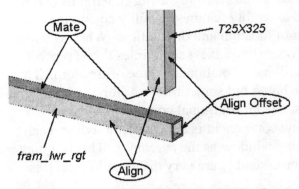

Figure 3 Assembling the vertical tube for a component pattern

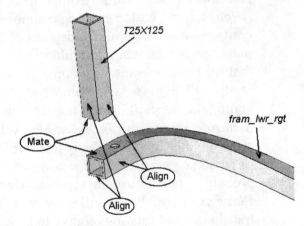

Figure 4 Assembling the front vertical tube

Bring in another instance (the **T25X125**) and constrain it as shown in Figure 4.

Assemble the top frame part *fram_upp_rgt* by constraining it using *Mate* and *Align* to the front vertical tube. (Why not the back one?)

Component Patterns

Now we can pattern the vertical tubes:

Component > Pattern

Click on the longer vertical tube, then on the offset dimension. The pattern increment is **275**mm. There are **4** instances in the pattern. The assembly should now look like Figure 5. Once patterned, change the offset dimension of the pattern leader to **0**.

Save the assembly. We are not quite finished with it yet, so don't remove it.

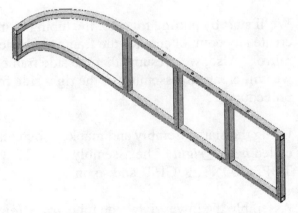

Figure 5 The pattern of 4 vertical tubes

Merging Components

Note that the *frame_right.asm* contains individual components that mate and align. Zoom in on one of the joints to see the edges formed by the individual components. As stated above, our intent for the cart is that these tubes will be welded together. We can do that in assembly mode by merging these tubes into a single solid. At the same time, we will create a new part file containing the merged tubes. Do not confuse this with the use of all the welding tools in Pro/E.

These tools allow you to specify full welding parameters (weld shape, rod type, weld parameters, and so) for the actual welds in an assembly. These welds can be identified along edges or surfaces in the assembly. See *Applications > Welding* some time to explore this capability. We will not do that here.

Create an empty part (using your start part mapkey) called *frame_right*. We have used the same name as the assembly. This is not necessary, but will help us keep everything organized. Pro/E will not get confused between the part and assembly files of the same name.

Activate the window containing the assembly *frame_right*. Bring in the empty part *frame_right* (pick it from the *In Session* button in the Open dialog window) and constrain it (using *Align Coincident*) to the assembly datum planes in the assembly *frame_right*. You may find *Sel by Menu* useful here to pick the correct datums in the assembly for the constraints.

Now we will perform the merge. Select

Component > Adv Utils > Merge

Follow the prompts in the message window. We have to identify two major items, in this order:

♦   the component to be merged to (our empty part *frame_right*)
♦   the components to be added to the merge set (all the tubes)

The first selected component is the one whose geometry will change as a result of the merge, in our case the empty part *frame_right*. Select that now, then *Done Sel*. Read the message window.

Now we select components that will be added to (ie merged with) the previous component. The easiest way to do this is to open the model tree and click on each of the tubing components - there are seven in all. Then *Done Sel*.

When merging components, you can either merge by *Reference* or *Copy*. The difference is that components merged by reference will maintain a link between the original components and the new merged part. This means, for example, that if we go back and move some of the holes in the horizontal tubes, then the holes in the merged part would move accordingly. We will actually do that later. Although this complicates the data structure a bit (meaning you have to be more careful with moving files and so on), it is ideal for managing design changes. If you have to change a feature in an individual part, it is much easier to do this at the part level than at the assembly level. If we merge using the copy option, the new part will have no link to the previous part.

We can also choose if we want to bring datums
into the merged part. Select (these are the
defaults)

Reference | No Datums | Done

This same option selection will be required for all
seven merged components. Remember that
clicking the middle mouse button is a shortcut for
selecting *Done*. Follow along in the message
window while doing this. Finally, the message
window will inform you that the parts have been
merged successfully. Activate the *frame_right*
part window. Zoom in on one of the tubing joints
- there are no lines showing between components. We have created one solid. See Figure 6.

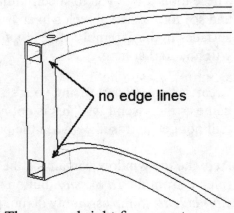

Figure 6 The merged right frame part

Open the model tree for the new part to see how the merged components have been identified.
Check out the *Feat Info* for one of the merged features.

Add some holes to the right side part according to the dimensions shown in Figures 7 and 8.
Make the hole through the vertical members (Figure 7) as a single hole going through both
members. This provides a single axis that we will use to assemble the brackets a bit later in the
lesson.

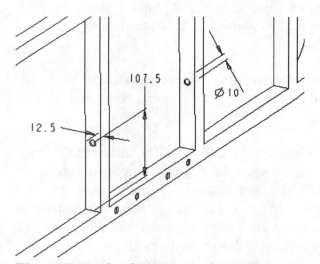

Figure 7 Bracket holes in vertical tubes

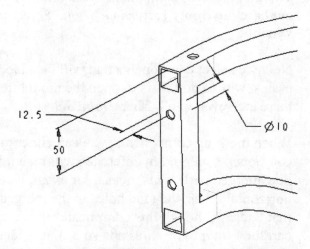

Figure 8 Holes for mounting the front frame

Save the part *frame_right*.

Open the model tree for the assembly file and observe the entries for the merged component
(*frame_right.prt*). Save the assembly file and remove it from your session.

Creating a Part using *Mirror*

A very useful tool for creating symmetric parts is using the mirror function. To do this, we have to create a dummy assembly file. Do that now using your start assembly mapkey; call the assembly something like *mirror*. We will not be keeping this permanently.

Assemble the merged part *frame_right* that we just created. You should be able to find this in session. Constrain it using *Align* to the default datum planes in the new *mirror* assembly.

Now we create the mirror copy

Component > Create

In the dialog window, in the TYPE area select *Part*, and in the SUBTYPE area select *Mirror*. Enter a name for the new part, *frame_left*. Accept the dialog.

We have a choice between a reference and copy mirror. These operate the same as discussed above for the merge function. Select *Reference*.

Pick on the existing right frame. It highlights. Now select the mirror plane. This is the vertical face of the short vertical tube at the front of the frame, as shown in Figure 9. Select *OK*. The part mirrors in the assembly. Note that the parts are not joined (as in merged). To prove that, *Open* the new part *frame_left* (using the *In Session* option) into a separate window. Have a look at the model tree for the new part.

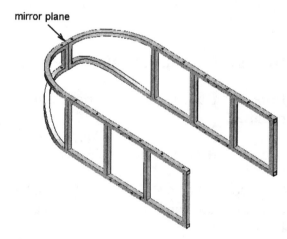

The new left part has not yet been saved to disk; do that now.

You do not need to save the *mirror.asm*.

Figure 9 Creating the mirrored frame part

Examining Dependencies

Let's examine the relationship between the original tube parts and the new merged and mirrored left frame part. Open the part file for the upper horizontal frame tube (*fram_upp_rgt*) which should (if you've been following along closely!) have a pattern of holes. In the upper tube part file, modify the increment value between the holes in the pattern (make it **100**) and *Regenerate* the part. Now go to the new part *frame_left* and *Regenerate*. Magic! The holes have moved. The change has propagated from the original tube *fram_upp_rgt.prt*, through the original assembly *frame_right.asm*, the merged part *frame_right.prt*, and into the mirrored part *frame_left.prt*. Go back to the upper tube part file and return the hole pattern to the original state (increment 100).

You can now remove all objects from your session.

The Side Frame Subassembly

The first subassembly of the cart is the side frame. These will include the side frame parts made above, and the brackets to hold the wheel suspension arms and spring. We will use a handy trick for constraining identical components in a number of places on the assembly. We will also add some assembly features that will be used to assemble the side wheels and make their position adjustable.

Start by creating a new assembly called *right_side*. Bring in the merged right side part using

>*Component > Assemble*

and select *frame_right.prt*. Make sure you pick the part and not the assembly of the same name. Align the part with the assembly default datum frames.

Now we'll bring in the brackets for the wheel mounts. The placement constraints for these are very similar and we will use a new command in assembly mode to expedite their placement.

Repeating Components

Bring in the bracket for the vertical frame members:

>*Component > Assemble*

and select the part *arm_vbrack*. Set up the assembly constraints for this first bracket as shown in Figure 10.

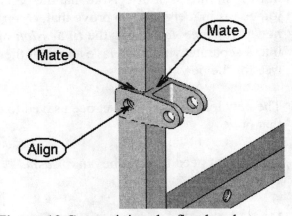

Figure 10 Constraining the first bracket

The only difference between the placement of this component and the bracket on the next vertical tube is the assembly reference for the *Mate* constraint on the side of the tube above the bolt hole - the *Mate* constraint on the front refers to the same surface at the other bracket location. We can save a lot of mouse clicks by using a special function for repeating the placement of components. In the COMPONENT menu, select

>*Adv Utils > Repeat*

This brings up the REPEAT COMPONENT dialog window shown in Figure 11. Follow the prompts in the message window. The first thing to do is to select the component to be repeated. Click on the first bracket. Its assembly constraints will appear in the dialog window. Click on each of these to see the assembly references highlight on the model (wireframe works best for this). Highlight only the **Mate** constraint that involves the inside vertical face. This chooses the constraint to be repeated and changed for the next component. Then select

Add

and pick on the corresponding surface on the next vertical tube in the frame. See the constraint indicated at the top of Figure 12. A new bracket appears at the new location. To accept this placement, select

Confirm

It's that easy!

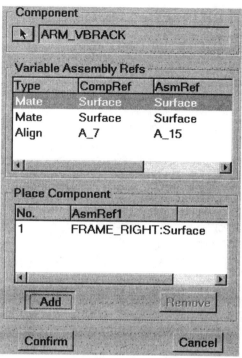

Figure 11 *Repeat* dialog window

Bring in the other bracket, *arm_brack*. We can place this with the constraints shown in Figure 12. Note that Pro/E will sometimes give you a message that the component is fully constrained, and when you select *Preview*, it ends up upside down. The "fully constrained" message is generated when Pro/E thinks it can locate the part but it is using some internal rules to determine the orientation. Sometimes it guesses wrong, usually involving a degree of freedom of rotation around an axis. You can fix the problem by turning off the *Allow Assumptions* box and then *Add*ing an additional **Align Oriented** or **Align Coincident** constraint.

Use the *Repeat* command to places duplicates of the *arm_brack* part at the other locations on the side frame shown in Figure 13. For the bracket on the lower tube, you actually only need a new axis reference since the same alignment surface applies. For the upper bracket, you need to select a new axis and new alignment surface.

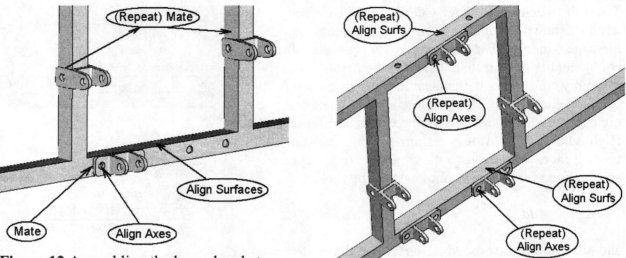

Figure 12 Assembling the lower bracket

Figure 13 Repeating the bracket

Creating a Skeleton Feature

We're going to add some assembly features (a datum curve and some axes) to the side frame to help us out later by supplying references when we assemble the side wheel assembly. The problem is that, for the side wheels, the S-shaped side arms, the mounting plate, and the frame form a parallel 4-bar linkage. Consider the difficulty involved in constraining these components, since the four links must be assembled to form a closed chain. Suppose you start with the frame and try to assemble one of the side arms. Without the wheel mounting plate already in the assembly, there is nothing to assemble the other end of the side arm to. And the mounting plate can't be assembled first without the side arm to constrain to. Try this out some time! We'll get around this sort of vicious circle by creating some assembly features that will allow us to constrain the components properly and also allow us to easily change the vertical position of the wheel using Pro/PROGRAM. These assembly features are typically datum planes and curves. It is possible to construct entire parts and subassemblies using datum features. These are called skeleton models. Such models are then used in the creation of solid features, the geometry of which is driven by the skeleton.

Start by creating an assembly datum curve in the right side frame assembly. Use the toolbar icon for a sketched datum curve. For the sketching plane, use *Make Datum > Through* and select the outside vertical plane of the bracket closest to the back of the assembly. For the sketching references required by Intent Manager, all you need to select are the axes of the two outer holes in the brackets. Note that these holes are 120mm apart (the height between the pins on the wheel mounting plate) - this will yield a parallel 4-bar linkage. The sketch for the datum curve is shown in Figure 14. Note that the length of each long edge in the curve corresponds to the dimensions of the side arms. Also, note the location of the vertical height dimension. We will be using this later to control the position of the entire suspension system. You can see the effect this will have by *Modify*ing this height dimension and regenerating the sketch.

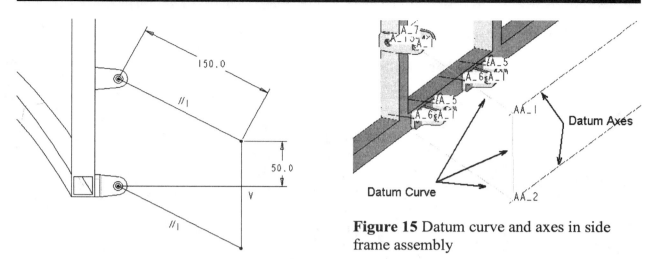

Figure 14 Sketch for datum curve

Figure 15 Datum curve and axes in side frame assembly

Finally, we need to create a couple of datum axes through the vertices at the outer corners of the datum curve:

Datum Axis > Pnt Norm Pln

Select a planar surface (assembly default datum?) parallel to the datum curve, then (toolbar icon)

Datum Point > On Vertex

and pick one of the corner vertices of the datum curves. Then middle click four times to return to the menus. Do this again for the other datum axis. See axes AA_1 and AA_2 in Figure 15.

We are finished with the right side subassembly. Save the assembly and remove it from the session. You can now do all this over again (for practice!) on the left side to create another subassembly called *left_side*. You will need to assemble the part *frame_left*, the five brackets, and create the datum curve and axes.

The Front Wheel Subassembly

We'll use the front wheel subassembly to illustrate another way of quickly adding a number of related components to an existing pattern of features. These are the bolts connecting the vertical pillar to the front wheel bracket. The parts involved in the subassembly are shown in Figure 16.

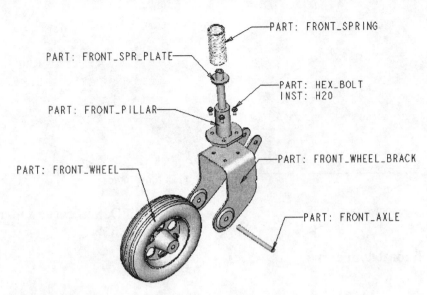

Figure 16 The *front_wheel* subassembly

Using your mapkey, start a new assembly called *front_wheel*. Again, Pro/E doesn't mind if you already have a part of that name. We'll start at the bottom of the assembly and work our way up. Bring in the part *front_wheel* and align it to the default datum planes. Then assemble the part *front_wheel_brack*. ***Align*** the hole axis and the symmetry datum plane (you do have one?) of the bracket to the wheel. You may have to add an ***Orient*** constraint to make sure the bracket is vertical. Next, bring in the part *front_axle* and constrain it to the wheel (***Align*** axes and symmetry plane). The assembly at this point should look like Figure 17.

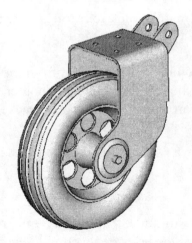

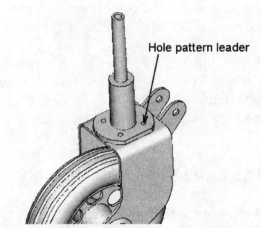

Figure 17 Front wheel subassembly in progress

Figure 18 Identify the hole pattern leader on the *front_pillar* part

Assemble the part *front_pillar* to the top surface of the bracket. You can ***Mate*** the relevant surfaces and align the axes of two of the bolt holes. Observe the orientation of the flats on the pillar base. IMPORTANT: Make a note of which hole in the pillar is the leader for the radial hole pattern, possibly the one shown in Figure 18.

Using a *Ref Pattern*

The next part to bring in is the instance **H20** in the part *hex_bolt*. Assemble this using a *Mate* of the underside of the bolt head with the pillar surface. *Align* the bolt axis with the axis of the hole pattern leader in the pillar. Make sure you pick this axis and not the axis in the hole in the bracket using *Query Select*. It is critical that all the bolt constraint references are to the same feature in the radial hole pattern.

Placing the remaining bolts is very slick. In the COMPONENT menu, select

> *Pattern*

and click on the bolt. Then select *Ref Pattern | Done*. A duplicate bolt will appear in each of the four holes in the radial pattern.

Bring in the final two parts for the front assembly. The first is the part *front_spr_plate*, which *Mate*s to the shoulder on the pillar about half way up and *Align*s with the pillar axis. Finally, the part *front_spring* can be assembled by aligning its axis with the pillar and using *Mate* on the flat end of the spring to the top of the spring plate. The completed assembly is shown in Figure 19.

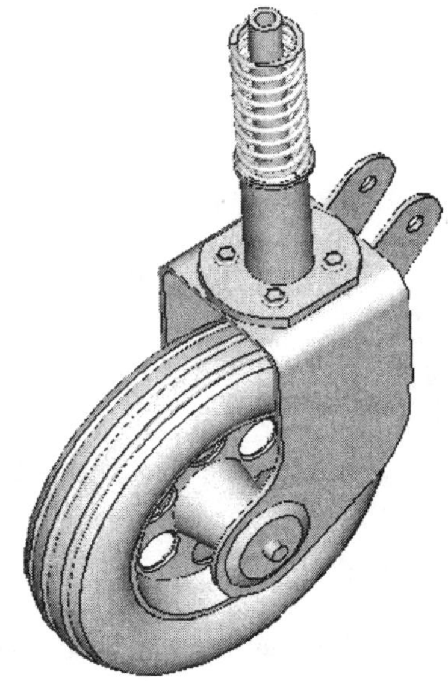

Figure 19 Completed *front_wheel* subassembly

Using *Measure*, determine the distance from the top flat surface of the spring to a parallel plane tangent to the bottom of the wheel. We will need this distance later when we do the total assembly. It should be about 620mm, depending on how you made the tread pattern on the wheel.

Save the assembly and remove it and all its components from the session.

The Side Wheel Subassembly

Start up a new assembly called *side_wheel*. The components are shown in Figure 20. Assembly of these components is going to be pretty routine, and won't be described in great detail here, except that you can use another *Ref Pattern* to place the lug nuts on the wheel if you constrain the first one to the hole pattern leader. IMPORTANT: You might like to create an named exploded view of this assembly for the drawing exercise at the end of the lesson.

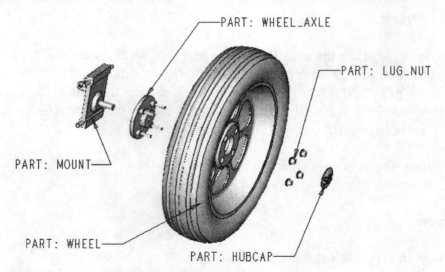

Figure 20 The *side_wheel* subassembly

To make it easier to locate the relevant assembly references, we will bring in the wheel first, then assemble the part *lug_nut* to the hole pattern leader. The lug nut is placed by aligning it to the hole axis and Mating the conical surface to the chamfer on the hole. You can than use ***Ref Pattern*** to place the additional lug nuts. The remaining components in the assembly are all ***Align***ed to the axis of the wheel. The part *wheel_axle* is placed using a ***Mate*** constraint between the shoulder on one of the mounting studs and the inside surface of the wheel (the side opposite the lug nuts). You will also need to ***Align*** one of the studs with one of the holes in the wheel. The studs should just protrude through the lug nuts. The part *mount* mates with the back surface of the wheel axle part. You may need an ***Orient*** constraint on this to get the proper orientation of the mounting plate. The outer lip on the hub cap mates with the outer surface of the wheel and aligns with its axis. You may have to use an ***Orient*** constraint on the hub cap if you have placed a design on the outer surface and you want it the right way up! The finished assembly is shown in Figure 21.

Figure 21 Finished *side_wheel* assembly

Save the assembly and remove it from the session. We will use an identical assembly on both sides of the cart, so you don't need to duplicate this subassembly.

The Frame Subassembly

The frame structure is our last subassembly. There is not anything new here, although you will get to use a component pattern again.

Create a new assembly called *main_frame*. The components are shown in Figure 22. Start by bringing in the part *frame_front* and aligning it to the default assembly datums. Bring in the subassemblies *right_side.asm* and *left_side.asm* and mate them to the surfaces of the pockets on the back of the *frame_front*. All the holes should line up!

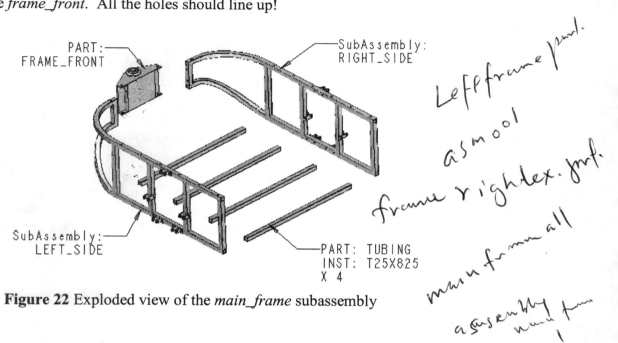

Figure 22 Exploded view of the *main_frame* subassembly

Now assemble the rear cross-frame member using the instance **T25X825** in the generic part *tubing*. Since we are going to pattern this, use an **Align Offset** dimension to the vertical back face on the right side subassembly. Any offset value will do, but note it will have to be entered as a negative value (try **-50**). The end of the tube can **Mate** with the inside surface of the right side subassembly, and the top of the tube can **Align** with the upper surface of the lower horizontal frame member. When the tube is placed, the frame should look something like Figure 23. The tube should just reach across to exactly meet the frame on the left side.

Pattern the tube using (starting from the ASSEMBLY menu)

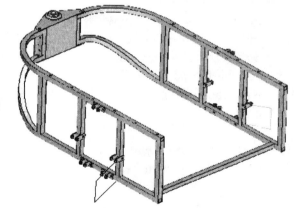

Figure 23 First cross member placed for patterning

Component > Pattern

and clicking on the cross member. Select the offset value. Enter the increment of **275**, and create **4** instances in the pattern. *Modify* the offset dimension to **0** so that the pattern leader is flush with the back end of the frame. This completes the frame, so save it and remove all objects from your session.

The Main Assembly

It's time to put the whole cart together. This involves putting together the subassemblies made previously and a few individual parts. We will use some additional assembly datums to help us position various components and subassemblies. One part is missing (can you figure out which one?) and we will create it in assembly mode. We will also introduce something called an evaluate feature to let Pro/E automatically compute the required length of the side wheel spring based on the position (height) of the side wheel relative to the cart.

Start up a new assembly called *cart_total*. Bring in the subassembly *main_frame*. **Align** the FRONT and SIDE assembly default datums in *main_frame* and *cart_total*. You will probably have to use **Sel by Menu** to pick these out of the crowd. We want the frame to "float" above the assembly datums so that when the front wheel assembly is added, the wheel will just touch the TOP assembly datum in *cart_total*. The third constraint is therefore a **Mate Offset** from the TOP datum in *cart_total* to the underside of the top plate in the *frame_front* part. The offset distance is the height of the *front_wheel* subassembly (from the bottom of the wheel to the top of the spring) that we measured previously. This dimension should be around 620mm. Don't worry if this number is not exact - getting the wheel to exactly touch the TOP datum is not critical.

Adding the Suspension Arms

Now we can bring in the side arms for the wheel suspension. Start on the right side and bring in the *arm_lower* part. The two lower arms face in opposite directions so that the separation between the arms at the outboard end is less than the separation at the bracket end. Start by aligning the axes in the bosses at each end of the arm. **Align** one end with the forward bracket axis and the other end with the lower datum axis. See Figure 24. The final constraint is a **Mate Offset** between the flat surface of the appropriate boss and the inside face of the bracket. The offset distance is **0.5**mm.

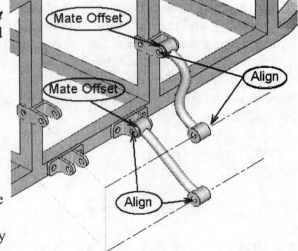

The next part, *arm_upper,* is assembled in the same way to the forward upper bracket.

The second lower and upper arms can be easily placed using the **Repeat** command. For each arm, all you have to do is pick a new assembly reference surface for the **Mate Offset**, since the other axes coincide for each part. The arms will automatically flip over if you pick the correct surface on the brackets.

Figure 24 Assembling the suspension arms

Just for fun, in the ASSEMBLY menu, go to

   Modify > Mod Dim

and click on the suspension datum curve. Change the height dimension to the upper vertex to 100 and *Regenerate > Automatic*. All four side arms should rotate with the new datum frame position. Put the height dimension back to **50** before proceeding.

Adding the Side Wheel Subassembly

Now bring in the *side_wheel* subassembly. Place this using two *Align* constraints between the assembly datum axes and the axes of the pins on the mount plate. Finally, *Mate* the forward side face of the mounting plate with the inside face of the lower suspension arm. See Figure 25.

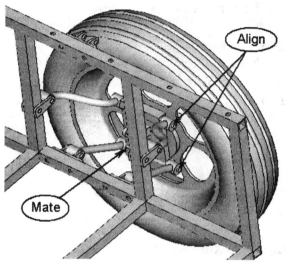

The side arms and the side wheel subassembly now need to be added to the left side of the frame. Your system performance will probably improve if you suppress these components on the right side. As we did above, add the side arms first, then the wheel subassembly. Use the *In Session* button (blue) in the **Open** dialog window when selecting components to be brought into the assembly.

Figure 25 Assembling the *side_wheel*

There is a small dimensional error in the suspension system. To see this, view the assembly from the side and zoom in to examine the clearance between the four side arm bosses and the wheel mounting plate. These are not all the same. Can you figure out the problem? Can you fix it? You will have to move one component and change one assembly constraint. This is not critical to what follows.

Now is a good time to save your *cart_total* assembly.

Adding the Front Wheel Subassembly and Parts

The next component to add is the *front_wheel* subassembly. Before starting that, suppress the side wheel assemblies and arms. To make the position of the front wheel adjustable, we will first create a new assembly datum plane at an angle to a vertical plane in the cart. The angle will be adjustable (we'll do that later with Pro/PROGRAM). We'll align the vertical datum of the front wheel assembly to this adjustable datum plane in *cart_total*.

To create this datum plane in *cart_total*, select the **Datum Plane** toolbar icon, then

> *Through* [pick the vertical axis through the hole in the *front_frame* part]
> *Angle* [use *Sel by Menu* to select the *cart_total.asm* SIDE datum]
> *Done > Enter Value*

Check the direction of rotation and enter an angle value of **30**.

Now bring in the subassembly *front_wheel*. This is constrained using **Align** between the symmetry datum in the subassembly to the new datum plane created above. **Align** the pillar axis with the hole axis in the *front_frame* part. Finally, **Mate** the top of the spring with the underside of the top plate in *front_frame*. See Figure 26.

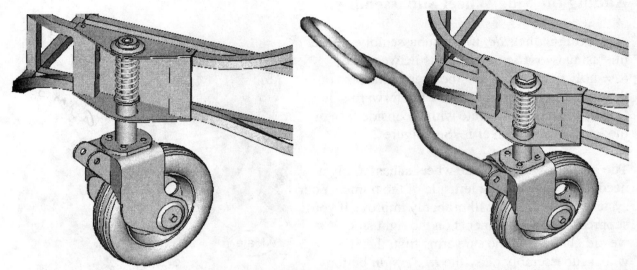

Figure 26 Subassembly *front_wheel* added   **Figure 27** Adding individual parts to the cart - handle, pin, cap

The next part to add is the handle. We also want to make the position of this adjustable by controlling the angle from a horizontal plane. Create another assembly datum through the axis of the horizontal hole on the front of the *front_brack* and at an angle of 45° above the top horizontal surface of *front_wheel_brack*. Bring in the handle and place it using three **Align** constraints: the hole axis on the handle boss with the hole axis in *front_brack*, the SIDE datum of the handle with the symmetry datum created for the *front_wheel_brack* part, the TOP handle datum with the assembly datum created here at 45° above horizontal.

Now bring in the part *handle_pin* and assemble it on the handle axis. If you created this as a both sides protrusion, you can **Align** the symmetry plane with the appropriate plane in the *front_wheel_brack*. Otherwise, you will have to use an **Align Offset** with a vertical plane in *front_wheel_brack*.

The last part on the front assembly is the *pillar_cap*. Bring this in and use **Mate** and **Align** to assemble it on the top of the *front_frame*. See Figure 27.

Just in case disaster strikes, save the assembly now.

Adding the Cargo Bin

The last major component is the cargo bin. Suppress all the other components except the frame. Bring the part *cargo* into the session. *Mate* the underside of the sweep that goes around the top of the bin with the top surface of the frame. *Align* the hole axes of the rear holes on both sides of the bin with the corresponding holes on the frame. See Figure 28.

Check to make sure that all the other holes in the bin and the frame are lined up.

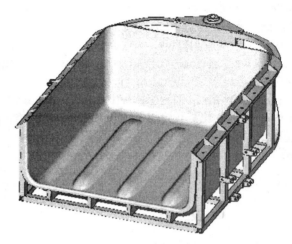

Figure 28 Assembly with the cargo bin

Creating a Part in Assembly Mode

Have you figured out which part is missing? We need a tubing frame member under the front edge of the cargo bin extending from one side frame to the other. This was not made previously due to the uncertainty in the length, which depends on where the cargo bin is (and its size) and the curvature of the side frame members. The easiest way to create this part has been to wait until the assembly was together and then make the part to suit the geometry. We will create the tube as a both sides protrusion from the SIDE datum of the assembly *cart_total*.

In the COMPONENT menu, select

> *Create > Part | Solid*

and enter the name *cross_tube*. In the next dialog window, check the button

> *Create First Feature | OK*

The message window states that the component has been created (it has been added to the assembly model tree) and we are looking at the usual feature creation menu for parts. Select

> *Solid | Protrusion*
> *Extrude | Solid | Done*
> *Both Sides | Done*

For the sketching plane, use *Sel By Menu* to pick from the top level assembly *cart_total* the datum plane named SIDE. Pick the TOP datum for the sketching reference.

In Sketcher, pick the following references: the top, bottom, and interior surfaces of the side frame, and the axis of the hole in the cargo bin. We'll center the sketch on this hole. To help position this, sketch a centerline on the vertical reference (this allows us to use a symmetry constraint in the sketch). Then sketch two rectangles using the existing references. You should not need any dimensions on this sketch (Figure 29). Note that sketcher constraints are turned off in this image. When the sketch is completed, select *Done* and specify *Up To Surface* for the depth specification. The terminating surface for the protrusion in each direction is the inside surface of the side frame.

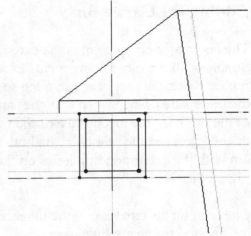

Figure 29 Sketch for *cross_tube* (constraints not displayed)

We need to make some holes in the *cross_tube* that line up with the holes in the cargo bin. Realizing that the cargo bin holes are a pattern, we will use a *Ref Pattern* to place the holes in the tube. To do this, we need to create the first hole at the location of the pattern leader in the cargo bin - find that location now. Starting in the ASSEMBLY menu, select

> *Modify* > *Mod Part* > [pick the cross_tube] > *Feature Create* > *Solid | Hole*

Make the hole *Straight*, diameter *10*, and *Thru All*. For the primary reference pick the axis of the pattern leader hole in the cargo bin. This automatically makes a *Coaxial* hole. The placement plane is the top surface of the part *cross_tube*.

Now, in the PART FEAT menu, select *Pattern* and pick the hole in the tube (probably using *Query Select*). Presto! All the holes in the tube are created. See Figure 30.

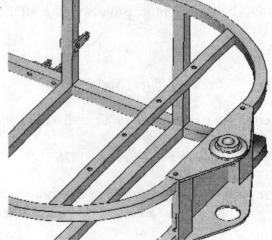

Figure 30 Cross tube member created

Setting a Display State

Have another look at Figure 30. Realizing that the cross-tube is a child of the cargo bin, which appears to not be in the assembly, how was this figure produced? Try to suppress the cargo bin to see what happens. The features of the *cross_tube* part are external children of the cargo bin. With these identified, you could (don't do this now!) get the desired view by *Suspending* the cross_tube. This keeps the tube visible, but it might require special attention if the assembly ever needed regeneration. Don't do that but instead go to

View > Model Setup > Component Display > Create

Enter a name like *no_cargo_bin* for the name of the display state. Open up the model tree. You can now select individual components (even within the subassemblies) and set how you want them displayed: *Blank*, *Hidden* line, *No Hidden* lines, *Shaded* and so on. Any component not specifically set with these options will assume the display state set by the controls on the main graphics window. Select *Blank* and pick on the cargo bin. To see the effect of your settings, select *Update Screen*. When you are happy with the display state, select *Done*.

Note that you can *Redefine* (or *Rename*, *Delete*, ...) the display state. For now, select *Set Current*. This opens a display list of the currently defined states. Select *Master Rep* to return to the default.

You can also get the same result (without the benefit of a named display state), by right clicking on the component in the model tree and selecting *Hide*. In this case, notice the change in the model tree component icon. To get the display turned back on, select *Unhide* (or *View > Unhide All*).

Assembling the Springs

We now want to add the springs on the side wheel suspensions. *Suppress* the cargo bin. You are notified that the cross tube is a child. To keep it in the assembly, select *Suspend All*. This keeps it from being suppressed and maintains its geometry. Resume the right side wheel subassembly.

Bring in the part *spring*. We'll assemble it to the right side wheel subassembly. Constrain the spring as follows: *Align* the lateral axis at one end of the spring to the axis in the top bracket on the right side, *Align* the lateral axis at the other end of the spring to the axis of the bracket on the back of the wheel mounting plate. Finally, *Align* the spring symmetry datum plane with the symmetry plane of the top bracket. If you look very carefully, you will see that the spring is not exactly the correct length to match the holes in the two brackets - it is too long by a couple of millimeters. We will fix this problem in a minute using an evaluate feature and a relation to automatically determine the required length of the spring.

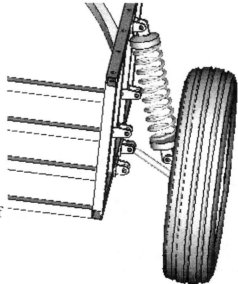

Resume the wheel subassembly on the other side of the cart and assemble another spring between the upper bracket and the wheel mounting plate.

Save the assembly.

Figure 31 Assembled *spring*

Using an Evaluate Feature

We want to set up a method to automatically compute the length of the spring in the suspension system for any position of the wheel. The wheel position is determined by a dimension in the datum curve in the side frame subassembly (our skeleton). When the wheel is repositioned by modifying this dimension, we can measure the distance between the two mounting axes for the spring, and use that to automatically update the spring length. We will implement this only on the right side of the cart. You can add a relation later so that the same effect occurs on the left side.

You can suppress all the components except the main frame and the side wheel (and the arm used to constrain it).

Creating the *Evaluate Feature*

An evaluate feature is a feature that contains the numerical value of some measured quantity in the assembly, like a distance, radius, curve length, area, and so on. We want to use an evaluate feature to measure the distance between the axis in the top bracket and the axis in the bracket on the wheel mounting plate. Starting in the pull-down menus, select

> *Insert > Datum > Evaluate*

Call the feature **spring_mount**. Then select

> *Create*

and enter a parameter name **axis_distance**. The GET MEASURE menu opens showing the items that can be measured, with the numerical result stored in *axis_distance* parameter. An evaluate feature can have several measured quantities in it, each with a unique parameter name. Select *Distance* and then, in the FROM menu select

> *Linear Ent*

and pick on the axis through the top bracket. In the TO menu, select

> *Linear Ent*

and pick on the axis through the bracket on the wheel mounting plate. The message window will report the current value of the measure, something like 348mm, a bit shorter than the current spring length. Close out the menus with *Done*. Open the model tree and observe the location of the new feature (NOTE: the model tree item display must be set to show features).

We will use this measure to control the length of the helical sweep in the spring using a relation. When referring to the evaluate feature in a relation, we use the syntax

> *{parameter_name}:FID_{feature_name}*

or, in our case, *axis_distance:FID_spring_mount*.

Before we implement the desired relation, we need
to find out some information about the symbolic
names for some dimensions, and the value of a
specific dimension in the spring.

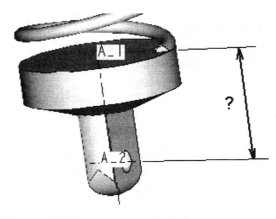

First, we need to find out how much of the distance
between the axes is taken up by the features at the
ends of the spring. See Figure 32. We will need to
subtract this from the evaluate feature value. Open
up the spring part, and use Measure to find the
distance indicated in Figure 32. It should be
something like 50mm. Make a note of this value.
We will double this value for the two ends.

Figure 32 Distance required in spring part

Returning to the assembly window, resume the spring on the right side and use *Modify* and *Info*
> *Switch Dims* to find the symbolic dimension name for the helix length in the spring, and the
vertical dimension in the datum frame. See Figures 33 and 34 where the spring dimension is
shown as *d0:38*, and the vertical datum dimension is *d2:5*. These are the original *d#* dimension
symbols in the parts, and the component number in the assembly.

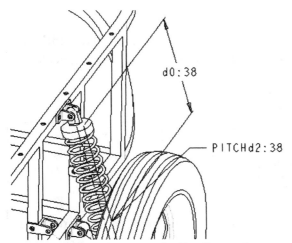

Figure 33 Finding symbolic dimension
names in the *spring* part

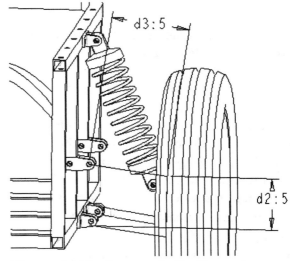

Figure 34 Finding symbolic dimension
names in the datum frame

We're now ready to set up our relation. In the ASSEMBLY menu, select

Relations > Add

and type in the following two lines (use the correct *d#:#* for your assembly):

```
/* spring helix length based on evaluate feature minus spring ends
d0:38 = axis_distance:FID_spring_mount - 100
```

Now use *Modify* to change the vertical dimension on the datum curve to **100**, and *Regenerate > Automatic*. You may get some warning messages about missing references (these might refer to the missing cargo bin and the suspended *cross_tube*). More importantly, you will get a message to the effect that there is a problem with some relations in the assembly *cart_total*, specifically for the dimension *d0:38* in the relation we entered above. What's happening?

When the assembly is regenerated, the parts are regenerated first, then the subassemblies, then the entire top level assembly containing the evaluate feature. So the evaluate feature is not updated until the very end of the regeneration. The new value was not available when the spring was regenerated and so its length does not change. This discrepancy in value is noted, and Pro/E reports that the current value of *d0:38* is not valid. You must regenerate the assembly again to propagate the new value "backwards" in the regeneration sequence, using *Regenerate > Automatic*. This should produce a spring of the correct length. This is not a bug in the program, just a consequence of the fact that the leaves of the assembly tree must be regenerated before moving up the branches.

You may also find that the assembly constraints have been broken - the spring has come off its mounts! Just select *Component > Redefine > {select the spring} > OK* and the spring should snap back to its proper constrained position. Return the datum curve dimension to **50**.

Using Pro/PROGRAM

Let's set up a parameter that we can easily adjust to change the suspension height. This will use Pro/PROGRAM, a function introduced in an earlier lesson[1]. In the ASSEMBLY menu, select

> *Program > Edit Design*

and enter the information shown in Figure 35. Note that the relation created above is already in the program. We only need to add the input statements and the additional relation to transfer the input value to the datum curve dimension.

When you leave your editor, incorporate the design changes into the model and use *Current Vals*. Since the parameter height is initially zero, the side wheel assembly position will change. You must use

```
LISTING FOR ASSEMBLY CART_TOTAL

INPUT
 HEIGHT NUMBER
 "Enter height for datum frame:"
END INPUT

RELATIONS
/* SET DATUM FRAME HEIGHT TO INPUT VALUE - RIGHT SIDE
D2:5 = HEIGHT
/* SPRING HELIX LENGTH BASED ON EVALUATE FEATURE
D0:38 = AXIS_DISTANCE:FID_SPRING_MOUNT - 100
END RELATIONS
```

Figure 35 PROGRAM design file first version

> *Regenerate > Automatic > Enter*

---

[1] You need a license for Pro/ASSEMBLY to use Pro/PROGRAM in assembly mode. If you cannot do this, continue on to the next section.

to set the value of height to 50. *Regenerate* again.

Let's check out something else with the new program. *Resume* all the features and components in the cart. Use *Relations > Show Rel* to open an information window that lists the component numbers (in the Coding Table at the top) and all the defined relations and parameters. The component numbers will have changed due to the resumed parts. Fortunately, Pro/E realizes this and changes the component numbers in the relations automatically.

We'll add a couple more input parameters to control the angle of the front wheel assembly and the handle. Open up the model tree and select *Modify > Mod Dim*. In the model tree look for the two assembly datums created just before the front wheel subassembly (probably called ADTM1) and just before the handle (probably ADTM2). Click on these entries in the model tree and the angle dimensions should show on the model, as in Figure 36. Use *Switch Dims* if necessary to get their symbolic names. The turn angle shown in the figure is *d9:1* and the handle angle is *d10:1*. Note that the *:1* refers to the main assembly level, a clue that these dimensions refer to assembly features and not part features.

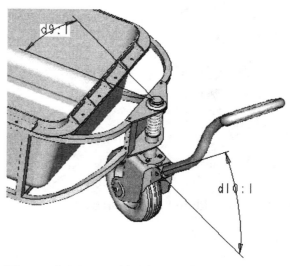

Figure 36 Assembly datum dimensions

Go to *Program > Edit Design* and modify the design file as shown in Figure 37. This involves adding two new input parameters for the turn and handle angles, and two relations to assign these values to the appropriate parameter. You will also have to come back later and add another relation to control the datum frame height on the left side, otherwise the spring part will not fit properly on the left side. Leave the design editor and incorporate the new design. Use *Enter* to set new values for the parameters, say **60** for the turn angle and **30** for the handle angle. What happens if you try to use a negative angle value?

```
LISTING FOR ASSEMBLY CART_TOTAL

INPUT
  HEIGHT NUMBER
  "Enter height for suspension datum frame:"
  TURN NUMBER
  "Enter turn angle (positive right):"
  HANDLE NUMBER
  "Enter handle angle (positive up):"
END INPUT

RELATIONS
/* SET DATUM FRAME HEIGHT TO INPUT VALUE - RIGHT SIDE
D2:5 = HEIGHT
/* SET DATUM FRAME HEIGHT TO INPUT VALUE - LEFT SIDE
D1:7 = HEIGHT
/* SPRING HELIX LENGTH BASED ON EVALUATE FEATURE
D0:40 = AXIS_DISTANCE:FID_SPRING_MOUNT - 100
/* TURN ANGLE FOR FRONT WHEEL SUBASSEMBLY
D9:1 = TURN
/* HANDLE ANGLE ABOVE HORIZONTAL
D10:1 = HANDLE
END RELATIONS
```

Figure 37 PROGRAM design file final version

Completing the Cart

We only have 50 more parts to add to the cart - the bolts! This should not be a big job, however, because we can make good use of the *Adv Utils > Repeat* and *Pattern > Ref Pattern* commands here. The bolts are all instances of the generic part *hex_bolt*. Use the part **H50** on the suspension brackets (see Figure 38) and the part **H40** for all holes in the cargo bin and the front frame (see

Figure 39). Remember that to use *Ref Pattern*, the first bolt must be constrained entirely to the pattern leader hole. This should all go pretty quickly.

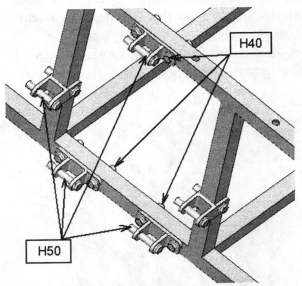

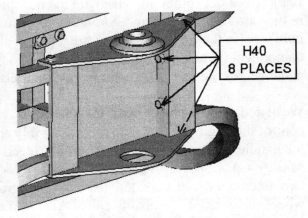

Figure 39 Adding bolts to *frame_front*

Figure 38 Adding bolts to brackets

The assembly is now completed. Save it! There are a few odds and ends missing, such as washers and nuts to put on the bottom of the bolts and some additional components on the axles. You might like to try to add these some time. Also, if you want to assign colors to the different parts and surfaces, go ahead and do that.

Performing an Interference Check

Let's see if we have any gross geometric problems with the design of the cart. We want to find out if any of the parts are overlapping, or interfering. We shouldn't be too concerned about the bolts, so it will speed up things considerably if we suppress all the bolts out of the assembly. Select

> *Component > Suppress > Range*

Open up the model tree and find the component numbers for the bolts at the end of the model tree. The range should be something like 26 through 75. Enter these numbers at the prompts then select *Done*.

To check for interference with the remaining components, select

> *Analysis > Model Analysis*

In the Model Analysis window that opens up, in the Type pull-down list select

> *Global Interference > Compute*

If all goes well, after a minute or two you will be informed that there are no interfering parts.

What happens if the wheel suspension moves to a new position? *Regenerate* the assembly with the suspension height variable set to **0**. Perform the interference analysis again. This time, you should be informed that there is interference in two places. In the Model Analysis window, a display box shows the pairs of parts involved. Highlighting one of these lines will cause the interfering parts, the spring and the wheel mount plate, to highlight in blue and yellow in the graphics window. Zoom in on the interfering area. The interference volume is shown in red. The actual volume of interference (something like 833 mm^3) is also indicated. There are a number of ways that you could eliminate this interference, and you can do that on your own. Set the suspension height back to 50.

Assembly Drawings

The essential commands for constructing drawings were discussed in the first Pro/E tutorial and in the previous lesson. You will find that, for assemblies, multi-model and multi-sheet drawings are critical to help you organize the task of presenting and detailing the design. As for creating the assembly, it would be a good idea to spend some time planning the layout of all the drawings first, before committing to any particular scheme. We are not going to do any of that here, since we have already covered many of the basic drawing functions. Also, the cart model could easily involve 20 to 30 drawings for a complete documentation package.

Before we proceed, *Resume* all the parts in the assembly.

One important item that has not been discussed is the creation of a bill of materials (BOM) for the assembly. When you are in assembly mode, you can easily create a BOM by selecting

> *Info > Bill of Materials > Top Level | OK*

An information window opens showing a listing of all parts in the assembly, broken down by subassemblies and a total part count at the end of the listing. Notice that the BOM file is automatically placed in your working directory with the file name *cart_total.bom*.

What we will do here is to create a BOM on a drawing of the assembly, and attach balloons to some of the components in one subassembly. This is essential design documentation.

Creating a Drawing BOM

Start up a new drawing called *cart*. Deselect the option "Use default template". Check the option "Empty with format" on the next window and select the format *tut_format* developed in the last lesson. Complete the prompts as required to specify any parameters in the drawing (like *drawn_by*). Add a general view of the cart assembly:

Views > Add
General | ... | No Scale | Done

Place the view slightly to the left of center on the drawing sheet. Set the orientation of the view as desired. If you happen to have a favorite view saved in the assembly (like a right isometric), you can select this directly. Use the *Edit > Value* command to change the sheet scale to **0.075**. The sheet should look like Figure 40.

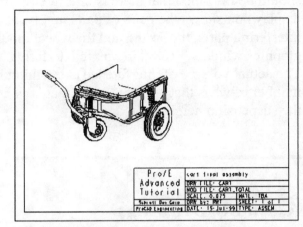

Figure 40 Drawing format and first view

Creating the BOM Table

Our BOM on the drawing will be created using a repeat region defined in a table. In the DRAWING menu, select

Table > Create
Descending > Rightward > By Length > Abs Coords

The top left starting point of the table is at coordinates X = **6.375**, Y = **8.125**. Enter the column widths as follows:

column 1	**0.625**
column 2	**1.5**
column 3	**1.5**
column 4	**0.625**

Hit *Enter* on a blank line to finish the column definition. Observe the tick marks as the columns are created. This should produce a table that is even with the right border of the sheet. Now enter the row heights: **0.25** for the first row, **0.2** for the second row. Hit *Enter* on a blank line to finish the definition. Now create the column headings. Select

Enter Text

Pick in the cells in the top row and enter the following text:

Figure 41 BOM column headings in table

column 1	**INDEX**
column 2	**Component Name**
column 3	**Component Type**
column 4	**QTY**

as shown in the figure at the right.

Creating the Repeat Region

Still in the TABLE menu, select

> *Repeat Region > Add > Simple*

and pick on the first and fourth cells in the second row. Now we add some text into the cells. Go to

> *Enter Text > Report Sym*

Enter the following sequences from the REPORT SYM menus into each cell:

column 1	**rpt.index**	
column 2	**asm.mbr.name**	
column 3	**asm.mbr.type**	
column 4	**rpt.qty**	

INDEX	Component Name	Component Type	QTY
rpt.index	asm.mbr.name	asm.mbr.type	rpt.qty

These text strings will appear in the table, overlapping the cells a bit. Don't worry about that now. See Figure 42.

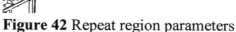

Figure 42 Repeat region parameters

Creating the BOM

We now have everything defined. Go to

> *Repeat Region > Update Tables*

The table will expand down considerably off the sheet. The table contains a large number of duplicated entities (especially the bolts). We'll combine these by selecting, in the TBL REGIONS menu

> *Attributes* > [pick on the region] > *No Duplicates | .. | Done/Return*

The table now collapses and will appear as shown in Figure 43. This is the BOM for the top level assembly. It identifies which components are parts and which are subassemblies, and how many components are involved.

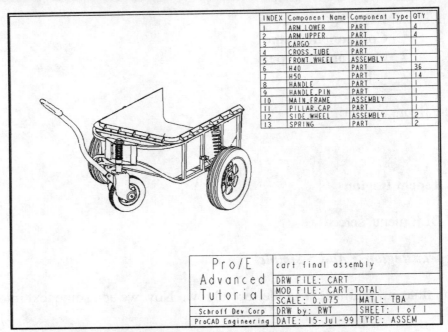

INDEX table:

INDEX	Component Name	Component Type	QTY
1	ARM_LOWER	PART	4
2	ARM_UPPER	PART	4
3	CARGO	PART	1
4	CROSS_TUBE	PART	1
5	FRONT_WHEEL	ASSEMBLY	1
6	H40	PART	36
7	H50	PART	14
8	HANDLE	PART	1
9	HANDLE_PIN	PART	1
10	MAIN_FRAME	ASSEMBLY	1
11	PILLAR_CAP	PART	1
12	SIDE_WHEEL	ASSEMBLY	2
13	SPRING	PART	2

Title block:

Pro/E Advanced Tutorial	cart final assembly
	DRW FILE: CART
	MOD FILE: CART_TOTAL
	SCALE: 0.075 MATL: TBA
Schroff Dev Corp	DRW by: RWT SHEET: 1 of 1
ProCAD Engineering	DATE: 15-Jul-99 TYPE: ASSEM

Figure 43 Assembly top level drawing with BOM

Adding Balloons

Add another sheet to the drawing and add another drawing model, for example the side wheel subassembly. Methods to do this were discussed in the previous tutorial. On the second sheet, create an exploded view with an appropriate scale. This is most easily done if the explode distances are defined in assembly mode and a named view created there, as suggested earlier. Update the format to show the correct model name (discussed in the last lesson). Create another BOM for the subassembly using the same procedure and repeat region parameters as on sheet 1, and remove duplicates. Use *Format > Text Style* to center the text in the cells.

Finally, in the TABLE menu select

> *BOM Balloon*

Pick on the region, then select *Show > By View* and pick on the exploded view. Pick on each balloon to drag it to a better position. The final drawing should look something like Figure 44. Save the drawing.

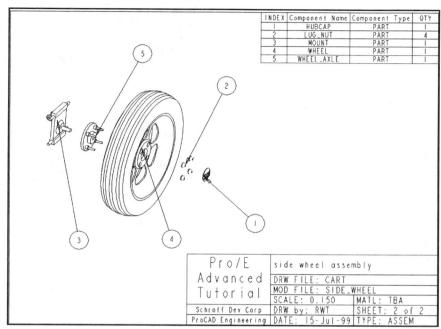

INDEX	Component Name	Component Type	QTY
1	HUBCAP	PART	1
2	LUG_NUT	PART	4
3	MOUNT	PART	1
4	WHEEL	PART	1
5	WHEEL_AXLE	PART	1

Pro/E Advanced Tutorial	side wheel assembly	
	DRW FILE: CART	
	MOD FILE: SIDE_WHEEL	
	SCALE: 0.150	MATL: TBA
Schroff Dev Corp	DRW by: RWT	SHEET: 2 of 2
ProCAD Engineering	DATE: 15-Jul-99	TYPE: ASSEM

Figure 44 BOM with balloons

There is considerably more you can do with the BOM. You can, for example, attach a cost to each component and sum the cost for all entries in the table. You can add **Bulk Items** such as paint, solder, glue, and so on. These are actually created as components in the top-level assembly. The repeat regions can also be nested so that the entire BOM contains components sorted by subassembly.

Conclusion

Well, this is the end of this tutorial. There are some exercises at the end of this lesson to give you some ideas for extending the cart project. Hopefully, the tutorial has shown you a number of new tools and techniques to allow you to take on more challenging and complex modeling projects, and to do them more efficiently. As always, there is lots more to learn about how the basic Pro/E modeling tools can be applied. Only with practice and experience will you become very adept at this task. You are certain to come across unique and tricky modeling tasks, and the more acquainted you are with the tools, the better you will able to succeed. You should be developing a feel for how these modeling tools can be employed to produce clean, flexible, and easy to use models, and how advanced modeling differs from simple geometry creation.

Questions for Review

1. What must you consider when planning to create a component pattern?
2. Where can you find the merge command?
3. What is the order of component selection when using **Merge**?
4. What is the difference between merging and mirroring **By Reference** and **Copy**?

5. What happens to the assembly file used to create a mirrored part?
6. How do you select the constraints to be used to repeat the placement of a component?
7. What restriction to you have to keep in mind when using *Ref Pattern* to place new components?
8. What was the purpose of the assembly datum curve in the side frame subassemblies?
9. Explain the purpose and explain how to use an evaluate feature in a relation.
10. Where does an evaluate feature appear on the model tree?
11. When you use an evaluate feature, why do you have to regenerate twice?
12. What happens if you edit a dimension of a family table instance in the assembly if (a) the dimension is driven by the family table? and (b) the dimension is not driven by the family table?
13. How do you determine if there are interfering parts in the assembly?
14. When you are in assembly mode, how do you create a bill of materials?
15. How do you get rid of repeated entries in a BOM on a drawing?

Some Final Project Exercises

1. Modify the cargo bin so that it will dump. Perhaps you could add a spring assisted lift for this.
2. Set up the model so that the location of the side wheels (front to back) is adjustable.
3. Determine the total weight of the cart and find its center of gravity - if it's behind the wheels we're in big trouble.
4. Design a canopy for the cart.
5. Design an easily removed tailgate.
6. Add parameters and relations to automatically change the lengths of the side arms on the suspension.
7. Add parameters and relations to change the size of the cargo bin and main frame.